Copyright Law and Transl

Arguing that the translation of scientific and technical learning materials, and the publication of these translations in a timely and affordable manner, is crucially important in promoting access to scientific and technical knowledge in the developing world, this book examines the relationship between copyright law, translation and access to knowledge.

Taking Sri Lanka as a case study in comparison with India and Bangladesh, it identifies factors that have contributed to the unfavourable relationship between copyright law and the timely and affordable translation of scientific and technical learning materials, such as colonisation, international copyright law, the trade interests of the developing economies and a lack of expertise and general lack of awareness surrounding copyright law in the developing world.

Highlighting the need to reform international copyright law to promote the needs and interests of developing countries such as Sri Lanka, the book points to a possible way forward for developing countries to achieve this and to address the problem of striking a proper and delicate balance in their copyright laws between the protection of translation rights and the ability of people to access translations of copyright protected scientific and technical learning materials.

Chamila S. Talagala is a member of the Australian Centre for Intellectual Property in Agriculture and an Attorney-at-Law of the Supreme Court of Sri Lanka.

Routledge Research in Intellectual Property

Available:

Patent Pools, Competition Law and Biotechnology
Devdatta Malshe

Copyright Law and Derivative Works
Regulating Creativity
Omri Rachum-Twaig

The Patentability of Software
Software as Mathematics
Anton Hughes

Annotated Leading Trademark Cases in Major Asian Jurisdictions
Edited by Kung-Chung Liu

SEPs, SSOs and FRAND
Asian and Global Perspectives on Fostering Innovation in Interconnectivity
Edited by Kung-Chung Liu and Reto M. Hilty

Towards an Ecological Intellectual Property
Reconfiguring Relationships Between People and Plants in Ecuador
David Jefferson

The Transformation of EU Geographical Indications Law
The Present, Past and Future of the Origin Link
Andrea Zappalaglio

Copyright Law and Translation
Access to Knowledge in Developing Economies
Chamila S. Talagala

For more information about this series, please visit www.routledge.com/Routledge-Research-in-Intellectual-Property/book-series/INTELLPROP

Copyright Law and Translation

Access to Knowledge in Developing Economies

Chamila S. Talagala

Routledge
Taylor & Francis Group
LONDON AND NEW YORK

First published 2021
by Routledge
2 Park Square, Milton Park, Abingdon, Oxon OX14 4RN

and by Routledge
605 Third Avenue, New York, NY 10158

Routledge is an imprint of the Taylor & Francis Group, an informa business

British Library Cataloguing-in-Publication Data
A catalogue record for this book is available from the British Library

Library of Congress Cataloging-in-Publication Data
Names: Talagala, Chamila S., author.
Title: Copyright law and translation : access to knowledge in developing economies / Chamila S. Talagala.
Description: Milton Park, Abingdon, Oxon ; New York, NY : Routledge, 2021. | Series: Routledge research in intellectual property | Includes bibliographical references and index.
Identifiers: LCCN 2020049282 (print) | LCCN 2020049283 (ebook) | ISBN 9780367861063 (hardback) | ISBN 9781003165446 (ebook)
Subjects: LCSH: Copyright—Translations—Developing countries. | Copyright, International. | World Intellectual Property Organization Copyright Treaty (1996 December 20) | Agreement on Trade-Related Aspects of Intellectual Property Rights (1994 April 15)
Classification: LCC K1447.7 .T35 2021 (print) | LCC K1447.7 (ebook) | DDC 346/.17240482—dc23
LC record available at https://lccn.loc.gov/2020049282
LC ebook record available at https://lccn.loc.gov/2020049283

ISBN: 978-0-367-86106-3 (hbk)
ISBN: 978-0-367-76094-6 (pbk)
ISBN: 978-1-003-16544-6 (ebk)

Typeset in Galliard
by Apex CoVantage, LLC

To my parents, Susiri Talagala and Indrani Talagala

Contents

Acknowledgements

I owe an enormous debt of gratitude to Professor Brad Sherman, who sparked my interest in the topic of this book. As the first Principal Supervisor of my PhD at Griffith University, he supported, guided and encouraged me immensely towards the completion of the thesis and this book. Without his support, this book could not have seen the light of day. I also express my deepest gratitude to Professor Leanne Wiseman, who was the second Principal Supervisor of my PhD, for her endless support and guidance. She has been a constant source of encouragement and inspiration. I am also grateful to my other PhD Supervisor, Professor Charles Lawson, and others who have helped and supported me in numerous ways, particularly Dr DM Karunaratna, Dr Tissa Hemaratne, Professor Shironica Karunanayaka, Dr Kanchana Kariyawasam, Mr Gayan Jayaweera. Professor WD Lakshman and the late Professor Buddhadasa Hewavitharana. Last, but certainly not least, I wish to extend my deepest appreciation to my parents, to whom I dedicate this work.

Abbreviations

Anglo-French Copyright Treaty	*Convention between Her Majesty and the French Republic for the Establishment of International Copyright 1851*
Berne Convention	*Berne Convention for the Protection of Literary and Artistic Works 1886* (As revised)
BIRPI	United International Bureaux for the Protection of Intellectual Property
Constitution 1972	*Constitution of the Republic of Sri Lanka 1972*
Constitution 1978	*Constitution of the Democratic Socialist Republic of Sri Lanka 1978*
FTA	Free Trade Agreement
GATT	General Agreement on Tariffs and Trade
ICCPR	*International Covenant on Civil and Political Rights 1966*
ICESCR	*International Covenant on Economic, Social and Cultural Rights 1966*
IP Code	*Code of Intellectual Property Act No 52 of 1979*
Marrakesh VIP Treaty	*Marrakesh Treaty to Facilitate Access to Published Works for Persons Who Are Blind, Visually Impaired, or Otherwise Print Disabled 2013*
MFA	*Multi-Fibre Agreement 1974*
NTM	National Translation Mission of India
Paris Convention	*Paris Convention for the Protection of Industrial Property 1883* (As revised)
Special Committee on Education	Special Committee appointed to investigate the defects of the present educational system and to recommend measures of reform necessitated by the changed conditions 1940
TIFA	Trade and Investment Framework Agreement

TRIPS Agreement	*Agreement on Trade-Related Aspects of Intellectual Property Rights 1994*
UCC	*Universal Copyright Convention 1952* (As revised)
UDHR	*Universal Declaration of Human Rights 1948*
UN	United Nations
UNDP	United Nations Development Programme
UNESCO	United Nations Educational, Scientific and Cultural Organisation
UNICEF	United Nations Children's Fund
USSLTIFA	*United States-Sri Lanka Trade and Investment Framework Agreement 2002*
US-Sri Lanka BIT	*Treaty between the United States of America and the Democratic Socialist Republic of Sri Lanka concerning the Encouragement and Reciprocal Protection of Investment 1991*
US-Sri Lanka IPR Agreement	*Agreement on the Protection and Enforcement of Intellectual Property Rights between the United States of America and the Democratic Socialist Republic of Sri Lanka 1991*
Uruguay Round	The 8th Round of Multilateral Trade Negotiations conducted within the framework of the General Agreement on Tariffs and Trade during 1986–1994
USTR	United States Trade Representative
WIPO	World Intellectual Property Organisation
WTO	World Trade Organisation

Table of international treaties, conventions and other instruments

Table of statutes and bills

Australia

Bangladesh

Britain

India

Sri Lanka

United States

Table of cases

Britain

India

Sri Lanka

United States

1 Introduction

1.1. Objective and scope of the book

This book is about why developing countries have failed to strike a proper balance in their copyright laws between the protection of translation rights and the ability of people to access translations of copyright protected scientific and technical books and learning materials. Timely and affordable translation of scientific and technical books and learning materials produced in developed countries is key to promoting access to scientific and technical knowledge in developing countries. However, the unbalanced manner in which copyright owners' translation rights are protected in the copyright laws of developing countries has the potential to impede the timely and affordable translation of these knowledge products.

For developing countries, copyright in general and the right to translate in particular is essentially a balancing act between the protection of copyright owners' rights and the people's (users') ability to access copyright protected works.[1] While on the one hand, it is necessary to provide protection to the legitimate interests of authors and publishers, on the other hand, it is equally important, if not more so, to ensure the free flow of information.[2] This means that stringent copyright protection standards that protect translation rights, without appropriate exceptions to balance these rights with the people's ability to access copyright protected works are unsuitable for developing countries. Strict protection of translation rights without commensurate attention to their exceptions not only prevents people from accessing translations of copyright protected works directly but can also increase the cost of translations and thereby impede access to them indirectly. Despite the clear need for timely and affordable translation of scientific and technical books and learning materials, many developing countries have failed to strike a proper balance between the protection of translation rights and the people's ability to access translations of copyright protected scientific and technical books and learning materials. This imbalance constrains access to scientific and technical knowledge in these countries.

1 See Frederick M Abbott, 'The WTO TRIPS Agreement and Global Economic Development' (1996) 72 *Chicago-Kent Law Review* 385, 386.
2 WD Rodrigo, 'Copyright Law in the Digital Era: A Comparative Study of Sri Lanka, Australia and the United States' (PhD Thesis, University of Queensland, 2007) 44.

In exploring the reason for this copyright imbalance, this book employs Sri Lanka as a case study. There are several reasons for selecting Sri Lanka for this purpose. Sri Lanka is a developing country that has many of the common characteristics of a typical developing country. It is a multilingual, multi-ethnic and multicultural country striving to maintain its diversity while promoting economic and social development. The local languages in Sri Lanka are geographically limited and the country has a colonial history. In addition, as will be seen later, up until 2003 Sri Lankan copyright law provided special exceptions to copyright owners' translation rights. However, the present copyright law, which came into force in 2003, does not provide for any special exceptions to copyright owners' translation rights. Thus, the copyright law of Sri Lanka protects translation rights of copyright owners in an unbalanced manner.

While the discussion in this book is predominantly focused on Sri Lanka, it indisputably relates to developing economies in general. Although the context and characteristics in every developing country concerning the need for translation of scientific and technical books and learning materials might not be identical, the need for such translation becomes crucial in countries where there is a multiplicity of languages or where one local language (which is not in general use in the world) dominates the spheres of culture, national identity, education, and so on. Sri Lanka shares many similarities with India and Bangladesh in this connection. All these countries are commonwealth nations and democracies. India is the largest commonwealth nation by population and Bangladesh is the fourth. Sri Lanka 'has been the prototype and model for the new Commonwealth of the latter part of the twentieth century'.[3] India is the second most populous country and the most populous democracy in the world,[4] which, together with Bangladesh and Sri Lanka, qualifies to make a broader representation of developing countries in general. While the *Constitution of India* prescribes that the 'official language of the Union shall be Hindi',[5] it also casts a duty on the Union 'to promote the spread of the Hindi language, to develop it so that it may serve as a medium of expression for all the elements of the composite culture of India'.[6] In addition, the Indian Constitution also specifies 22 local languages in its Eighth Schedule. The *Constitution of the People's Republic of Bangladesh 1972* stipulates Bangla [Bengali] as the state language of Bangladesh,[7] and stresses that the 'unity and solidarity of the Bangalee nation, which deriving its identity from its language and culture . . . shall be the basis of Bangalee nationalism.'[8] While Sinhala and Tamil constitute the official and national languages in Sri Lanka in terms of the *Constitution of the Democratic Socialist Republic of Sri Lanka 1978*,[9] the Constitution

3 Sir Charles Jeffries, *Ceylon: The Path to Independence* (Pall Mall Press, 1962) ix.
4 Claire O'Kane et al., 'Protection in Action: Regional Evaluation of the Effectiveness of Community Based Child Protection Mechanisms' (Report, Plan International, September 2014) 11.
5 *The Constitution of India*, art 343 (1).
6 Ibid., art 351.
7 *The Constitution of the People's Republic of Bangladesh 1972*, art 3.
8 Ibid., art 9.
9 *The Constitution of the Democratic Socialist Republic of Sri Lanka 1978*, arts 18 & 19.

also obliges the State to assist 'the development of the cultures and languages of the People.'[10] Thus, the local languages play a prominent role in all these three countries which form an intrinsic part of culture, self-identity and nationalism. As in the case of Sri Lanka, the copyright laws of India and Bangladesh are of British origin, and they follow the British tradition of copyright owing to the effects of colonisation. The comparative approach adopted in the ensuing discussion will further reveal how the facts and findings relating to Sri Lanka throughout this book relate to India, Bangladesh and other developing economies in general.

1.2. Importance of access to knowledge

Knowledge is the single most important underlying factor in the tremendous development that humankind has achieved to date. As Khan noted:

> Knowledge has always been crucial to human development. Since the dawn of humankind, the creation and application of new knowledge, in every sphere of human activities, have contributed to the evolution of societies and economic welfare of people. Knowledge of how to do things, how to communicate and how to work with other people has always been regarded as the most precious 'wealth' that humans possess.[11]

Knowledge is a key catalyst for economic development in the modern world. As a 2008 World Bank report noted, 'A knowledge economy is one that creates, disseminates, and uses knowledge to enhance its growth and development.'[12] While the term 'knowledge economy' is said to have first been used by Peter Drucker in his 1969 book *The Age of Discontinuity: The Guidelines to Our Changing Society*,[13] the vital contribution of knowledge to economic development has long been recognised. For example, in the 1950s Robert Solow (who was awarded the Nobel Prize in Economics in 1987) posited a relationship between knowledge and economic growth, arguing that 'the vast proportion of gains in productivity in [the] early twentieth-century [United States] could be attributed not to factors related to the use of labour or capital, but to a "residual" that he described as technical change'.[14] This residual 'came to be

10 Ibid., art 27(10).
11 Abdul Waheed Khan, 'Universal Access to Knowledge as a Global Public Good' on Global Policy Forum (June 2009) <www.globalpolicy.org/social-and-economic-policy/global-public-goods-1-101/50437-universal-access-to-knowledge-as-a-global-public-good.html?itemid=id#1017>.
12 Ismail Radwan et al., 'Building the Sri Lankan Knowledge Economy' (Report, World Bank, March 2008) 16.
13 See Mark A Langley, 'The Power of Knowledge' in 'Pulse of Profession: Capturing the Value of Project Management through Knowledge Transfer' (Report, Project Management Institute, March 2015) 2.
14 Amy Kapczynski, 'Access to Knowledge: A Conceptual Genealogy' in Gaelle Krikorian and Amy Kapczynski (eds), *Access to Knowledge in the Age of Intellectual Property* (Zone Books, 2010) 17, 18.

understood as a range of advances in knowledge . . . that made processes of production more efficient'.[15] Solow's findings were followed by '[m]ainstream economists [who] soon began to contend that knowledge is not only important, but increasingly important to economic growth, positing that the world's most developed economies have been becoming more knowledge intensive'.[16] Proving these contentions true, in the late twentieth century the global economy increasingly came to be driven by knowledge. As Waitley commented, 'Yesterday natural resources defined power. Today knowledge is power.'[17] Thus, it is clear that access to knowledge is crucially important for human and economic development.

In view of its importance for human and economic development, it is not surprising that access to knowledge is increasingly being recognised as a human right. As the United Nations Development Program (UNDP) states:

> Access to knowledge is a human right. It is a prerequisite for achieving full human potentials and inclusive development, as it opens the door for education, employment, improved health, social and political participation, and access to justice.[18]

The roots of the contention that access to knowledge is a human right lie in provisions of the *Universal Declaration of Human Rights 1948* (*UDHR*) and the *International Covenant on Economic, Social and Cultural Rights 1966* (*ICESCR*). In particular, Article 27(1) of the *UDHR* states:

> Everyone has the right freely to participate in the cultural life of the community, to enjoy the arts and to share in scientific advancement and its benefits.

Likewise, Article 15(1) of the *ICESCR* states that everyone has a right to 'take part in cultural life' and to 'enjoy the benefits of scientific progress and its applications'. Other instruments in the international human rights field, such as the *Convention on the Rights of the Child 1989*, also provide for a right to information of certain persons.[19]

In broad terms, access to knowledge is required for the effective realisation and enforcement of all human rights. This is because access to knowledge 'has a claim on our humanity that stands with other basic rights, whether to life, liberty, justice, or respect' and 'is closely associated with the ability to defend,

15 Ibid., 18–19.
16 Ibid., 19 (emphasis added).
17 Denis Waitley, *Empires of the Mind: Lessons to Lead and Succeed in a Knowledge-Based World* (William Morrow and Company, 1995) 2.
18 See UNDP, 'Individual Consultant Procurement Notice' (Procurement Notice, 27 January 2015) <http://procurement-notices.undp.org/view_file.cfm?doc_id=45894>.
19 See *Convention on the Rights of the Child 1989*, art 17.

as well as to advocate for other rights'.[20] Simply said, knowledge affects the ways in which individuals exercise their rights and also whether they are aware of those rights.

There is also a close connection between access to knowledge and human rights such as the right to freedom of expression. Access to knowledge is a prerequisite for freedom of expression, since expression is often, if not always, based on the understanding of the available knowledge. Many international human rights instruments like the *UDHR* and the *International Covenant on Civil and Political Rights 1966* (*ICCPR*) articulate the right to freedom of expression to encapsulate freedom to seek, receive and impart information.[21] This makes the right to freedom of expression dependent on access to knowledge. Jonker observed that 'increased access to knowledge may be seen as a prerequisite for freedom of expression, since participating in certain discourses (such as that of science) requires access to the existing knowledge base'.[22] Access to knowledge is also dependent on freedom of expression. Shaver stated that 'freedom of expression protects the ability to communicate existing knowledge to new parties and enables collaboration for the development of new knowledge'.[23] As such, 'upholding freedom of expression is important in promoting access to knowledge'.[24] In the same way, factors that impede freedom of expression also impede access to knowledge.[25]

Access to knowledge is closely interrelated with the right to education. The right to education envisages providing students with access to knowledge to facilitate their learning. This includes teaching as well as the provision of educational materials. Helfer and Austin argued that '[t]he provision of [educational materials] is also an integral part of the human right to education'.[26] In particular, they contended:

> [T]he human right to education imposes public law obligations on governments, including the provision of free educational materials (particularly

20 John Willinsky, *The Access Principle: The Case for Open Access to Research and Scholarship* (MIT Press, 2006) 143.

21 See *Universal Declaration of Human Rights 1948*, art 19; *International Covenant on Civil and Political Rights 1966*, art 19; *American Convention on Human Rights 1969*, art 13; *European Convention on Human Rights 1950*, art 10.

22 Julian Jonker, 'Access to Learning Materials in South Africa: The Convergence of Development and Right-Based Arguments for Access to Knowledge' in Andrew Rens and Rebecca Kahn (eds), *Access to Knowledge in South Africa* (Intellectual Property Research Unit, University of Cape Town and Information Society Project at Yale Law School, 2009) 113.

23 Lea Bishop Shaver, 'Defining and Measuring A2K: A Blueprint for an Index of Access to Knowledge' (2008) 4(2) *I/S: A Journal of Law and Policy* 1, 23.

24 Frederick Noronha and Jeremy Malcolm (eds), *Access to Knowledge: A Guide for Everyone* (Consumers International, 2010) 94.

25 Ibid.

26 Laurence R Helfer and Graeme W Austin, *Human Rights and Intellectual Property: Mapping the Global Interface* (Cambridge University Press, 2011) 318.

> to primary school children). The human right to education must therefore mean something other than the existence of markets for [educational materials], which anticipate that [these] materials will be sold rather than distributed free of charge.[27]

This contention is supported by the *Convention on the Rights of the Child 1989*, which requires State Parties to make educational and vocational information 'available and accessible to children', with a view to achieving the right of the child to education guaranteed under it.[28] The *Convention* also requires Parties to promote and encourage international cooperation in matters relating to education with a view to 'facilitating access to scientific and technical knowledge'.[29]

It is clear that access to knowledge, both in terms of imparting knowledge through teaching and the provision of educational materials, is essential for the realisation of the right to education. Conversely, since education promotes knowledge, a right to education broadens access to knowledge.

1.3. Developing countries and access to knowledge

Access to knowledge is particularly important for developing countries or those that, according to the World Bank, have low and middle incomes. As of 2020, there are 135 countries around the world that are classified as developing countries.[30] India, Bangladesh and Sri Lanka are three examples. Developing countries have particular problems in ensuring that citizens are able to get access to knowledge. These problems are primarily a result of the knowledge gap that exists between developing and developed countries as well as the dominance of the English language in knowledge distribution.

1.3.1. Knowledge gap

One of the key reasons that developing countries face so many problems in ensuring that citizens are able to get access to knowledge is the knowledge gap that exists between developed and developing countries. This gap is most marked in the field of science and technology. Because of this, developing countries are dependent on developed countries for access to scientific and technical knowledge. UNESCO noted that 'scientific and technological knowledge . . . is mostly

27 Ibid., 316–317.

28 *Convention on the Rights of the Child, 1989*, art 28(d).

29 Ibid., art 28(3). See also UN Committee on Economic, Social and Cultural Rights, *General Comment No.13: The Right to Education (Art 13 of the Covenant)*, 21st sess. UN Doc E/C.12/1999/10 (8 December 1999).

30 World Bank, *Country and Lending Groups* <http://data.worldbank.org/about/country-and-lending-groups>.

concentrated in the [developed countries]'.[31] This problem is compounded by the fact that the level of education and research in developed countries is far more advanced than in most developing countries. Deckelbaum, Ntambi and Wolgemoth observed that there are tremendous gaps between developed and developing countries with regard to science education and research.[32] Alarmingly, this gap appears to be widening.[33]

The knowledge gap between developed and developing countries in the field of science and technology is manifested in three ways: (1) the amount of books produced, (2) the number of journals published and (3) the materials available on the internet.

Inadequate production of scientific and technical books in developing countries and the resultant dependency of developing countries on the developed world for scientific and technical knowledge products is a long-standing phenomenon.[34] The 1973 UNESCO publication *The Book Hunger* observed:

> Two-thirds of the men, women and children in the world today are handicapped in their search for a better and fuller life by lack of one of the essential tools of progress: books and reading material. . . . In Asia, Africa, Latin America and the Arab States, in varying degrees, there is an acute shortage of books. . . . Only one title out of every five produced today originates in a developing country. Of the more than 500,000 titles which are issued every year—a new book a minute—80 per cent come from the countries of Europe, plus Japan, the Soviet Union and the United States.[35]

The situation described by UNESCO has changed little over the years. There is still a large disparity between developed and developing countries with regard to the production and distribution of scientific and technical knowledge products. In particular, the extent of scientific and technical book publishing in developing countries (especially in the African region) is negligible, which, in turn,

31 UNESCO, 'Towards Knowledge Societies' (World Report, UNESCO, 2005) 26. In contrast, most developing countries lack scientific and technological knowledge when compared with the developed countries. M Saiful Karim, 'Implementation of the MARPOL Convention in Developing Countries' (2010) 79 *Nordic Journal of International Law* 303, 330.

32 Richard J Deckelbaum, James M Ntambi and Debra J Wolgemuth, 'Basic Science Research and Education: A Priority for Training and Capacity Building in Developing Countries' (2011) 25(3) *Infectious Disease Clinics of North America* 669 <www.id.theclinics.com/article/S0891-5520%2811%2900044-4/abstract>.

33 See, e.g., Anthony N Ezeife and T Arivalagan, 'Technology Education and Economic Competitiveness in Developing Countries: The Sri Lankan Experience' (2006) 35(1) *Canadian and International Education Journal* 12, 15.

34 See Leah A Lievrouw and Sharon E Farb, 'Information and Equity' (2003) 37 *Annual Review of Information Science and Technology* 499, 499–500.

35 Ronald Barker and Robert Escarpit (eds), *The Book Hunger* (UNESCO, 1973) 6 (emphasis added).

makes developing countries heavily dependent on scientific and technical books and reading materials published in developed countries.[36] Shaver observed that '[i]n many developing countries, it remains difficult to locate a bookstore [and] [a]cademics and university students in developing countries experience great difficulty [in] meeting their book needs'.[37] Although one text book per student (in any subject) is the norm, in most developing countries this is the exception rather than the norm.[38]

The number of academic journals published and their rankings offer a useful estimate of scientific and technical knowledge production and distribution in countries around the world. This is an area where the disparity between developed and developing countries with regard to the production and distribution of scientific and technical knowledge is most marked. A 2011 research study titled *Geographies of World Knowledge* revealed that there is 'a staggering amount of inequality in the geography of the production of academic knowledge' between the West and the rest of the world.[39] 'The United States and the United Kingdom publish more indexed journals than the rest of the world combined.'[40] This is followed by 'Western Europe, in particular Germany and the Netherlands', which 'scores relatively well'.[41] However, '[m]ost of the rest of the world . . . scarcely shows up in these rankings'.[42] 'The non-Western world is not only under-represented in these rankings, but also ranks poorly on average citation score measures.'[43] The result of this is that:

> [T]he world's codified knowledge remain[s] concentrated among educated and affluent people in industrialised nations. This concentration span[s] all phases in the cycle of information—from the production of knowledge to its distribution and access. Changing these patterns is inevitably hard, as access to knowledge is often a prerequisite to create new knowledge. . . . [A]lthough information can now be produced almost

36 Susan Isiko Strba, *International Copyright Law and Access to Education in Developing Countries: Exploring Multilateral Legal and Quasi-Legal Solutions* (Martinus Nijhoff Publishers, 2012) 35–36.

37 Lea Shaver, 'Copyright and Inequality' (2014) 92 *Washington University Law Review* 117, 119. Similarly, Askerud stated that '[t]extbooks are a rare commodity in most developing countries.' Pernille Askerud, *A Guide to Sustainable Book Provision* (UNESCO, 1997) 16.

38 Pernille Askerud, *A Guide to Sustainable Book Provision* (UNESCO, 1997) 16. 'Even middle-income countries such as Brazil, Uruguay, and Venezuela, have failed to maintain a regular supply of textbooks over the past fifteen years': at 16.

39 M Graham, SA Hale and M Stephens, *Geographies of the World Knowledge*, Corinne M Flick (ed), (Corinne M Flick, Convoco Foundation and Oxford Internet Institute, Convoco! ed, 2011) 14.

40 Ibid.

41 Ibid.

42 Ibid.

43 Ibid.

> anywhere, we should never assume that information is produced everywhere. Much of the world remains, both literally and figuratively, absent from the global map of knowledge.[44]

The internet plays a key role in the distribution of scientific and technical knowledge in the modern world. Sorosky stated that 'the Internet has become a primary means of communication and an indispensable tool for gathering information and exchanging ideas'.[45] For many, '[t]he Internet raised hopes that knowledge might become more accessible, reaching less affluent groups, as well as those farther away from the producers and sources of information'.[46] However, the internet is another area where the disparity between developed and developing countries with regard to production and distribution of scientific and technical knowledge is marked. As the *Geographies of World Knowledge* found, '[T]here are very few countries in the Global South with high internet penetration rates.'[47] More importantly, referring to the '[k]nowledge [the user-generated content] indexed by Google', the *Geographies of World Knowledge* highlighted the fact that there was a 'staggering amount of unevenness in the production and dissemination of information' between the developed and the developing countries. In particular, it revealed that the 'United States, and to a lesser extent Europe and Japan, are home to the bulk of the world's [user-generated] content', which is about 90 percent.[48]

The gap that exists between developed and developing countries in terms of the availability of scientific and technical knowledge is a severe problem in developing countries. This is because science and technology are key to economic development. Khan observed that '[d]ependence on Science [and] Technology as an instrument for attainment of national developmental goals, is a phenomenon seen all over the world.'[49] Also, Enderby noted that '[s]cience, engineering, technology, and innovation . . . are the bedrock of a successful economy, particularly as nations are moving toward knowledge-based economies.'[50]

There are a number of reasons for the knowledge gap between developed and developing countries in the field of science and technology. The primary reasons are the lack of financial resources invested in developing countries in scientific and technological research that would create knowledge in these fields and the

44 Ibid., 7.
45 Schuyler Sorosky, 'United States v Forrester: An Unwarranted Narrowing of the Fourth Amendment' (2008) 41 *Loyola of Los Angeles Law Review* 1121, 1121.
46 Graham, Hale and Stephens, above n 39, 7.
47 Ibid., 10.
48 Ibid., 26.
49 Hameed Ahmed Khan, *Education, Science and Technology in Developing Countries: Some Thoughts and Recollections* (COMSATS, 2004) 62.
50 John Enderby, 'Knowledge, Validation, and Transfer: Science, Communication, and Economic Development' in Glenn Schweitzer (ed), *Science and Technology and the Future Development of Societies, International Workshop Proceedings* (The National Academic Press, 2008) 5.

lack of expertise in these countries to carry out these activities. Suter stated, 'Ninety-seven percent of all the world's scientists are in the developed western and former communist nations. Eighty percent of humankind [only] have 3 percent of the world's scientists.'[51]

To bridge the knowledge gap in the field of science and technology, developing countries need to have improved access to scientific and technical knowledge created in developed countries. To overcome their lack of scientific and technical expertise, developing countries also need to promote scientific and technical education.[52] This also requires increased access to the stock of scientific and technical knowledge that is available in developed countries.

1.3.2. Dominance of English language in knowledge distribution

Another factor that creates problems for developing countries in ensuring that citizens are able to get access to knowledge is the dominance of the English language. English is the global *lingua franca* and, as such, dominates knowledge distribution around the world. According to *Geographies of World Knowledge*:

> English is a dominant language in academic publishing not only because of large number of journals published in the United States and United Kingdom. . . . English-language journals are also published from much of the rest of the world (English accounts for 86% of academic journals in the dataset).[53]

The dominance of English is particularly evident in the field of science and technology. There are two main reason for this. Firstly, the English-speaking world, particularly the Anglo-American countries, dominates the world in the field of science and technology.[54] Almost all of the material produced by scientists and academics in these countries is published in English. Secondly, given that English is the *lingua franca* of science, scientists and academics in the non-English-speaking world publish their writings in English in order to gain international recognition and to reach a wider audience. As Smith noted, leading academics, scholars and book authors in developing countries not only write in English but they also tend to give their books to internationally reputed publishers in London, Paris or New York.[55]

51 Keith Suter, *Global Order and Global Disorder: Globalization and the Nation-State* (Praeger Publishers, 2003) 186.

52 See, e.g., Ezeife and Arivalagan, above n 33, 13.

53 Graham, Hale and Stephens, above n 39, 16.

54 Rogerio Meneghini and Abel L Packer, 'Is there Science Beyond English?' (2007) 8(2) *EMBO Reports* 112.

55 Datus C Smith Jr, 'The Economics of Book Publishing' in Philip G Altbach and Edith S Hoshino (eds), *International Book Publishing: An Encyclopedia* (Garland Publishing, 1995) 71, 72.

The ramifications of British colonisation have also had an impact on the frequent use of English by authors in developing countries. Smith observed:

> Developing countries have for decades, or even centuries, depended on books written and published by their imperial masters, so there has been a very limited tradition of local authorship or of books written in their own languages and published in their own countries.[56]

Although English is the global *lingua franca*, English is not a language of general use in many developing countries. Instead, these countries use a multiplicity of local languages and dialects. For instance, while India is home to 1,652 languages belonging to several distinct language families,[57] there are 460 local languages currently in use in that country.[58] Of these, the 'Indian Constitution accords official status to only 22 languages, and . . . 43 languages function as instructional medium in schools.'[59] It is important to keep in mind that at least these constitutionally recognised languages are full-fledged languages, 'each spoken and cultivated for centuries by millions, and some, like Tamil, a contemporary of the classical Sanskrit, having a rich and continuous literary history for over two thousand years'.[60] According to a UNESCO publication, the publication and dissemination of knowledge products in India are inseparably related to the multilingual, multicultural and multi-ethnic realities of the country.[61]

Although English is used in India, the literacy in that language is only about 10 percent. Also, as the India Human Development Survey 2005 revealed:

> Among men, 72 percent do not speak English, 28 percent speak at least some English, and 5 percent are fluent. Among women, the corresponding proportions are 83 percent, 17 percent and 3 percent.[62]

This is despite the fact that this language had been imported into the country more than 200 years ago.

In contrast to India, Bangladesh is by and large considered to be a monolingual country. Yet a sizeable minority in Bangladesh are speakers of more than ten

56 Ibid., 71.
57 Usree Bhattacharya, 'Mediating Inequalities: Exploring English-Medium Instruction in a Suburban Indian Village School' (2013) 14(1) *Current Issues in Language Planning* 164, 165.
58 Lewis M Paul, Gary F Simons and Charles D Fennig (eds), *Ethnologue: Language of the World* (SIL International, 18th ed, 2015) <www.ethnologue.com>.
59 Bhattacharya, above n 57, 165.
60 Lokenath Bhattacharya, *Books and Reading in India* (UNESCO, 1985) 1.
61 Ibid.
62 Sonalde B Desai et al., *Human Development in India: Challenge for a Society* (Oxford University Press, 2010) 85.

additional languages such as Urdu, Monipuri, Chakma, Santali, Garo, Rakhain and Tipra.[63] Bangladesh, perhaps, provides the best example for the sacrosanctity of a mother tongue to its people, as well as its power and potential. The emergence of Bangladesh is essentially a result of a language. While the territory currently designated as Bangladesh constituted part of British India during the British colonial rule, at the end of this rule, it was established as one of two wings of the Dominion of Pakistan, then called East Pakistan.[64] Although Bengali (an Indo-European language which is the world's sixth or seventh largest language in terms of speakers)[65] was the mother tongue of the majority of the population in this territory, the government imposed Urdu as the State language on this population. Protest and a war of independence ensued against this, culminating in the independence of Bangladesh in 1971.[66]

Bangladesh made its own Constitution: *The Constitution of the People's Republic of Bangladesh 1972* within one year of its independence. While this Constitution 'reflected the aspiration of the heroic people who dedicated themselves to and the brave martyrs who sacrificed their lives in the liberation struggle', it adopted Bengali as the State language.[67] The subsequently enacted *Bengali Language Introduction Act 1987* further strengthened the power and use of Bengali, making the language a crucially important factor in national planning of the country, including the National Educational Policy.[68] While these initiatives have come at the expense of the use of English, Bengali has taken over almost all major domains, including education and administration which previously belonged to English.[69] The effects of this are particularly evident from the English literacy rate in the country. According to a Report of the Asian Development Bank, the 'English literacy rate in Bangladesh is less than in its neighbouring countries of India and Pakistan.'[70] As in the case of almost all national languages in developing countries, Bengali too has not been able to make its mark in or at least localize the global scientific and technical knowledgebase.

The dominance of the English language in the dissemination of scientific and technical knowledge products, especially those published in developed countries, is a problem for non-English-speaking developing countries. Given that English

63 MN Islam, 'Historical Evolution of English in Bangladesh' (2019) 10(2) *Journal of Language Teaching and Research*, 247.
64 See Elizabeth J Erling, 'Language Planning, English Language Education and Development Aid in Bangladesh' (2017) 18(4) *Current Issues in Language Planning* 388.
65 MN Islam, above n 63, 247.
66 Ibid.
67 Ibid.
68 Ibid., 251.
69 Ibid.
70 Asian Development Bank, *Innovative Strategies for Accelerated Human Resource Development in South Asia: Teacher Professional Development* (Report, ADB, 2017) 82.

is not a widely spoken language in these countries, scientific and technical knowledge products published in English are of very little use to these countries.[71]

1.4. Translation

It is clear from the preceding discussion that access to scientific and technical knowledge is essential for economic and human development, which is a key goal of developing countries. Given that science and technology are crucial for economic and human development, developing countries need to promote science and technology to further economic and human development. For this to occur, developing countries need to be able to access scientific and technical books and learning materials produced in developed countries. Ricketson and Ginsburg noted:

> Ways of achieving [economic development] are through the promotion of literacy and through technical and vocational training, and these programmes, in turn, necessitate ready access to a wide range of educational and informational materials.[72]

Because scientific and technical books and learning materials are mostly published in English or other languages that are commonly used in developed countries, to promote access to scientific and technical knowledge, developing countries need to translate these materials into the local languages.

Translation facilitates access to knowledge.[73] Translation basically involves rewriting knowledge from one language to another. This is perhaps particularly the case with regard to the translation of scientific and technical information. Translation enables people to access knowledge in a language in which they are conversant. If not for translation, people who are not conversant in the language in which knowledge is made available would be deprived of that knowledge. As diversity of languages is a natural and common phenomenon, translation is necessary if people around the world are to have meaningful access to knowledge.

There are two main arguments against translation. One is that as translation involves the rewriting of an original text from one language to another, the act of translating can misinterpret or even manipulate the thoughts and ideas in the original text.[74] The other argument is that the need for translation will not arise

71 See Farida Shaheed, Special Rapporteur in field of Cultural Rights, *Report on Copyright Policy and the Right to Science and Culture* UN Doc A/HRC/28/57 (24 December 2014) 14.

72 Sam Ricketson and Jane Ginsburg, *International Copyright and Neighbouring Rights: The Berne Convention and Beyond* (Oxford University Press, 2nd ed, 2006) vol 2, 882.

73 See European Commission Directorate-General for Translation, *Contribution of Translation to the Multilingual Society in the EU* (2010) 2.

74 See L Venuti, *The Translator's Invisibility: A History of Translation* (Routledge, 1995) vii. Also see Lionel Bently, 'Copyright and Translations in the English Speaking World' (1993) 12(4) *Translatio—FIT Newsletter* 491, 495.

at all when bilingualism (or multilingualism) is promoted—so that people can use one global language to communicate with each other. However, as will be seen later, these arguments are not persuasive, because the first is only a 'possible technicality' attributed to the process of translation, while the second is still far from reality.

The concern that translation can alter the original author's intended meaning is more or less related to the quality of the translation. The impact of poor translations can be disastrous. Yet it may not be prudent to attribute anything negative to the translation process in general by referring to idiosyncratic characteristics of a particular category of translations. Moreover, it is not possible to ignore the fact that quality translations are achievable, though this depends on various factors, one factor being the knowledge and skill of the translator.

Many commentators have pointed out that English is the global language of the modern world. However, this is not something that will necessarily be the case forever. For instance, Latin occupied the same position which English occupies today at a certain period in time.[75] Human society has existed for thousands of years, and yet the majority of people still do not speak a common language. Moreover, there are a significant number of people around the world who are not even literate in their own language. This is especially so in the developing world. For instance, India, which has the second largest population in the world, had 287 million adults who lacked basic literacy skills in 2010. In Bangladesh, this number was 44 million.[76] It is not realistic for such people to achieve literacy in another language (for example in English). Even if it is assumed that a global language was a possibility, it would have an adverse impact on aspects of human development, such as the right to self-determination, culture and language.

Given that developing countries are dependent on developed countries for scientific and technical knowledge, and that English is the dominant language in the field of science and technology, translation is needed for developing countries to promote access to scientific and technical knowledge.

Many developing countries have recognised the importance of translation in facilitating access to knowledge. India provides a good example in this connection. The National Translation Mission of India (NTM) observes that '[t]ranslation has a chequered history in India'.[77] While '[t]he Colonial period saw a spurt in translations between European languages and Indian languages', the 'British attempts in translation were determined by the Orientalist ideology and the need

75 See European Commission Directorate-General for Translation, *Lingua Franca: Chimera or Reality?* (2011) 9–26. Also see E Cary, 'Translation in the Modern World' *The UNESCO Courier*, April 1958, 9, 9.

76 UNESCO, *Adult and Youth Literacy, 1990–2015: Analysis of Data for 41 Selected Countries* (UNESCO Institute for Statistics, 2012) 6.

77 The National Translation Mission, *A Detailed Project Report* (Central Institute of Indian Languages, February 2008) 1.

for the new rulers to grasp, define, categorise and control India'.[78] 'Translations between Indian languages also began around this time, though in a limited way.'[79]

A 1985 UNESCO publication pointed out that the Ministry of Education in India was 'considering a proposal to chalk out [a] programme for translation and low-priced publication of university-level textbooks including teaching aids and materials of the same standard, particularly in the fields pertaining to natural sciences and technology'.[80] By this time, various programmes for the translation of low-priced editions of suitable university-level books of foreign origin into Indian languages and their publication were already in place at the State government level.[81] The Indian central government supported and aided 'the state governments for facilitating and co-ordinating the task of obtaining translation rights from the foreign copyright owners with regard to such university-level books as may have been selected by the state governments in question under these programmes.'[82]

The Government of India has taken further initiatives to promote access to knowledge through translation in recent times. Of these, quite significant is the establishment of the NTM, which is an initiative to make knowledge products accessible in all the languages listed in the Eighth Schedule of the Indian Constitution through translation. The idea of the NTM came originally from Prime Minister Dr Manmohan Singh:[83]

> In the first meeting of the National Knowledge Commission (NKC), he mentioned how it was vital to access translated materials for increasing access to knowledge in many critical areas and broadening and strengthening people's participation in education and continuous learning.[84]

Sri Sam Pitroda who chaired the Commission took note of the suggestion and felt the immediate need to have a separate institution or mission to promote the cause of translation for education in India.[85]

The NTM, which has sprung out of the firm belief that knowledge should be available to the common men and women in India who are anxious to access the highest knowledge through their mother tongues,[86] has identified that '[t]here is an unrecognised demand for translation in diverse existing and emerging

78 Ibid.
79 Ibid.
80 Bhattacharya, above n 60, 20.
81 Ibid.
82 Ibid.
83 The National Translation Mission, above n 77, 4.
84 The National Translation Mission, 'Origin' <www.ntm.org.in/languages/english/origin.aspx>.
85 Ibid.
86 The National Translation Mission, above n 77, 3.

domains like literature, pure sciences, applied sciences, social sciences, law, medicine, management, technology and more'.[87] While there is a broad range of target beneficiaries of the NTM, the first and foremost are the students from the weaker sections of the society who have very little or no access to scientific and technical knowledge, which is available mainly in English.[88] The NTM has clearly emphasized that 'the Mission will attain its true objective only if and when the translated texts from diverse disciplines reach these seekers of knowledge from the marginalized sections of [the Indian] society'.[89]

1.4.1. Special needs of developing countries

Developing countries have certain special needs when it comes to translation of knowledge products for the purpose of promoting access to scientific and technical knowledge. Developing countries need scientific and technical books and learning materials from developed countries for use in mass educational, technical and vocational training programs. Because of this, developing countries need to translate the whole (as opposed to parts) of these knowledge products into local languages. Developing countries also need to reproduce translations in large quantities in order for students and teachers to have proper access to them. Okediji observed:

> Bulk access . . . is . . . critical to developing countries where education is a top development priority. For such countries, the freedom to quote from [knowledge products] is secondary to the need for affordable access to educational texts, scientific journals and other learning materials.[90]

One of the key characteristics of modern science and technology is the speed of change. Given that scientific and technical books and learning materials are rendered obsolete very quickly, it is important that these materials are translated within a very short period after their publication.[91] For developing countries to have meaningful access to scientific and technical knowledge, the translations of scientific and technical books and learning materials produced in developed countries must also be affordable. Developing countries should be able to translate books and learning materials and reproduce the translations at an affordable cost to the public.

87 Ibid., 4.
88 Ibid., 12.
89 Ibid.
90 Ruth L Okediji, 'Africa and the Global Intellectual Property System: Beyond the Agency Model' (2004) 12 *African Year Book of International Law* 207, 230.
91 Chamila Talagala and Leanne Wiseman, 'Copyright, Open Access and Translation' (2015) 37(8) *European Intellectual Property Review* 498, 499.

1.5. Copyright

Many factors affect the translation of scientific and technical books and learning materials in developing countries. One of these, which is the focus of this book, is copyright law. In particular, copyright protection of translation rights has the potential to constrain the ability of developing countries to translate scientific and technical books and learning materials produced in developed countries in a timely and affordable manner.

Copyright law confers an exclusive right on copyright owners of original literary and scientific works to translate their works. Protection of the exclusive right to translate can restrict translation. This is because no other person can translate copyright protected works without the authorisation of the copyright owner. It may be argued that extending copyright protection to include translation encourages the translation of works. Although this is theoretically correct, in reality translation rights have not encouraged copyright owners to translate their works into local languages in developing countries. The reason is that translation often only occurs where there is a lucrative market for translations.[92]

Translations are generally protected as original literary and scientific works under copyright law. Protection of translations as original literary and scientific works under copyright law can restrict the dissemination of a particular translation. In particular, if A translates a book, A receives copyright protection for that translation. No other person can use A's translation without authorisation. However, copyright protection for A's translation does not prevent someone else from translating the original book. Because of this, protection of translations as original literary and scientific works under copyright law is not as serious an issue as protection of copyright owners' translation rights for persons or countries who need to translate the original copyright protected works.

The primary objective of copyright law (at least in common law countries) is public benefit.[93] To this end, copyright performs a balancing act between (1) protecting the rights of creators of literary and scientific works and (2) the ability of the public to use these works. More specifically, copyright law grants certain legal rights to the creators of literary and scientific works in order to encourage them to create more of these works, which will ultimately benefit the public. At the same time, copyright law provides for certain exceptions to these legal rights in order to ensure that the public has the ability to use these works.

Although copyright law is a balancing act, the trend that has prevailed over the past two centuries has been to expand and to add to the rights of owners of copyright protected works without commensurate attention being given to

92 See Lea Shaver, 'Local Language Limitations: Copyright and the Commons' (Working Paper, August 2014) <www.law.berkeley.edu/files/Shaver_Lea_IPSC_paper_2014.pdf>; Farida Shaheed, Special Rapporteur in field of Cultural Rights, *Report on Copyright Policy and the Right to Science and Culture* UN Doc A/HRC/28/57 (24 December 2014); Lea Shaver, 'Copyright and Inequality' (2014) 92 *Washington University Law Review* 117.

93 Bently, above n 74, 491.

the exceptions to these rights which promote the interests of the users of these works.[94] Absorption of translation rights into the bundle of rights granted to the owners of copyright protected works is a classic example of this situation. In particular, copyright law in the English-speaking world did not protect the translation rights of the authors of copyright protected works up until the second half of the nineteenth century. More specifically, Britain only started to protect translation rights in 1852 through the *International Copyright Act 1852*. However, the translation rights protected by the 1852 Act were extremely limited and only applied to foreign authors. Eventually, it was only via the *Imperial Copyright Act 1911* that Britain protected the translation rights of all authors for the full duration of the term of copyright protection. At its inception, the *Berne Convention for the Protection of Literary and Artistic Works 1886* (*Berne Convention*), which is the most important instrument determining international copyright, did not protect the translation rights of authors for the full duration of the term of copyright protection. Instead, this *Convention* only started to protect the translation rights of authors for the full duration of the term of copyright protection from 1908.

Copyright laws of many developing countries are of British origin. This is because of British colonisation which started in the eighteenth century. India, Bangladesh and Sri Lanka are examples in this connection. For instance, the domestic copyright law in India can be traced back to 1847, when the English East India Company enacted the first copyright statute in India.[95] In 1914, the *Indian Copyright Act* was enacted, and its provisions were largely based on the *Imperial Copyright Act 1911*.[96] Bangladesh also has inherited the copyright system from Great Britain. In fact, the *Imperial Copyright Act 1911* of Great Britain 'was extended to Bangladesh (then part of British India) in 1914'.[97] As will be seen later, British copyright law began to be applied in Sri Lanka at least from 1842 and the *Imperial Copyright Act 1911* was extended to Sri Lanka in 1912. While the current Indian law dealing with copyright protection, namely, the *Indian Copyright Act 1957*, is based on the *Copyright Act 1914*, it also extensively borrows provisions from the *Copyright Act 1956* of Great Britain.[98] The current copyright law in Bangladesh, which is provided for in the *Copyright Act 2000*,[99] is predominantly based on the British model of copyright. The present copyright law applicable in Sri Lanka, which is provided in the *Intellectual Property Act*

94 Strba, above n 36, 2.
95 Daniel Seng, 'WIPO Study on the Copyright Exceptions for the Benefit of Educational Activities for Asia and Australia' (SCCR/19/7, WIPO, 29 October 2009) 64.
96 *Copyright Act 1911*, 1 & 2 Geo 5, c 46; Daniel Seng, 'WIPO Study on the Copyright Exceptions for the Benefit of Educational Activities for Asia and Australia' (SCCR/19/7, WIPO, 29 October 2009) 64.
97 Daniel Seng, 'WIPO Study on the Copyright Exceptions for the Benefit of Educational Activities for Asia and Australia' (SCCR/19/7, WIPO, 29 October 2009) 44.
98 Ibid., 64.
99 Ibid., 44.

2003, also follows the British tradition of copyright, though certain provisions therein have been taken verbatim from the United States *Copyright Act 1976*.[100]

India was one of the first Asian countries to join the *Berne Convention* in 1928, and Bangladesh became a Member State to this *Convention* in 1999.[101] Sri Lanka, as an independent nation, took the Berne membership in 1959.[102] Copyright statutes in these three countries have been substantially revised to ensure that they adhere to the *Berne Convention* and its revisions.[103]

1.5.1. Translation rights and their effect on translation

International copyright law[104] and the national copyright laws of most countries around the world protect the translation rights of owners of original literary and scientific works. Article 8 of the *Berne Convention* (*Paris Act 1971*) states:

> Authors of literary and artistic works protected by this Convention shall enjoy the exclusive right of making and of authorising the translation of their works throughout the term of protection of their rights in the original works.

The *Agreement on Trade Related Aspects of Intellectual Property Rights 1994* (*TRIPS Agreement*) obliges Member Countries to comply with, inter alia, Article 8 of the *Berne Convention* (*Paris Act 1971*).[105] As of 2020, the *Berne Convention* has 171 Member Countries, and the *TRIPS Agreement* has 164 Member Countries. All these countries are obliged to protect translation rights in their national copyright laws.

India, Bangladesh and Sri Lanka are Member Countries to both the *Berne Convention* and the *TRIPS Agreement*. The Indian *Copyright Act 1957* provides that translation of the copyright protected work without the consent or license of the owner of the copyright will constitute copyright infringement.[106] In terms of the Bangladeshi *Copyright Act 2000*, copyright covers the right to 'produce, reproduce, perform or publish' any translation of a copyright protected work or

100 See, e.g., *Intellectual Property Act No.36 of 2003*, s 11.
101 WIPO, *WIPO-Administered Treaties—Contracting Parties: Berne Convention* <www.wipo.int/treaties/en/ShowResults.jsp?treaty_id=15>.
102 WIPO, *Treaties and Contracting Parties: Contracting Parties—Berne Convention—Sri Lanka* <www.wipo.int/treaties/en/remarks.jsp?cnty_id=1028C>.
103 Daniel Seng, 'WIPO Study on the Copyright Exceptions for the Benefit of Educational Activities for Asia and Australia' (SCCR/19/7, WIPO, 29 October 2009) 64.
104 As determined by the *Berne Convention* and the *Agreement on Trade Related Aspects of Intellectual Property Rights 1994* (*TRIPS Agreement*).
105 See Christopher May and Susan K Sell, *Intellectual Property Rights: A Critical History* (Lynne Rienner Publishers, 2006) 4.
106 See *Copyright Act No.14 of 1957* (India) s 14(a)(v); *Blackwood v. Parasuraman* 1959 AIR 410.

to authorise the doing of the same.[107] The Sri Lankan *Intellectual Property Act 2003*, also prohibits translation of a copyright protected work without the consent or license of the owner of the copyright.[108] As such, authors' (copyright owners') translation rights are protected under the copyright laws of India, Bangladesh and Sri Lanka.

Translation rights give the owners of copyright protected works the right to exclude or prohibit people from translating their works. This means that people who want to translate copyright protected works first need to obtain permission for the translation from the owners of these works. Translation rights (together with the right of reproduction) enable the copyright owners to exclude or prohibit others from reproducing translations of their works. As the authors of *Copinger and Skone James on Copyright* observed, the owners of copyright protected works have the right to restrain the reproduction of their works in 'original or any translated form.' As such, '[a]nyone wishing to reproduce a particular translation should therefore obtain a license from the owner of the copyright in . . . the original'.[109] While it is not clear whether this position is accurate,[110] nonetheless, in practice, copyright owners can restrain translators and other parties from reproducing translations of their works by imposing conditions in the license agreements. Translation rights ensure that copyright owners can exercise control over the process of translating their works, as well as over the resulting translations. In particular, copyright owners can exercise control over whether to translate their works, who should translate them, how and when it should be done, whether the translations should be reproduced (in printed format or online), who should reproduce the translations and what the cost should be.

Translation rights potentially impact on translation in three main ways. Firstly, translation rights can prevent the translation of copyright protected works altogether (when copyright owners refuse to allow their works to be translated).[111]

107 See *Copyright Act 2000* (Bangladesh) s 14(1)(d) & (h).

108 See *Intellectual Property Act No.36 of 2003* (Sri Lanka) s 9(1)(b).

109 Gillian Davies, Nicholas Caddick and Gwilym Harbottle, *Copinger and Skone James on Copyright* (Sweet & Maxwell, 17th ed South Asian, 2019) vol 1, 664; Kevin Garnett, Gillian Davies and Gwilym Harbottle, *Copinger and Skone James on Copyright* (Sweet & Maxwell, 16th ed, 2011) 515.

110 The authority cited in support of this proposition is *Murray v Bogue* (1853) 1 Drew 353. However, the ratio decidendi of this case appears to be that '[i]f a foreigner translates an English work, and then an Englishman retranslates that foreign work into English, that would be an infringement of the original copyright'—*Murray v Bogue* (1853) 1 Drew 353, 353.

Also see Bently, above n 74, 491, 508, where Bently, citing this case as authority, stated that:

> If A wrote a novel in English and B translated it into French, then in the absence of such a right C could translate B's translation into English and directly compete with A's original work. In this case, however, there might simply be an indirect infringement of A's reproduction rights.

111 Bently, above n 74, 491, 496.

Secondly, translation rights can impose a financial burden on those who wish to translate copyright protected works and reproduce translations. As copyright owners can charge license fees for allowing others to translate copyright protected works and to reproduce the translations, translation rights can 'increase the cost of translations to the public'.[112] Thirdly, translation rights can impose an administrative burden on those who wish to translate copyright protected works and to reproduce translations. This is particularly the case with copyright protected works published in foreign countries. In particular, parties who wish to translate these works and to reproduce the translations have to obtain the consent of copyright owners who are usually resident in foreign countries. Locating the copyright owners and communicating with them can sometimes be difficult, time-consuming and expensive. The effect of these three factors is that translation rights may be a constraint on translation of copyright protected works and reproduction of translations. This is particularly the case in developing countries, where there is a pressing need for translations of copyright protected scientific and technical books and learning materials to be made available in a timely and affordable manner.

1.5.2. Exceptions to translation rights

Over the years, copyright law has recognised certain exceptions to translation rights. These exceptions have the objective of ensuring that the public has a chance to translate copyright protected works (and reproducing the translations so made) without the authorisation of the copyright owner. International copyright law and the national copyright laws of countries (which follow international copyright obligations) provide for two general types of exceptions to translation rights: general exceptions to translation rights and special exceptions to translation rights.

1.5.2.1. General exceptions

The *Berne Convention* does not expressly provide for general exceptions to translation rights. By implication, however, the general exceptions therein applicable to the right of reproduction may be applicable to translation rights as well.[113] In contrast, the *TRIPS Agreement* explicitly allows general exceptions to be applicable to all exclusive rights of the copyright owners, including translation rights.[114]

Article 9(2) of the *Berne Convention* (*Paris Act 1971*) which provides for the main general exception to authors' rights reads:

> It shall be a matter for legislation in the countries of the Union to permit the reproduction of [literary and artistic] works in certain special cases, provided

112 Ibid.
113 See *Berne Convention* (*Paris Act 1971*) art 9.
114 *TRIPS Agreement*, art 13.

> that such reproduction does not conflict with a normal exploitation of the work and does not unreasonably prejudice the legitimate interests of the author.

Although this exception does not expressly refer to translation, it is arguable that the exception applies equally to translation rights by implication.

The *TRIPS Agreement* is clearer than the *Berne Convention* on the issue of the coverage of translation rights under the general exception to authors' rights. In particular, Article 13 of the *TRIPS Agreement* states the following:

> Members shall confine limitations or exceptions to exclusive rights to certain special cases which do not conflict with a normal exploitation of the work and do not unreasonably prejudice the legitimate interests of the right holder.

Although Article 9(2) of the *Berne Convention* (*Paris Act 1971*) and Article 13 of the *TRIPS Agreement* set out certain conditions upon which the general exceptions to translation rights should be based, these provisions leave the determination of the exact scope of these exceptions to Member Countries.[115] As a result, the exact scope of the general exceptions to translation rights remains uncertain. In any event, it is unlikely that Article 9(2) of the *Berne Convention* (*Paris Act 1971*) and Article 13 of the *TRIPS Agreement* would allow Member Countries to adopt broad exceptions which would enable the copyright protected scientific and technical books and learning materials to be translated in a timely and affordable manner.[116]

In practice, the most common way in which Article 9(2) of the *Berne Convention* (*Paris Act 1971*) and Article 13 of the *TRIPS Agreement* are implemented into national copyright laws is through fair dealing or fair use exceptions.[117] For instance, while India and Bangladesh employ the fair dealing exception,[118] Sri Lanka uses the fair use exception.[119] There is much uncertainty attached to the

115 Also, these conditions are ill-defined. See especially Ruth L Okediji, 'The International Copyright System: Limitations, Exceptions and Public Interest Considerations for Developing Countries' (Issue Paper No 15, ICTSD and UNCTAD, March 2006) <http://unctad.org/en/Docs/iteipc200610_en.pdf>; Ricketson and Ginsburg, above n 72, vol 1, 763–783; Justin Malbon, Charles Lawson and Mark Davison, *The WTO Agreement on Trade-Related Aspects of Intellectual Property Rights: A Commentary* (Edward Elgar, 2014) 256–264; Daniel Gervais, *The TRIPS Agreement: Drafting History and Analysis* (Sweet & Maxwell, 3rd ed, 2008) 236–243.

116 See especially Okediji, above n 115.

117 The United States *Copyright Act 1976* provides for fair use. The British *Copyright, Designs and Patents Act 1988* and the *Australian Copyright Act 1968* (Cth) provide for fair dealing. *Copyright Act 1976* (United States), s 107; *Copyright, Designs and Patents Act 1988*, ss 29, 30; *Copyright Act 1968* (Cth) ss 40, 41, 41A, 42, 43(2), 103A, 103AA, 103B, 103C.

118 See *Copyright Act No.14 of 1957* (India) s 52; See *Copyright Act 2000* (Bangladesh) s 72.

119 See *Intellectual Property Act No.36 of 2003* (Sri Lanka) ss 11 & 12.

scope of fair dealing and fair use exceptions, particularly in countries that follow the legal traditions of Britain and the United States. As Lord Denning said in *Hubbard v Vosper*,[120] '[i]t is impossible to define what is "fair dealing". It must be a question of degree.'[121] First, 'the number and extent of the quotations and extracts' must be considered in order to decide whether 'they [are] altogether too many and too long to be fair?'[122] Then 'the use made of them' must be considered. 'If they are used as a basis for comment, criticism or review, that may be fair dealing. If they are used to convey the same information as the author, for a rival purpose, that may be unfair.'[123] Next, 'the proportions' that were taken must be considered. 'To take long extracts and attach short comments may be unfair. But, short extracts and long comments may be fair.'[124] While there may also be other matters that would have to be considered, 'after all is said and done, it must be a matter of impression'.[125]

The fair use exception used in the United States is also an ill-defined defence. In *Triangle Publications v Knight-Ridder Newspapers*,[126] the United States Court of Appeals (Fifth Circuit) observed that '[t]he question of fair use has been appropriately described as "the most troublesome in the whole law of copyright" '.[127] Although there does not exist 'a definition of fair use that is workable in every case', it has been frequently used to refer to 'a privilege in [persons other] than the owner of a copyright to use the copyrighted material in a reasonable manner without his consent, notwithstanding the monopoly granted to the owner [by the copyright].'[128]

It is also questionable whether the fair dealing and fair use exceptions would allow all of a copyright protected work to be translated and the resulting translation to be reproduced in large quantities. As such, the fair dealing and fair use exceptions are unlikely to address the needs of developing countries with regard to the translation of scientific and technical books and learning materials produced in developed countries.

1.5.2.2. Special exceptions

The Appendix to the *Paris Act 1971* of the *Berne Convention* contains special exceptions to translation rights that developing countries can adopt in their national copyright laws. This allows a developing country to either limit the duration of translation rights to a period of ten years or to issue compulsory licenses

120 [1972] 2 QB 84.
121 Ibid., 94.
122 Ibid.
123 Ibid.
124 Ibid.
125 Ibid.
126 626 F.2d 1171 (1980).
127 Ibid., 1174 (citations omitted).
128 Ibid., (citations omitted).

for translations.[129] Both India and Bangladesh have made use of the special faculties provided in the *Berne Appendix*, whereas the Copyright Boards established under the Indian *Copyright Act 1957* and Bangladeshi *Copyright Act 2000* are empowered to issue compulsory licenses to produce and publish translations of copyright protected works.[130] Accordingly, both in India and Bangladesh, a license to produce and publish a translation of a copyright protected foreign work in any language in general use in those countries may be obtained from the Copyright Board by any person after a period of three years from the first publication of such work.[131] Where such translation is in a language not in general use in any developed country, however, the application for license may be made after a period of one year from such publication.[132] But there are numerous conditions that are needed to be satisfied by an applicant for the granting of such a license by the Copyright Board, which makes the entire process cumbersome and rigid.[133] As will be seen in chapter 4 of this book, these special exceptions were introduced to appease the interests of developing countries in relation to translation rights. It was hoped that these provisions would promote translation and thus improve access to knowledge in developing countries. Despite this, there are two main drawbacks to these special exceptions: the long delays and the administrative and procedural burdens involved in translating copyright protected works. Under the *Berne Convention*, a developing country is required to wait for three years and six months before issuing a compulsory license for translation.[134] Obviously, this waiting period for issuing translation licenses, and the 10-year limit on the duration of translation rights, are too long when dealing with the translation of scientific and technical books and learning materials. In addition, the various administrative and procedural requirements involved in the process of applying for compulsory licenses not only cause delays but also increase the cost of translation. The result is that these exceptions do not address the needs of developing countries.

1.6. Structure of the book

The introductory chapter of this book has set out how translation of copyright protected works is crucially important for promoting access to scientific and technical knowledge in developing countries in general. It has also portrayed the

129 See Appendix to the *Berne Convention* (*Paris Act, 1971*) arts I, II and V. Also see *Berne Convention* (*Paris Act 1971*) art 30.

130 See *Copyright Act No.14 of 1957* (India) s 32; See *Copyright Act 2000* (Bangladesh) s 52.

131 Ibid.

132 Ibid.

133 Ibid.

134 Appendix to the *Berne Convention* (*Paris Act 1971*) arts II(2)(a) and II(4)(a). However, in the case of translations into a language which is not in general use in one or more developed countries that are members of the Berne Union, the waiting period could be one year and nine months. See Appendix to the *Berne Convention* (*Paris Act 1971*) arts II(3)(a) and II(4)(a).

existing imbalance in copyright laws of developing countries between the protection of translation rights and the ability of people to access translations of copyright protected scientific and technical books and learning materials.

As the main objective of this book is to expound why developing countries have failed to strike a proper balance in their copyright laws between the protection of translation rights and the ability of people to access translations of copyright protected scientific and technical books and learning materials by taking Sri Lanka as a case study, the second chapter of this book explores the importance of access to scientific and technical knowledge for Sri Lanka, the role of translation in relation to improving access to scientific and technical knowledge in Sri Lanka and the impact of copyright law in Sri Lanka on translation. In particular, the second chapter examines: the characteristics of Sri Lanka, why access to scientific and technical knowledge is important to Sri Lanka, why translation is important to promoting access to scientific and technical knowledge in Sri Lanka and how the present copyright law in Sri Lanka affects translation. In doing so, chapter 2 demonstrates that access to scientific and technical knowledge is essential for Sri Lanka to meet its development goals. To promote access to scientific and technical knowledge, Sri Lanka needs to translate and publish scientific and technical books and learning materials (which are mostly produced in developed countries). This needs to be done quickly, in large quantities and at prices that are affordable. However, the way in which the present copyright law in Sri Lanka (as determined by the *Intellectual Property Act 2003*) protects translation rights impedes translation of copyright protected scientific and technical books and learning materials and their reproduction in a timely and affordable manner.

The third, fourth and fifth chapters of this book examine—through the lens of the history of Sri Lankan copyright law—the reason that the copyright law in Sri Lanka protects translation rights stringently. As demonstrated in chapters 3, 4 and 5, the history of the copyright law of Sri Lanka can be divided into three stages, namely, the 'British model of copyright law', the 'WIPO model of copyright law' and the 'TRIPS model of copyright law'.

The third chapter examines the British model of copyright law which was in force in Sri Lanka from 1908 to 1979. In particular, it examines how translation rights were protected under the *Copyright Ordinance 1908* and the *Imperial Copyright Act 1911*, which determined the copyright law of Sri Lanka during this period. Since both of these statutes were of British origin, in order to identify how and why translation rights came to be recognised as copyright owners' rights under these statutes, chapter 3 traces the history of translation rights in the copyright law of Britain from 1476 to 1911. This chapter also demonstrates that the British model of copyright law in Sri Lanka did not facilitate translation of copyright protected scientific and technical books and learning materials on time and their reproduction in large quantities at affordable prices because it protected translation rights stringently. Despite this, Sri Lanka implemented the British model of copyright law because of its colonial legacy.

The fourth chapter focuses on how and why the copyright law which was in force in Sri Lanka from 1979 to 2003 (the WIPO model of copyright law) protected translation rights. In particular, chapter 4 demonstrates that the *Code of Intellectual Property Act 1979* (*IP Code*), which exclusively determined the copyright law of Sri Lanka during this period, protected translation rights extensively and as a result did not facilitate the translation of copyright protected scientific and technical books and learning materials. The *IP Code* protected translation rights extensively because it was based on the *WIPO Model Law on Copyright for Developing Countries*,[135] which was, in turn, based on the obligations of the *Berne Convention*. More specifically, at the time Sri Lanka enacted the *IP Code*, it was a Member to the *Berne Convention*. This *Convention* requires Member Countries to protect translation rights rigorously. The *WIPO Model Law on Copyright for Developing Countries* is a model law which was prepared in 1976 for the benefit of developing countries that need to comply with the obligations of the *Berne Convention* but lack necessary expertise in formulating copyright laws on their own. Because Sri Lanka did not have the required expertise to formulate its copyright law on its own, it adopted the provisions of the *WIPO Model Law on Copyright for Developing Countries* in the *IP Code*.

The fifth chapter of this book examines the TRIPS model of copyright law, which has been in force in Sri Lanka since 2003. As it is pointed out in chapter 2 that the current copyright law of Sri Lanka (as determined by the *Intellectual Property Act 2003*) protects copyright owners' translation rights in a manner that inhibit access to scientific and technical knowledge, chapter 5 examines the reasons for Sri Lanka enacting the TRIPS model of copyright law.

Chapter 6 concludes the book by focusing on the necessity to reform international copyright law (*Berne Convention*, *TRIPS Agreement* and other initiatives) to promote the needs and interests of developing countries. It also emphasises a possible way forward for developing countries to achieve this and to address the problem of striking a proper balance in their copyright laws between the protection of translation rights and the ability of people to access translations of copyright protected scientific and technical books and learning materials.

135 Also referred to as the *Tunis Model Law on Copyright for Developing Countries*.

II Access to scientific and technical knowledge, translation and copyright in Sri Lanka

2.1. Introduction

The purpose of this chapter is to examine the interrelation between access to scientific and technical knowledge, translation and copyright law in Sri Lanka. More specifically, this chapter examines three issues in connection to this: the reasons why access to scientific and technical knowledge is important for Sri Lanka, the role of translation in relation to access to scientific and technical knowledge in Sri Lanka and the way in which copyright law in Sri Lanka affects translation.

This chapter will argue that in order to develop economically and to raise the living standards of its people, Sri Lanka needs to promote access to scientific and technical knowledge. To this end, timely and affordable translation of scientific and technical knowledge products (books and learning materials) produced in developed countries is vital for Sri Lanka. However, the way in which translation rights are protected by copyright law of Sri Lanka is a constraint on timely and affordable translation of scientific and technical knowledge products. This means that the way in which the Sri Lankan copyright law protects translation rights restricts access to scientific and technical knowledge in Sri Lanka.

2.2. Importance of access to scientific and technical knowledge

Access to scientific and technical knowledge is crucially important for Sri Lanka's efforts to further human and economic development, as well as to fulfil its constitutional and international human rights obligations.

Sri Lanka is highly regarded for its notable achievements in human development.[1] Yet, it has much more to achieve in terms of economic development. According to the World Bank, 'Sri Lanka is a lower middle-income country with a GDP per capita of USD 3853' for the year 2019.[2] To further economic

1 See especially UNDP, *Sri Lanka National Human Development Report 2014: Youth and Development: Towards a More Inclusive Future* (2014) vii.

2 World Bank, 'Sri Lanka Home: Overview' <www.worldbank.org/en/country/srilanka/overview>.

development, Sri Lanka needs to promote education, literacy in science and technology, creativity and innovation. For this, Sri Lanka requires greater access to scientific and technical knowledge. Promoting access to scientific and technical knowledge is also important to ensure that Sri Lanka meets its constitutional and international human rights obligations.

2.2.1. Economic development

Economic development has been an overriding goal for Sri Lanka ever since it became a sovereign nation in 1948. Sri Lanka believes that building a knowledge economy is fundamental for the country's economic development. In particular, the manifesto of the newly elected President in 2019 places much emphasis on the importance of having a knowledge-centred economy for the country's advancement.[3] This echoes the 2010 *Development Policy Framework of the Government of Sri Lanka*, which envisioned 'policies and measures to be implemented . . . to reposition Sri Lanka in the global arena as a knowledge based strong middle income country with better and improved living standards.'[4]

In order to build a knowledge economy, it is vital for Sri Lanka to promote science and technology, education and research.[5] Indisputably, developing science and technology, and strengthening education, training, skills and human resources requires increased access to scientific and technical knowledge.

2.2.2. Constitutional obligations

Promoting access to scientific and technical knowledge is also important in order to allow Sri Lanka to meet its constitutional obligations under the *Constitution of the Democratic Socialist Republic of Sri Lanka 1978* (*Constitution 1978*). While access to scientific and technical knowledge is not a human right guaranteed under the *Constitution 1978*, its provisions relating to fundamental human rights and directive principles do require the Sri Lankan State to ensure access to scientific and technical knowledge in the country.

The *Constitution 1978*, which is the supreme law of the land, declares the fundamental human rights protected in Sri Lanka. These rights, which are part of the 'Sovereignty of the People', must be 'respected, secured and advanced by all organs of government and shall not be abridged, restricted or denied, save in the manner and to the extent [provided by the *Constitution*]'.[6]

The fundamental human rights recognised in the *Constitution 1978* include freedom of thought, conscience and religion; freedom from torture; the right to equality; freedom from arbitrary arrest, detention and punishment; prohibition

3 Gotabaya Rajapaksa, *Vistas of Prosperity and Splendour* (2019) 20, 50.
4 Ministry of Finance and Planning, *Mahinda Chinthana—Vision for the Future: The Development Policy Framework, Government of Sri Lanka* (2010) 2.
5 See Ali Madanipour, *Knowledge Economy and the City: Spaces of Knowledge* (Routledge, 2011) 11.
6 *Constitution of the Democratic Socialist Republic of Sri Lanka 1978*, arts 3 & 4(d).

of retrospective penal legislation; freedom of speech, expression, assembly, association, occupation and movement; and the right to access to information.[7] Although not explicitly enshrined in the *Constitution 1978*, the human right to education is also recognised. As observed by the Supreme Court of Sri Lanka in *Kavirathne and Others v Commissioner General of Examinations and Others*:[8]

> [A]lthough there is no specific provision dealing with the right to Education in [the Sri Lankan] Constitution as such in the Universal Declaration of Human Rights, the said right has been accepted and acknowledged by [the Sri Lankan] Courts through the provisions embodied in Article 12 (1) of the Constitution.[9]

Although access to scientific and technical knowledge is not recognised as a human right in the *Constitution 1978*, it affects the realisation of certain human rights guaranteed under the Constitution, such as the right to education.

Access to scientific and technical knowledge is a corollary of the right to education guaranteed under the *Constitution 1978*. As observed in the previous chapter, the right to education envisages providing students with access to scientific and technical knowledge for their learning, which includes teaching as well as provision of scientific and technical educational and learning materials. In recognising this, the government of Sri Lanka has been providing free textbooks for education (including science and technical education) at the primary and secondary level (Grade 1 to 11) since 1980.[10]

Apart from its provisions guaranteeing human rights, the *Constitution 1978* also has certain provisions in its Directive Principles of State Policy which address matters regarding access to scientific and technical knowledge. In particular, these provisions state that Sri Lanka is pledged to establish 'a Democratic Socialist Society', the objectives of which include, inter alia:

> [T]he realisation by all citizens of an adequate standard of living for themselves and their families, including . . . the full enjoyment of . . . social and cultural opportunities;[11]
>
> [T]he equitable distribution among all citizens of the material resources of the community and the social product, so as best to subserve the common good;[12]
>
> [T]he rapid development of the whole country by means of public and private economic activity . . . [13]

7 Ibid., arts 10–14.
8 (2012) BLR 139.
9 Ibid., 150 (emphasis added).
10 Swarna Jayaweera and Chandra Gunawardena, *Social Inclusion: Gender and Equity in Education SWAPS in South Asia: Sri Lanka Case Study* (UNICEF, 2007) 74.
11 *Constitution of the Democratic Socialist Republic of Sri Lanka 1978*, art 27(2)(c).
12 Ibid., art 27(2)(e).
13 Ibid., art 27(1)(d).

> [T]he complete eradication of illiteracy and the assurance to all persons of the right to universal and equal access to education at all levels.[14]

Access to scientific and technical knowledge is vital if Sri Lanka is to realise these objectives. In particular, living standards can only be raised through economic and social development, which itself requires wider access to scientific and technical knowledge. Also, wider access to scientific and technical knowledge is essential for the full enjoyment of social and cultural opportunities, the rapid development of the whole country, the eradication of illiteracy and promoting access to scientific and technical education.[15] Moreover, since scientific and technical knowledge is one of the most valuable resources in the modern world, equal distribution of material resources of the community among all citizens entails equal distribution of scientific and technical knowledge in material form, such as books and leaning materials.

Although the objectives under the Directive Principles of State Policy are not strict obligations imposed on the State of Sri Lanka,[16] the *Constitution 1978* nevertheless confers a duty on Sri Lanka to be at least mindful of these objectives in the governance and enactment of laws. In particular, the *Constitution* states that Directive Principles of State Policy 'shall guide Parliament, the President and the Cabinet of Ministers in the enactment of laws and governance of Sri Lanka for the establishment of a just and free society'.[17] Also, the Supreme Court of Sri Lanka has declared that the Directive Principles of State Policy 'must be given due recognition, and proper allowance [must be] made for their operation and functioning as part and parcel of the constitution'.[18] The Supreme Court has further stated that the Directive Principles of State Policy 'are in the nature of an instrument of instructions which both the legislature and executive must respect and follow'.[19] The upshot of this is that there is a duty on the Sri Lankan State to be mindful of ensuring wider access to scientific and technical knowledge when enacting legislation and governing the country.

2.2.3. *International human rights obligations*

Promoting access to scientific and technical knowledge is also important if Sri Lanka is going to be able to meet its international human rights obligations. In

14 Ibid., art 27(1)(h).

15 As Jawaharlal Nehru, the first Prime Minister of India, stated, '[i]t is science alone that can solve the problems of hunger and poverty, of insanitation and illiteracy.' Quoted in T Sorell, *Scientism: Philosophy and the Infatuation with Science* (Routledge, 1991) 2.

16 *Constitution of the Democratic Socialist Republic of Sri Lanka 1978*, art 29.

17 Ibid., art 27(1).

18 *Seveviratne and Another v University Grants Commission and Another* 1978–79–80 (1) SLR 182, 183.

19 1978–79–80 (1) SLR 182, 183. See also in *In Re the Thirteenth Amendment to the Constitution* 1987 (2) SLR 312, 326.

addition to the fundamental human rights guaranteed under the *Constitution 1978*, several international instruments also impose obligations on Sri Lanka to protect certain human rights. Sri Lanka is a State Party to some of these instruments. In particular, it has signed the *International Covenant on Civil and Political Rights 1966*, the *International Covenant on Economic, Social and Cultural Rights 1966* and the *Convention on the Rights of the Child 1989*.[20] As observed in the previous chapter, these three instruments either directly or indirectly require State Parties to promote access to scientific and technical knowledge. Therefore, Sri Lanka has an obligation to promote access to scientific and technical knowledge under these instruments. Apart from this, the *Universal Declaration of Human Rights 1948* (*UDHR*), which is the pioneer instrument declaring the human right of access to scientific and technical knowledge, is also applicable in Sri Lanka. Although the *UDHR* has no binding force in Sri Lanka, the Supreme Court of Sri Lanka has held that it is the 'highest moral authority'.[21] In view of this, Sri Lanka also has a moral duty to promote access to scientific and technical knowledge in the country.

2.3. Issues with regard to access to scientific and technical knowledge

There are three interrelated issues that adversely affect access to scientific and technical knowledge in Sri Lanka. These are knowledge dependency, low income levels and the dominance of the English language in knowledge dissemination. Before proceeding to examine these issues, it is necessary for us to understand what the term 'access to scientific and technical knowledge' means in the context of Sri Lanka.

For Sri Lanka, access to scientific and technical knowledge primarily means four things: the availability, affordability, timeliness and comprehensibility of scientific and technical knowledge. What is meant by 'availability' here is that scientific and technical knowledge is produced in sufficient quantities and that there are adequate scientific and technical knowledge products to meet the needs of people in Sri Lanka. 'Affordability' refers to the general financial ability of people in Sri Lanka to purchase scientific and technical knowledge products. 'Timeliness' means that scientific and technical knowledge products are available for the use of the people in Sri Lanka instantaneously or within a reasonable time frame from their creation.[22] 'Comprehensibility' mainly means that scientific and technical knowledge products needed by Sri Lankan people are available in the language/s in which Sri Lankans are fluent. Thus it is important to bear in mind that any issue which adversely impacts on availability, affordability, timeliness, and

20 Sri Lanka signed both the *International Covenant on Civil and Political Rights 1966* (*ICCPR*) and the *International Covenant on Economic, Social and Cultural Rights 1966* (*ICESCR*) on 11 June 1980. It signed the *Convention on the Rights of the Child 1989* (*CRC*) on 26 January 1990.

21 *Leelawathie v The Minister of Defence and External Affairs* (1965) 68 NLR 487, 490.

22 This would ensure that people in Sri Lanka could use knowledge products as soon as they are needed, as well as that these products are relevant and up to date.

comprehensibility of scientific and technical knowledge products will adversely affect access to scientific and technical knowledge in Sri Lanka.

As noted earlier, the main problems that Sri Lanka encounters with regard to access to scientific and technical knowledge are knowledge dependency, low income levels, and the dominance of the English language in knowledge dissemination. Knowledge dependency in Sri Lanka primarily affects the availability and the comprehensibility of scientific and technical knowledge. The low income levels in Sri Lanka primarily impacts upon the affordability of scientific and technical knowledge. The dominance of the English language in knowledge dissemination primarily affects the comprehensibility of scientific and technical knowledge.

2.3.1. ***Knowledge dependency***

Sri Lanka does not produce sufficient knowledge in the field of science and technology to meet the needs of its people. As a result, Sri Lanka has to import scientific and technical knowledge products from developed countries which lead in the field of science and technology. In other words, Sri Lanka is dependent on developed countries for scientific and technical knowledge products.

Sri Lanka is unable to produce sufficient scientific and technical knowledge products as a result of many factors. The most important of these are the after-effects of European colonisation and the lack of local research and innovation.

2.3.1.1. European colonisation and its after-effects

European colonial rule in Sri Lanka from the sixteenth to the mid-twentieth century linked Sri Lanka to the Western world. In particular, it replaced the existing political, economic, social and cultural landscape of Sri Lanka with transplanted Western systems and institutions. These changes benefited the interests of the colonial rulers, especially in their governance and administration of the country. Therefore, they were justified as a process of civilising the local population on the basis that the imposed Western systems and institutions were superior to those that existed. However, these transplanted systems and institutions had a devastating impact on the indigenous knowledge production systems in Sri Lanka. Moreover, the newly introduced Western systems and institutions needed Western knowledge for their proper functioning. This need was largely catered through Western knowledge production systems rather than creating independent knowledge production systems in Sri Lanka. The result of this was that Sri Lanka became increasingly dependent on Western knowledge and Western knowledge production systems.

From 1505 to 1948, Sri Lanka was under the colonial rule of three European nations: the Portuguese, the Dutch and the British. European colonisation in Sri Lanka started with the Portuguese intrusion in 1505.[23] However, the Portuguese were only able to rule a part of Sri Lanka, that is, the maritime regions, and the

23 See KM de Silva, *A History of Sri Lanka* (C Hurst, 1981) 100.

centre of the country was still ruled by the local kings. In the mid-seventeenth century, the Portuguese were expelled from Sri Lanka by the Dutch, who later established their rule in the maritime regions of the country. The Dutch rule gave way to the British in 1796, and in 1802 the former Dutch possessions in Sri Lanka became the 'British Crown Colony of Ceylon'.[24] In 1815, the British conquered the centre of Sri Lanka by defeating the local king, and thenceforth the entire country became a British colony until it was granted independence from Britain in 1948.

The British rule in Sri Lanka was a period that saw an overall change in the economic and sociopolitical characteristics of the country. The effect of many of these changes was that Sri Lanka became linked to the Western world.[25] KM de Silva noted:

> Because of the rapid shrinkage of the world in the nineteenth century, Sri Lanka would have faced westernisation anyway, but the British, in fact, deliberately started the process in the 1830s after some hesitation in the early years of their rule in the island.[26]

Westernisation that was started by the British in Sri Lanka overturned the systems and institutions that were already in place in Sri Lanka. A complicated new economic structure based on free trade and a laissez-faire approach was introduced, replacing the simple economy based on subsistence agriculture. A democratic government, which upheld constitutionalism and human rights, was gradually implemented in lieu of a monarchy. English law was introduced in many matters of trade and commerce, including copyright, patents and trademarks. English became the dominant language, marginalising the status and importance of the local languages. The education system became completely aligned with the West. These changes had a huge impact in terms of making Sri Lanka dependent on the developed countries of the West for knowledge. This can be explained in relation to the changes that took place in Sri Lanka's economic structure and the education system as a result of colonisation and westernisation.

2.3.1.1.1. CHANGES IN THE ECONOMY

Changes in the economic structure of Sri Lanka, especially those that took place during British rule, had a devastating impact on the country's indigenous knowledge base. Amarasuriya and Witharana observed:

> The plantation economy that was established during the colonial times dramatically changed the entire social, economic and political landscape of the

24 Ibid., 210.
25 PE Peiris, *Ceylon: The Portuguese Era: Being a History of the Island for the Period 1505–1658* (Tisara Prakashakayo, 2nd ed, 1992) v.
26 de Silva, above n 23, 479.

> country handicapping the knowledge base available for innovation in the pre-colonial Sri Lanka.[27]

Prior to European colonisation, Sri Lanka had a less complicated, closed economic system that was based on agriculture for consumption needs.[28] The primary form of agriculture (as even today) was rice cultivation.[29] The scientific and technical knowledge required for rice cultivation was sufficiently available in Sri Lanka in the form of traditional knowledge. In fact, this is evidenced by the 'large number of [traditional] rice varieties [that] were developed and selected by [Sri Lankan] farmers to suit to various agro-climatic conditions and to the preferable characteristics, such as colour, smell, taste and nutritive values'[30] and the advanced irrigation systems that were built to support rice cultivation in ancient Sri Lanka. In particular, it has been recorded that a collection of over 300 local varieties of rice was exhibited at the Kandy Agro-horticultural and Industrial Exhibition in 1902.[31] Moreover, out of the more than 3,000 rice varieties that were collected and conserved by the Agriculture Department of Sri Lanka in 1993, a significant percentage consisted of traditional varieties.[32]

The advanced irrigation systems built during the hydraulic civilisation in ancient Sri Lanka (300 BC–1200 AD) also highlight the nature and extent of the developed status of scientific and technical knowledge that Sri Lanka possessed at the time. According to Brohier:

> Extensive works of irrigation [in ancient Sri Lanka], secured with an immense amount of labour, skill and science had transformed arid plains to areas of plentiful prosperity at a period when agriculture in Europe was in the rudest and most primitive state.[33]

Although the fall of the hydraulic civilisation in the thirteenth century may have had an adverse impact on the stock of scientific and technical knowledge in Sri Lanka, particularly in the field of irrigation,[34] the indigenous knowledge systems

27 Harini Amarasuriya and Dileepa Witharana, 'Conflicting Agendas: Implications of Intellectual Property Rights on Access to Knowledge in Education and Research' (Paper presented at the 7th National Conference on Library and Information Science, Colombo, 25 June 2009) 4 <http://eprints.rclis.org/13385/>.

28 Patrick Peebles, *The History of Sri Lanka* (Greenwood Press, 2006) 2.

29 See, e.g., MKL Irangani and Yoshiharu Shiratake, 'Indigenous Techniques Used in Rice Cultivation in Sri Lanka: An Analysis from an Agricultural History Perspective' (2013) 12(4) *Indian Journal of Traditional Knowledge* 638.

30 Udaya Rajapaksha, 'Ancient Food and Farming Systems in Sri Lanka' (1997) 19(1) *Vidurava* 41.

31 Ibid.

32 Ibid.

33 RL Brohier, *Ancient Irrigation Works in Ceylon* (Government Publications Bureau, 1934) vol 1, 1. Also see JE Tennent, *Ceylon: An Account of the Island* (Longman, Green, Longman and Roberts, 1860) vol 2, 468.

34 However, Toynbee said that 'the cause of the decline and fall of the Indic Civilization in Ceylon' 'was not any decline in engineering technique but the social decline'. Arnold J Toynbee, *A Study of History* (Oxford University Press, first published 1939, 1951 ed) vol 4, 46.

in precolonial Sri Lanka were still sufficient to meet the needs of its economy, which was based on subsistence agriculture.

The indigenous knowledge creation systems in precolonial Sri Lanka were linked with '*Rajakariya*'—the traditional compulsory service system and the caste system.[35] MU De Silva observed, '*Rajakariya* was the mechanism which combined land tenure and the caste services for the state and the well-being of the community.'[36] That is, people in precolonial Sri Lanka got their land from the king. In return for their land tenure, people were obliged under *Rajakariya* to perform a caste-specific compulsory service to the king.[37] As such, *Rajakariya* ensured that the castes had a direct impact on the various professions in Sri Lanka (such as farmers, irrigation engineers, goldsmiths, blacksmiths and so on). *Rajakariya* also enabled industries and professions in Sri Lanka to be monopolised by individual castes. As this monopoly led to work specialisation, it generated a wealth of knowledge (now known as traditional knowledge) among the members of the individual castes with regard to their specialised work. This traditional knowledge was transferred from generation to generation, but only within the individual castes.[38] In this way, *Rajakariya*, together with the caste system, played an important role in Sri Lankan indigenous knowledge creation systems.

The era of European colonisation, particularly British rule, saw dramatic changes to the economic structure of Sri Lanka. One of the most fundamental changes that took place during British rule was the transformation of the Sri Lankan economy into a market economy based on the concept of a laissez-faire state.[39] The laissez-faire market economy was seen as an essential requirement to further British interests in Sri Lanka, particularly to promote the trade in plantation crops. The British administration saw the *Rajakariya* system as 'an obstacle to the free movement of labour, and to the creation of a land-market, both of which were vitally important in the establishment of the laissez-faire [market economy]'.[40] As a result, they abolished the *Rajakariya* system in 1833, following the recommendation of the Colebrooke-Cameron Commission, which was appointed by the British Government to inquire into the administration of the government, revenues and the judicial establishments and procedure in Sri Lanka.[41]

35 See GC Mendis, *Ceylon Under the British* (Asian Educational Services, first published 1952, 2005 ed) 46–47.
36 MU De Silva, 'Land Tenure, Caste System and the Rajakariya under Foreign Rule: A Review of Change in Sri Lanka under Western Powers, 1597–1832' (1992–1993) 37 *Journal of the Royal Asiatic Society of Sri Lanka* 1, 1.
37 Chandima D Daskon, 'Are Cultural Traditions Real "Assets" for Rural People? An Analysis from A Livelihood Perspective' (2010) 10(3) *Global Journal of Human Social Science* 13, 22.
38 See, e.g., CR de Silva, 'Education' in KM de Silva (ed), *Sri Lanka: A Survey* (University Press of Hawaii, 1977) 403.
39 See de Silva, above n 23, 246.
40 Ibid., 248 (emphasis added).
41 Ibid., 247–248.

The abolition of *Rajakariya* had a stifling effect on the growth and dissemination of traditional knowledge in Sri Lanka. It adversely affected the existing system of work specialisation through the caste system and thus the creation of new traditional knowledge.[42] It also affected the dissemination of traditional knowledge, because the free movement of labour meant that there was less scope for transferring that knowledge between generations.[43] The ultimate result of this was that Sri Lanka came to rely on Western knowledge to satisfy the country's new knowledge requirements.

Sri Lanka's independence from Britain in 1948 did not necessarily bring about changes in the economic structure implemented by the British.[44] The same was true for many other former British colonies in South and Southeast Asia. Moreover, at the time of Sri Lanka's independence, its economic structure was on the verge of a crisis. KM de Silva noted:

> The crux of the problem was that foreign income which 'directly or indirectly constituted the bulk of the national income began to fall rapidly', while there was a rise in the cost of imports. This was reflected in the country's balance of payments, which fell consistently from 'a handsome surplus in 1945 to a heavy deficit in 1947'. 'For a country which practically lives by foreign trade,' . . . 'no economic indices could be more significant. It represented a fall in national income and a march towards greater poverty and insecurity'.[45]

Thus, pursuant to its independence, economic development surfaced as the biggest hurdle for Sri Lanka, and promoting access to scientific and technical knowledge became crucial in this connection. The result of this was the increasing dependence of Sri Lanka on the developed countries for access to scientific and technical knowledge.

2.3.1.1.2. CHANGES IN THE EDUCATION SYSTEM

Another important transformation that took place during British rule in Sri Lanka was the introduction of a new education system based on the Western (British) model of education. As will be seen in the ensuing discussion, this made Sri Lanka

42 See Mendis, above n 35, 55–56, 67.

43 For instance, when the new generation belonging to a particular caste embarked on a different profession than what was specific to that caste, there was no room for the older generation to transfer professional knowledge specific to that caste (traditional knowledge) to the new generation. At the same time, the older generation was reluctant to share traditional knowledge with members of the new generation when they did not belong to the same caste.

44 LA Wickremeratne, 'The Economy in 1948' in KM de Silva (ed), *Sri Lanka: A Survey* (University Press of Hawaii, 1977) 131.

45 KM de Silva, 'Introduction' in KM de Silva (ed), *Sri Lanka: A Survey* (University Press of Hawaii, 1977) xi, xiii–xiv (emphasis added) (citations omitted).

dependent on scientific and technical knowledge produced in developed countries for educational purposes.

The formal education system that existed in precolonial Sri Lanka was not necessarily linked to science and technology. CR de Silva noted:

> The traditional education system was . . . fashioned and controlled by the religious order and education generally was regarded as a means of religious edification. Education imparted at the temple had a strong academic or literary bias. On the other hand, technical skills such as those needed to construct the ancient irrigation reservoirs and canals were transmitted from generation to generation, either by traditional instruction given by father to son or by craft apprenticeships, both outside the system of temple instruction.[46]

Formal education in precolonial Sri Lanka was restricted to members of the elite class, who were limited in numbers.[47] Thus, it is implausible to assume that the formal education system in precolonial Sri Lanka was the bedrock of indigenous knowledge systems or even that it constituted an important part of these systems. Besides, Lieutenant-Colonel Colebrooke, one of the commissioners of the Colebrooke-Cameron Commission, condemned and unhesitatingly dismissed the formal education system that was in place in precolonial Sri Lanka as one that 'scarcely merits any notice'.[48]

Until the recommendations of the Colebrooke-Cameron Commission, the British administration in Sri Lanka had no coherent policy on education. Neither was education regarded as a 'service normally provided by the state'.[49] However, with the implementation of the Commission's recommendations on education in 1832, 'State intervention in education . . . assumed a regular and definite form.'[50] Despite that, the British education policy in Sri Lanka predominantly addressed the needs and interests of the colonial rulers rather than those of Sri Lankans.[51]

The objective of the system of education introduced in Sri Lanka by the British was not to produce a well-informed and literate public. Instead, it was designed to create an elite class, limited in number, which would assist the rulers in matters

46 de Silva, above n 36, 403.
47 For a more detailed account of the formal education system in precolonial Sri Lanka, see, for instance, JE Jayasuriya, *Educational Policies and Progress During British Rule in Ceylon (Sri Lanka) 1796–1948* (Associated Educational Publishers, 1977) 1–23.
48 Ceylon, Royal Commission to Examine and Report upon the Present State of the Laws, Regulations and Usages in the Settlements of the Cape of Good Hope and the Island of Mauritius and Ceylon, *Report of Lieutenant-Colonel Colebrooke, One of His Majesty's Commissioners of Inquiry, upon the Administration and Government of Ceylon* (1831) 32.
49 de Silva, above n 23, 252.
50 Ibid., 253.
51 KD Ariyadasa, *The Curriculum Development Centre of Sri Lanka* (UNESCO, 1977) 1.

of local administration and other related affairs.[52] To implement this objective, the general education system was designed in two forms: (1) English education, which catered to a narrow elite class and (2) vernacular education, which catered to the general masses. What is important to note here is that neither the English nor the vernacular education systems facilitated the production and diffusion of indigenous knowledge in the country.[53] On the contrary, the English education system completely ignored indigenous knowledge and linked the country's education system with Western knowledge. Canagarajah observed that English education 'meant not only teaching [the] English language, but also adopting the medium, modes of instruction, curriculum, and teaching materials of the British public schools for general education'.[54] Thus, the system of education introduced during British rule in Sri Lanka paved the way for the undiscriminating assimilation of the country's educational system to that of Britain.[55]

Since English education provided the most effective mechanism for access to Western knowledge, it was able to produce a set of people who could easily connect with the Western world. Because of this, English-educated people were able to receive special privileges, such as better employment and higher education prospects. As a result, the general conception among the people in Sri Lanka was that English education was superior to vernacular education. Thus, English education became an important aspiration of almost everyone in the country.[56]

Although English education was in great demand among the local population in Sri Lanka, the objective of the British administration was to limit the number of people who were educated in English.[57] Thus, there were significant obstacles to access to English education, the main obstacle being the fees charged, and English education became a privilege which was confined to a small fraction of the local population. This created a severe imbalance with regard to people's access to Western knowledge.[58] This, in turn, affected people's prospects of being connected with the Western world. The result of this was that English education became a major factor that created economic and social inequality within the Sri Lankan population.

With the constitutional reforms in the 1930s that augmented local representation in the government of colonial Sri Lanka,[59] the economic and social inequality

52 WA Wiswa Warnapala, *The Making of the System of Higher Education in Sri Lanka: An Evaluative Study* (2011) ii–iv.

53 See especially Sandagomi Coperahewa, 'Colonialism and Problems of Language Policy: Formulation of a Colonial Language Policy in Sri Lanka' (2011) 1(1) *Sri Lanka Journal of Advanced Social Studies* 27, 45.

54 AS Canagarajah, 'Dilemmas in Planning English/Vernacular Relations in Post-Colonial Communities' (2005) 9(3) *Journal of Sociolinguistics* 418, 422.

55 Special Committee on Education, *Report of the Special Committee on Education*, State Council of Ceylon Sessional Paper XXIV (1943) 10.

56 Ibid., 22.

57 Ralph Pieris, *Social Development and Planning in Asia* (Shakti Malik Abhinav Publications, 1976) 239.

58 See, e.g., Warnapala, above n 52, vi–vii.

59 See KM de Silva, 'The Transfer of Power in Sri Lanka—A Review of British Perspectives' (1974) 4(1&2) *The Ceylon Journal of Historical and Social Studies* 8.

created by the English and vernacular education systems was identified as a severe drawback.[60] Thus, the government appointed a Special Committee on Education in 1940 to 'investigate the defects of the present educational system and to recommend measures of reform necessitated by the changed conditions'.[61] In order to eliminate the economic and social inequalities created by the two education systems, this Committee (among other things) recommended that English education should be made available free of charge.[62] This made English education open to all. However, the Committee recommended a single type of school for the primary stage where the medium of instruction should be the mother tongues of the pupils.[63] Although the objective of these steps was to make the Sri Lankan education system more suitable for the local people, in fact the effect of these steps was to establish a permanent link between Western knowledge and the Sri Lankan education system, making Sri Lanka overwhelmingly dependent on Western knowledge for education. Even after Sri Lanka's independence from Britain in 1948 and its breakaway from the dominion status in 1972, the education system has largely remained Western-oriented. This is particularly so with regard to scientific and technical education.

2.3.1.2. Lack of research and innovation

Research and innovation is an important knowledge production mechanism. Lack of research and innovation is a major factor which affects scientific and technical knowledge production in Sri Lanka.

Two indicators that are commonly used to measure the level of research and innovation in the field of science and technology are the journal articles published and the patents registered. The status of these indicators with regard to Sri Lanka is not impressive. According to the 2015 *Sri Lanka Science, Technology & Innovation Statistical Handbook* (2015 *STI Handbook*) published in 2018, the number of publications by Sri Lankan scientists in the Science Citation Index (SCI) journals for the year 2015 was only 396, of which 83.6 percent had been co-authored with foreigners.[64] In a study which analyses the performance of Sri Lanka's science and technology as reflected in their publications output during 2001–2010 (based on the publication data derived from the Scopus citation database), Gupta notes that Sri Lanka produced 5,301 papers during the period under study.[65]

60 See WD Rodrigo, 'Copyright Law in the Digital Era: A Comparative Study of Sri Lanka, Australia and the United States' (PhD Thesis, University of Queensland, 2007) 271 (citations omitted).
61 Special Committee on Education, *Report of the Special Committee on Education*, State Council of Ceylon Sessional Paper XXIV (1943) 9.
62 Ibid., 141.
63 Ibid., 35.
64 National Science Foundation, *Sri Lanka Science, Technology & Innovation: Statistical Handbook 2015* (National Science Foundation, 2018) 41.
65 BM Gupta, 'Sri Lanka S & T Output During 2001–2010: A Scientometric Assessment' (2012) 17(3) *Malaysian Journal of Library & Information Science* 49, 51.

However, this only amounted to a global publication share of 0.030 percent.[66] In a study which looks into the historical development of scholarly journal publishing in Sri Lanka from 1845 to 2010, Yapa finds that despite the steady increase in the number of scholarly journals published locally during this period, Sri Lanka published only 114 journals in 2010.[67] Of this figure, 35 percent is in Humanities and Social Sciences. The rest belongs to the fields of medicine (28 percent), natural and physical sciences (24 percent) and agriculture (14 percent).[68] In contrast, in the field of science alone, the United States published 6,771 scholarly journals in 1995.[69]

When considering the local output of scholarly scientific and technical journals in Sri Lanka, one needs to be mindful of the quality of these journals. In particular, a national survey report on publishing scientific and technical journals in Sri Lanka published in 1987 raised a number of serious issues about the quality of the locally published journals and their contents.[70] Firstly, many journals published in Sri Lanka failed or neglected to adhere to international standards, which render these journals of substandard quality.[71] Secondly, many journals were published irregularly or had suspended publication due to lack of material.[72] Thirdly, some journals had 'a low article/journal ratio' and there was a marked difficulty in obtaining articles.[73] Fourthly, more than one-half of the journals lacked quality contributions.[74]

The position in relation to published journal articles is similar with regard to patent registrations in Sri Lanka. According to the National Intellectual Property Office of Sri Lanka, the total number of patent registrations for the year 2019 was only 175, out of which 136 were registered by non-residents. Sri Lankan residents had only 39 patents registered for the year 2019.[75] The total number of patent registrations in Sri Lanka from 2000 to 2019 was 4,013. Of this figure, 2,720 were registered by non-residents and only 1,293 have been registered by residents of Sri Lanka.[76]

66 Ibid.
67 Geetha Yapa, 'The Historical Development of Sri Lanka Scholarly Journal Publishing (1845–2010)' (2011) 4(3&4) *Sri Lankan Journal of Librarianship and Information Management* <http://sllim.sljol.info/article/abstract/10.4038/sllim.v4i3-4.4253/>.
68 Ibid.
69 Carol Tenopir and Donald W King, 'Trends in Scientific Scholarly Journal Publishing in the United States' (1997) 28(3) *Journal of Scholarly Publishing* 135.
70 Nirmala R Amarasuriya, *Publishing Scientific & Technical Journals in Sri Lanka: Report of a National Survey* (Natural Resources, Energy and Science Authority, 1987).
71 Ibid., 57.
72 Ibid., 62.
73 Ibid., 57.
74 Ibid., 3, 49. Many of the observations in this report are equally valid today. See P Ranasinghe, YS Perera and AM Abeygunasekara, 'The Process and Costs of Publishing Medical Journals in Sri Lanka: An Economic Evaluation' (2011) 1(1) *BMJ Open* <http://bmjopen.bmj.com/content/1/1/e000057.full>.
75 National Intellectual Property Office of Sri Lanka, 'Statistics' <www.nipo.gov.lk/>.
76 Ibid.

2.3.1.2.1. FACTORS AFFECTING RESEARCH AND INNOVATION

Many factors have affected research and innovation in Sri Lanka, the most important being the lack of human capital and inadequate investment in research and innovation.[77] Lack of human capital severely affects research and innovation in Sri Lanka, particularly in the field of science and technology. There is a marked shortage of experts, such as research scientists and technicians, in this field. The major contributing factors to this situation are the shortcomings in the Sri Lankan university education system and the brain drain.

The university education system in Sri Lanka does not adequately cater to the human capital requirements of a knowledge economy. Perera and Dasanayaka stated that '[e]ven though Sri Lankan universities provide valuable human capital for the country's technology development, their contribution is at a lower level compared to other developing and newly industrialised countries'.[78] There are a number of reasons for this situation. Firstly, all the local universities in Sri Lanka are primarily teaching universities.[79] As a result, these universities do not create a strong research culture that develops human capital required for research and innovation in all fields, including science and technology. In particular, research output of local universities is very limited in terms of quantity and quality when compared with the universities in the developed countries.[80] According to Gunasena, '[t]he research output of [Sri Lankan] universities is pathetically low [even] compared to the leading universities of the region'.[81] More specifically, the research outputs of academics in local universities 'are well below the academic norms and the publications in peer reviewed journals rarely exceed 125, even less than one paper per academic. The number of inventions also remains below 10'.[82]

Secondly, local universities are too heavily focused on non-science and non-technical disciplines. As the UNDP's 2012 *Sri Lanka Human Development Report* noted, '[t]he study areas of Sri Lanka's undergraduates reveal a heavy concentration on Arts and Management'.[83] In 2009, only 21 percent

77 It is important to note that in order to overcome these deficiencies, Sri Lanka needs to promote access to knowledge (particularly in the field of science and technology) more and more. In particular, building human capital requires upgrading and expanding education which in turn requires increased access to knowledge. Also, to increase investment of funds in research and innovation, Sri Lanka needs to promote economic growth, which in turn requires increased access to knowledge.

78 Chandana Perera and Sarath Dasanayaka, 'Technology Development: Key Issues in Productivity' in Saman Kelegama (ed), *Economic Policy in Sri Lanka: Issues and Debates* (Sage Publications, 2004) 248–249.

79 UNESCO, *World Social Science Report 2010: Knowledge Divides* (UNESCO, 2010) 80.

80 Ibid.

81 HPM Gunasena, 'Universities Should Focus More on Researches Meant for Public Good' *The Island* (online), 25 May 2014 <www.island.lk/index.php?page_cat=article-details&page=article-details&code_title=103920>.

82 Ibid.

83 UNDP, *Sri Lanka Human Development Report 2012: Bridging Regional Disparities for Human Development* (UNDP, 2012) 75.

of undergraduates were studying engineering and mathematics, compared to 42 percent in Singapore which is 'ranked as one [of] the world's most scientifically oriented countries'.[84] The lower output of graduates in the science and technology field compared to arts and management affects the amount of skilled human resources available for research and innovation in the field of science and technology.

Thirdly, the capacity of the university education system in Sri Lanka 'is inadequate and it serves only a very small proportion of the population. In 2009, only 3.6 percent of 20–24-year-olds were enrolled in a university'.[85] The low enrolment rates in university education also affect the amount of skilled human resources available for research and innovation in all fields, including science and technology.

As UNESCO's 2010 *World Science Report* noted, 'brain drain' is a serious issue that affects scientific research in Sri Lanka.[86] Sri Lanka has experienced a considerable loss of human capital because of brain drain. In particular, the 2004 National Survey of Research and Development by the Sri Lankan National Science Foundation (published in 2007) found that 'the total number of economically active scientists [in Sri Lanka] has decreased substantially from 13,286 in 1996 to 9,746 in 2004. The number of technicians also has decreased from 14,514 in 1996 to 12,302 in 2004'.[87] This survey also noted that the brain drain 'can be identified as one of the main reasons for the decline in the number of scientists shown in [the] survey' because 'there is a considerable number of scientists and scientific professionals leaving the country annually for better job prospects, working conditions, recognition and more stable socio-economic environments'.[88] Apart from these reasons, better access to scientific and technical knowledge in developed countries is also another reason for the brain drain from Sri Lanka to these countries.

Sri Lanka also suffers from a lack of investment in research and innovation, especially in the field of science and technology, as well as in education. This directly hinders research and innovation activities, and it also limits the building of human capital that is required for these activities. According to the 2015 *STI Handbook*, the gross expenditure on research and development in Sri Lanka for the year 2015 was only 0.11 percent of the Gross Domestic Product (GDP). This is in comparison with 1.70 percent in Britain, 2.88 percent in Germany and 2.79 percent in the United States for the same year.[89]

According to the Central Bank of Sri Lanka, the government expenditure on education for the year 2013 was about 1.58 percent of the GDP. In 2018, this

84 Ibid.
85 Ibid.
86 UNESCO, above n 79, 6–7.
87 National Science Foundation, *National Survey of Research and Development in Sri Lanka 2004* (National Science Foundation, 2007) 32 (emphasis added).
88 Ibid. See also UNESCO, above n 79, 7.
89 National Science Foundation, above n 64, 4.

figure was 1.85 percent.[90] A World Bank study noted, referring to the figure in 2013, '[t]his is one of the lowest shares of public investment among countries.'[91] The public investment in education (which includes expenditures on general and higher education, as well as technical and vocational education and training) as a share of government expenditure is also 'well below the share of investment for lower-middle income countries and upper-middle income countries'.[92]

The insufficient investment in education in Sri Lanka has adversely impacted on its research and innovation, particularly in the field of science and technology. The lack of investment in education has severely restricted the production of human capital required for research and innovation in this field. It has also adversely affected the quality of the human capital so produced. In particular, because of the insufficient investment in education, there is a lack of teachers and other required resources for learning in Sri Lankan schools. Alarmingly, '[o]nly 10 percent of secondary schools have facilities to teach advanced science streams'.[93] This has severely limited the number of students qualifying for science and technical education. The other outcome of the lack of investment in education is the substandard quality of education. The 2012 *Sri Lanka Human Development Report* noted, 'Both poor facilities and resource constraints have spurred a decline in the quality of education.'[94] All these adversely impact on 'skills development programmes and the training of engineers and scientists' required for the production of scientific and technical knowledge.[95]

2.3.2. Low income levels

Low purchasing power resulting from low income levels in Sri Lanka affects the affordability of scientific and technical knowledge products that are produced in developed countries. Given that Sri Lanka lacks sufficient knowledge production (and knowledge products) in the field of science and technology, it needs to import scientific and technical knowledge products from overseas. However, these knowledge products come with a price that is often unaffordable to Sri Lanka.[96] Insufficient investment in education resulting from low GNP and GDP levels affects the purchasing power of educational institutions in Sri Lanka to acquire scientific and technical knowledge products. Amarasuriya and Witharana

90 Central Bank of Sri Lanka, *Sri Lanka Socio-Economic Data 2019* (Central Bank of Sri Lanka, 2019) 59.
91 Harsha Aturupane et al., 'Sri Lanka: Investment in Human Capital' (Report No 69, World Bank, 2014) 20.
92 Ibid., 19.
93 UNDP, above n 83, 67.
94 Ibid.
95 UNESCO, above n 79, 344.
96 See Susan Isiko Strba, *International Copyright Law and Access to Education in Developing Countries: Exploring Multilateral Legal and Quasi-Legal Solutions* (Martinus Nijhoff Publishers, 2012) 29.

observed that the annual budget for the year 2009 for the library of the Open University, which is one of the main State universities in Sri Lanka, was only Sri Lankan Rupees (SLRs)1 million (roughly US$ 7,700).[97] The low level of GDP per capita (which is about US$ 3,853) also affects the purchasing power of people in Sri Lanka to obtain scientific and technical knowledge products.

2.3.3. Dominance of English in knowledge dissemination

The dominance of the English language in the dissemination of knowledge products affects the ability of the people in Sri Lanka to understand these products. Since most of the knowledge products in the field of science and technology are produced and disseminated in English, the language barriers deprive Sri Lankan students of access to these knowledge products.

English dominates in the publication of scientific and technical knowledge products, not only overseas but also in Sri Lanka. As the 1987 national survey report on publishing scientific and technical journals in Sri Lanka pointed out, all the science and technology journals that were being published in Sri Lanka at that time were published in English. Indeed, there were no primary research journals published in the national languages of the country.[98] Alarmingly, this position has hardly changed subsequently. For instance, in their study in 2011, Ranasinghe, Perera and Abeygunasekara noted that all the medical journals that were identified as published in Sri Lanka were published in English.[99] Moreover, as Fernando noted, only a few textbooks in science have been produced in Sri Lanka in languages other than English for the use of secondary school students and university undergraduates.[100] One main reason for this is that 'English language publications have immediate access to an international readership and to the largest markets.'[101] Thus, the use of English in science and technology publications gives their authors an 'immediate advantage'.[102]

Despite this, English is not a generally used language in Sri Lanka. One reason for this is the ethnic composition of Sri Lanka. In particular, the total population in Sri Lanka was about 21.8 million in 2019.[103] There are three major ethnicities living in Sri Lanka, namely, Sinhalese, Tamils and Moors. According to the 2012 census, the Sinhalese, which form the majority ethnic group in Sri Lanka, make up 74.9 percent of the total population. Tamils and Muslims, which are the

97 Amarasuriya and Witharana, above n 27, 7.
98 Amarasuriya, above n 70, 56.
99 Ranasinghe, Perera and Abeygunasekara, above n 74.
100 JN Oleap Fernando, 'Sri Lankan Experience in School Science Education' (Proceedings of the Asian Regional IAP Seminar on the Generation of Experimental Materials and Learning Modules for Science Education, New Delhi, 24–25 October 2002) <http://insaindia.org/pdf/proceeding.pdf>.
101 Amarasuriya, above n 70, 56.
102 Ibid.
103 World Bank, above n 2.

minority ethnic groups in Sri Lanka, make up 15.3 percent and 9.3 percent of the total population respectively.[104]

The three main ethnic groups in Sri Lanka widely use two local languages, namely, Sinhala and Tamil. While Sinhala is the mother tongue of the Sinhalese, Tamil is the mother tongue of both Tamils and Moors. Sinhala is only used in Sri Lanka, whereas Tamil is also used in India.[105] Although English is used in Sri Lanka, it is only spoken competently by about 10 percent of the population.[106] As such, a clear majority of the Sri Lankan population do not have meaningful access to scientific and technical knowledge products published in English.

English is also not the general language of education in Sri Lanka. This is especially so in schools and universities run by the government, which is the major provider of education in Sri Lanka.[107] The reason for this is the education policy introduced by the British in Sri Lanka and the subsequent education policy which was implemented during the 1940s and 1950s to mitigate the injustice created by the British education policy. In particular, the education policy during British rule in Sri Lanka was not only unable to produce an educated public in the country but was also unsuccessful in creating widespread literacy in English, despite the fact that English was the official language of the country during that time.[108] As observed earlier, this resulted in social and economic inequality, which was sought to be remedied by education reforms implementing the recommendations of the Special Committee of Education. Accordingly, these education reforms made education in English free of charge and open to all, while making Sinhala and Tamil languages the media of instruction in the primary classes of English schools. In post-primary classes, the medium could be either of these languages or English at the option of the school.[109] Referring to these reforms, Ariyadasa noted: '[t]he most important change that resulted for the curriculum on the recommendations of the Special Committee was the change of the medium of instruction in the English schools.'[110] While 'Sinhala and Tamil replaced English as the medium of instruction in grade 1 in 1945' this 'was progressively carried through grade 10 for most schools in 1954'.[111] In 1957, Sinhala and Tamil were introduced in all schools for all subjects, and 'thereafter to the higher senior secondary grades and

104 Department of Census & Statistics, *Census of Population and Housing 2012* (Final Report, 2015) 141.
105 Sandagomi Coperahewa, 'The Language Planning Situation in Sri Lanka' (2009) 10(1) *Current Issues in Language Planning* 69, 78.
106 Central Intelligence Agency, *The World Fact Book: Sri Lanka* (18 May 2015) <www.cia.gov/library/publications/the-world-factbook/geos/ce.html>.
107 See Harsha Aturupane et al., *Transforming School Education in Sri Lanka: From Cut Stones to Polished Jewels* (World Bank, 2011) 2.
108 Ralph Pieris, *Social Development and Planning in Asia* (Shakti Malik Abhinav Publications, 1976) 241.
109 Jayasuriya, above n 47, 488.
110 Ariyadasa, above n 51, 3–4.
111 Ibid., 4.

the university'.[112] The effect of these educational reforms was that local languages came to be widely used in education, including in the universities.

The provision of education in local languages has remained an essential characteristic in the education policy of Sri Lanka to date. This is particularly the case in government schools. The effect of this is that Sri Lanka has 'a highly literate population who, however, for no fault of theirs, have not been sufficiently motivated to acquire competency in English, so necessary for many vocations in life'.[113]

Sri Lankan students' lack of proficiency in English means that they do not have meaningful access to scientific and technical knowledge products published in English. Therefore, it is difficult for them to acquire the necessary scientific and technical knowledge and skills they need. Fernando noted: '[d]ue to the lack of adequate competency in English, secondary school children as well as university undergraduates have insufficient and inadequate reading and reference material in all scientific fields.'[114] Although, '[a] few text-books have been produced in the local languages to cater to this need', 'these are grossly insufficient when one considers the wealth of material that is necessary for a complete education'.[115] As a result, '[s]cience education in Sri Lanka at the secondary and tertiary levels . . . has therefore been adversely affected'.[116]

2.4. Importance of translation

Given that the majority of the knowledge products in science and technology are published in English and that a majority of people in Sri Lanka do not have adequate competency in English, translation of these knowledge products into Sinhala and Tamil is essential in order to ensure that they are accessible. Although it may be argued that promoting English literacy among Sri Lankans would be a better solution than translation, there are many barriers to doing that. Also, it is improbable to assume that English literacy of all people in the country could be promoted within a short span of time. Thus, the need for translation of scientific and technical knowledge products into Sinhala and Tamil remains significant for the foreseeable future. Apart from this, the language rights in the *Constitution 1978* and past practices of the government have shown that translation is important for promoting scientific and technical education.

2.4.1. Barriers to promoting English

English was first introduced to Sri Lanka in 1796. During 1815–1956, it was the official language of Sri Lanka. From the 1950s onwards, English has been taught

112 Ibid.
113 Fernando, above n 100.
114 Ibid., (emphasis added).
115 Ibid.
116 Ibid.

as a language in all Sri Lankan schools.[117] In 1987, English was constitutionally recognised as a link language in Sri Lanka.[118] From the 1980s onwards, the government of Sri Lanka has repeatedly emphasised the importance of promoting English literacy, especially at the school level.[119] It has also taken many significant steps to promote English. Despite this, only about 10 percent of the population in Sri Lanka speak English.[120] As a study conducted for the National Education Commission revealed, 'After more than half a century of teaching English in Sri Lanka and assuming that all students have learnt English for at least eight years of learning, the results are not satisfactory.'[121] English proficiency is very low even among university students.[122] The pass rate in English is the lowest in the General Certificate of Education–Ordinary Level (GCE O/L) examination. In particular, only 37 percent of students have passed English in 2009.[123] Also, only about 10 percent of the Grade 4 students are mastering English.[124] This shows that promoting English in Sri Lanka has not been an easy task. This is particularly so in view of the barriers to promoting English in Sri Lanka, such as linguistic nationalism, language rights in the *Constitution 1978* and the lack of facilities for teaching English.

2.4.1.1. Linguistic nationalism

Language is an extremely sensitive issue in Sri Lanka because of the linguistic nationalism of both the Sinhala and Tamil ethnic communities. In particular, the issue relating to the use of Sinhala and Tamil as the national languages of Sri Lanka was one of the important factors which paved the way to Sri Lanka's recently ended three-decade civil war. Also, it is the main contributing factor to the ethnic conflict between these two communities that prevails to date.

The linguistic nationalism of Sinhalese and Tamils has undermined the use of English in Sri Lanka. This was particularly so in the wake of Sri Lanka's independence. With the declaration of Sinhala as the only official language of Sri Lanka in

117 See especially Marie Perera, 'Coping with Student Heterogeneity in the English Language Classrooms: A Collaborative Action Research' (Report, National Education Commission, February 2010) 1.
118 *Constitution of the Democratic Socialist Republic of Sri Lanka1978*, art 18(3).
119 See S Rupasinghe, 'The Role of English in Education, at School Level in Sri Lanka, as Perceived by Parents' (1983) *University of Colombo Review* 71.
120 Central Intelligence Agency, above n 106.
121 Marie Perera, 'Coping with Student Heterogeneity in the English Language Classrooms: A Collaborative Action Research' (Report, National Education Commission, February 2010) 1.
122 Dasun Edirisinghe, 'SL Undergrads' English Proficiency Woefully Low, A Study Reveals' *The Island* (online), 30 May 2013 <www.island.lk/index.php?page_cat=article-details&page=article-details&code_title=80148>.
123 Aturupane et al., above n 107, 12.
124 Rocio Castro et al., 'Sri Lanka Development Forum: The Economy, Regional Disparities, and Global Opportunities' (Report No 38388-LK, World Bank, 12 January 2007) 8.

1956, '[t]he official status of English underwent a dramatic change'.[125] Coperahewa observed, '[t]he use of English [in Sri Lanka] has declined since independence, [although] at present it is commonly viewed as a gateway to international communication and knowledge.'[126]

Even though it is now accepted that English is crucial to bridging the knowledge gap between Sri Lanka and the developed countries and to promoting greater access to knowledge in the country, the language conflict between Sinhalese and Tamils is important to the task of promoting English in the country. In particular, it is highly doubtful whether Sri Lanka would be able to replace the use of its local languages with English, especially in light of the linguistic nationalism that both the Sinhalese and Tamil ethnic groups have displayed over the years and the tensions between these two groups with regard to language.

The rise of linguistic nationalism in the Sinhala and Tamil communities was an important phenomenon that came to light in the immediate period after Sri Lanka's independence.[127] As observed earlier, English was the official language in Sri Lanka during British rule. Apart from the use of English in education, its use in government administration created many problems for a majority of people in the country during this period. For instance, 'since the country's legal codes and judicial and administrative decisions were . . . written in English, the majority of the population could comprehend judicial and administrative transactions only through translators and intermediaries.'[128] With the country's independence, the need to quickly address these issues came to the forefront. To overcome these issues, it was commonly accepted that English should be replaced with local languages of the country. However, once this was accepted, there arose another issue as to the status that should be conferred to each local language; in particular, whether Sinhala and Tamil should be given equal status ('parity of status'), or whether Sinhala should be preferred over Tamil. Tambiah stated that this issue 'proved to be unexpectedly contentious' between Sinhalese and Tamils.[129] One reason for this was that the Sinhalese were the overwhelming majority of the country. The other reason was the way in which the Sinhalese majority viewed the Tamil minority in the wake of Sri Lanka's independence. In particular, the Sinhalese majority's impression of the Tamil minority was that the latter received preferential treatment from British rulers and enjoyed prestigious positions and better jobs in the public service because

125 Coperahewa, above n 105, 69, 93.
126 Ibid.
127 The rise of linguistic nationalism is a common factor that can be seen in many other developing countries that have gained their independence from Britain. See, e.g., Ze'ev Sher, 'Reflections on Copyright in Developing Countries' (1968–1969) 16 *Bulletin of the Copyright Society of the USA* 201, 206.
128 SJ Tambiah, *Sri Lanka: Ethnic Fratricide and the Dismantling of Democracy* (IB Tauris, 1986) 74.
129 Ibid.

of their knowledge of and education in English.[130] Therefore, many Sinhalese believed that Sinhala should be given preference over Tamil in the administration of the country which, in turn, would provide the Sinhala majority with the means to occupy a majority of better employment positions in proportion to their demographic share.

However, the Tamils were not willing to concede to the Sinhalese proposals that Sinhala should be given preference over Tamil. As a result, a series of debates ensued between the two communities with regard to the language issue in the immediate period after Sri Lanka's independence. Notably, these debates showed victory for the Sinhalese, with the electoral victory in 1956 of the government under the prime ministership of SWRD Bandaranaike.[131] As Wilson observed, the most significant outcome of the electoral victory in 1956 was that 'the rural masses and the Sinhalese Buddhist intelligentsia now came to grips with the realities of political power.'[132] One of the main demands of these groups was conferring Sinhala its due place in Sri Lanka. In particular, the Buddhist pressure groups at that time, particularly the organisations of Buddhist monks, vociferously 'campaigned for the adoption of Sinhala as the sole official language'.[133] According to Wilson, 'Bandaranaike, who had reflected as well as articulated their needs and aspirations, found it difficult at times to hold the more militant sections in check.'[134] In fact, Prime Minister Bandaranaike himself had said at the general election of 1956 that 'if returned to power, he would affect a switchover from English in "twenty four hours"'.[135] As Coperahewa observed, 'Bandaranaike was elected Prime Minister at least in part based on his main election promise to establish Sinhala as the *only* Official language of the country, replacing English, and indeed, his first official action after his election was to fulfil his promise.'[136]

Soon after the electoral victory, the Bandaranaike government enacted the *Official Language Act 1956*, declaring Sinhala to be the only official language throughout Sri Lanka. However, it 'allowed for a transitional period of five years, with January 1961 as the date when the Act would be implemented in all its rigour.'[137] In the years to come, the declaration of Sinhala as the only official language widened the language and ethnic conflicts between the Sinhalese and Tamils, which remain unresolved to this day, and was an important factor that paved the way to Sri Lanka's recently ended three-decade civil war.

130 de Silva, above n 45, xi, xii.
131 Tambiah, above n 128, 75.
132 AJ Wilson, 'Politics and Political Development Since 1948' in KM de Silva (ed), *Sri Lanka: A Survey* (University Press of Hawaii, 1977) 281, 301.
133 Coperahewa, above n 105, 69, 112.
134 Wilson, above n 132, 281, 301.
135 Coperahewa, above n 105, 69, 111.
136 Ibid., 113.
137 A Jeyaratnam Wilson, *The Break-up of Sri Lanka: The Sinhalese-Tamil Conflict* (Orient Longman, 1988) 112.

Although the *Official Language Act 1956* was a 'triumph of linguistic nationalism' for the Sinhalese,[138] it was a defeat for the Tamils. From the point of view of the Sinhalese people, the declaration of Sinhala as the only official language 'reflected their aspirations to retrieve their cultural heritage, which they felt was endangered by the incursions of the West, and to reassert their position and prerogatives as the majority of the [country's] population'.[139] However, for the Tamils this foreshadowed

> the dangers of political domination by the Sinhala majority, which could lead to the undermining of Tamil language and culture in [Sri] Lanka and the eventual extermination of the [Sri Lankan] Tamil community as a distinctive and unique ethnic entity.[140]

As such, the Tamil community was vehemently opposed to the *Official Language Act*.[141]

As a response to the Tamil agitations over the *Official Language Act 1956*, the Bandaranaike government subsequently enacted the *Tamil Language (Special Provisions) Act 1958*. This Act provided for the use of Tamil as a medium of instruction in government and assisted schools, a medium of examination for admission to the public service and for correspondence and prescribed administrative purposes in the Northern and Eastern Provinces of Sri Lanka (where the majority of Tamil-speaking people are resident).[142] However, this did not satisfy Tamil aspirations, and their distress remained alive.[143] Moreover, as will be seen later, it took another eight years for the Regulations under the *Tamil Language (Special Provisions) Act* to be made and approved by Parliament.[144]

After a short period of unstable government following the assassination of Prime Minister SWRD Bandaranaike in 1959 (by a Buddhist monk), general elections were held in 1960 at which a new government was formed under the prime ministership of Sirimavo Bandaranaike, the widow of SWRD Bandaranaike. The new government, which 'pursued pro-Sinhalese policies',[145] brought the *Official Language Act 1956* into full operation in 1961 while ignoring the provisions of the *Tamil Language (Special Provisions) Act 1958*.[146] Moreover, it declared in

138 de Silva, above n 23, 10–524.
139 Robert N Kearney, 'Language and the Rise of Tamil Separatism in Sri Lanka' (1978) 15(5) *Asian Survey* 521, 528.
140 Ibid.
141 Neil DeVotta, 'Ethnolinguistic Nationalism and Ethnic Conflict in Sri Lanka' in Michael E Brown and Sumit Ganguly (eds), *Fighting Words: Language Policy and Ethnic Relations in Asia* (MIT Press, 2003) 105, 124 (emphasis added) (citations omitted).
142 *Tamil Language (Special Provisions) Act No 28 of 1958* (Sri Lanka), ss 2, 3, 4, 5.
143 Wilson, above n 137, 111.
144 Coperahewa, above n 105, 69, 118.
145 Christine Sixta Rinehart, *Volatile Social Movements and the Origins of Terrorism: The Radicalization of Change* (Lexington Books, 2013) 112.
146 Wilson, above n 137, 112.

1962 'that all entrance exams should be conducted in Sinhala, which was called the standardization policy'.[147] These events led to further agitations by the Tamils. However, pursuant to the defeat of Sirimavo Bandaranaike's government at the general elections held in 1965, a new government came into power under the prime ministership of Dudley Senanayake in coalition with a major Tamil political party (Federal Party). This government made the regulations under the *Tamil Language (Special Provisions) Act* that were approved by Parliament in 1966.[148] The effect of these regulations was that Tamil was recognised as a 'language of administration' along with Sinhala in the Northern and Eastern Provinces.[149] Yet the main opposition in Parliament (the Sri Lanka Freedom Party, led by Sirimavo Bandaranaike) and certain leftist parties were bitterly opposed to this move.[150] Apart from this, neither the *Tamil Language (Special Provisions) Act* nor the Regulations made under it satisfied the Tamils. As such, their grievances continued.

In 1972, for the first time in the history of Sri Lanka, the language policy of the country was given constitutional recognition. In particular, the *Constitution of the Republic of Sri Lanka 1972* (*Constitution 1972*), which was the first autochthonous constitution in postcolonial Sri Lanka, provided that '[t]he Official Language of Sri Lanka shall be Sinhala as provided by the Official Language Act, No.33 of 1956'[151] and that '[t]he use of Tamil language shall be in accordance with the Tamil Language (Special Provisions) Act, No.28 of 1958'.[152] However, it also stated:

> Any regulation for the use of the Tamil language made under the Tamil Language (Special Provisions) Act, No. 28 of 1958, and in force immediately before the commencement of the Constitution shall not in any manner be interpreted as being a provision of the Constitution but shall be deemed to be subordinate legislation.[153]

As Wijeyeratne observed, the last-mentioned provision confirmed the subordinate status of Tamil. Certain other provisions in the *Constitution 1972* relating to language, such as Articles 9, 10 and 11, reinforced this 'hierarchical subordination of the Tamil language'.[154] As such, the language policy envisaged in the

147 Rinehart, above n 145, 112.
148 A Jeyaratnam Wilson, 'Nation-Building in a Demotic State: The Failure of Political Leadership in Sri Lanka' in Amita Shastri and A Jeyaratnam Wilson (eds), *The Post-Colonial States of South Asia: Democracy, Identity, Development and Security* (Routledge, 2001) 88, 97.
149 Ibid.
150 Neil DeVotta, *Blowback: Linguistic Nationalism, Institutional Decay and Ethnic Conflict in Sri Lanka* (Stanford University Press, 2004) 133.
151 *Constitution of the Republic of Sri Lanka 1972*, art 7.
152 Ibid., art 8(1).
153 Ibid., art 8(2).
154 Roshan de Silva Wijeyeratne, *Nation, Constitutionalism and Buddhism in Sri Lanka* (Routledge, 2014) 138.

Constitution 1972 did not appease the Tamils. As Wilson observed, '[t]he Tamils felt indignant that it was specifically stated in the constitution that the provisions relating to the Tamil language could be amended by ordinary legislation whereas the provisions relating to Sinhalese were constitutionally entrenched.'[155] In short, it was believed that the *Constitution 1972* was a 'triumph of Sinhalese Buddhist linguistic nationalism'.[156]

Apart from the language policy, which was in favour of the Sinhalese, the *Constitution 1972* also contained certain new provisions that irked the Tamil community. In particular, the *Constitution 1972* declared Sri Lanka a unitary state for the first time and gave "foremost" place to Buddhism—the primary religion of the Sinhalese.[157] It also expressly precluded judicial review of legislation and 'removed an important safeguard for minorities that was in the previous constitution'.[158]

Given that the *Constitution 1972* clearly went against the aspirations of Tamils, it was not surprising that the Tamil United Front (TUF),[159] which was formed in 1972 with the participation of several influential Tamil political groups, rejected the *Constitution*.[160] In particular, they said:

> [T]he Republican Constitution of 1972 has made the Tamils a slave nation ruled by the new colonial masters, the Sinhalese, who are using the power they have wrongly usurped to deprive the Tamil Nation of its territory, language, citizenship, economic life, opportunities of employment and education, thereby destroying all the attributes of nationhood of the Tamil people.[161]

As Kearney noted, the *Constitution 1972* 'fuelled the swift growth of sentiment' of the Tamil people for separation.[162] Moreover, Gomez observed that '[a]t around this time, the language based "standardization" with regard to entry to Sri Lankan universities had angered Tamil youth'.[163] Ultimately, the Tamil agitations became more and more aggressive and eventually turned into an extremist militant combat.

The immediate aftermath of the *Constitution 1972* showed clear signs of preparation of the Tamils towards separatism and for an armed struggle for this purpose, if needed. In particular, the Vaddukoddai Resolution, the resolution

155 A Jeyaratnam Wilson, *Politics in Sri Lanka 1947–79* (Palgrave Macmillan, 2nd ed, 1979) 22 (citations omitted).
156 Wijeyeratne, above n 154, 138.
157 Mario Gomez, 'Keeping Rights Alive: Reform and Reconciliation in Post-War Sri Lanka' (2011) 17 *Asian Yearbook of International Law* 117, 122.
158 Ibid.
159 The Tamil United Front was later renamed as Tamil United Liberation Front (TULF).
160 See Kearney, above n 139, 521, 529.
161 Vaddukoddai Resolution: The Resolution unanimously adopted at the First National Convention of the Tamil United Liberation Front held at Vaddukoddai on 14 May 1976.
162 Kearney, above n 139, 521, 529.
163 Gomez, above n 157, 117, 122.

unanimously adopted at the first National Convention of the Tamil United Liberation Front (TULF) at Vaddukoddai on 14 May 1976, clearly advocated for a separate state called 'Tamil Eelam' in the Northern and Eastern Provinces of Sri Lanka. In particular, the Resolution declared:

> Tamils of [Sri Lanka] by virtue of their great language, their religions, their separate culture and heritage, their history of independent existence as a separate state over a distinct territory for several centuries till they were conquered by the armed might of the European invaders and above all by their will to exist as a separate entity ruling themselves in their own territory, are a nation distinct and apart from Sinhalese.[164]

Accordingly, the National Convention resolved that

> the restoration and reconstitution of the Free, Sovereign, Secular, Socialist State of [Tamil Eelam], based on the right of self-determination inherent to every nation, has become inevitable in order to safeguard the very existence of the Tamil Nation in this Country.[165]

Moreover, it called upon the 'Tamil Nation in general and the Tamil youth in particular to come forward to throw themselves fully into the sacred fight for freedom and to flinch not till the goal of a sovereign state of [Tamil Eelam] is reached.'[166]

Certainly, one of the most important reasons for the separatism advocated by the Vaddukoddai Resolution was the inferior status accorded to the Tamil language in Sri Lanka. In particular, it specifically said:

> [S]uccessive Sinhalese governments since independence have always encouraged and fostered the aggressive nationalism of the Sinhalese people and have used their political power to the detriment of the Tamils by . . . [m]aking Sinhala the only official language throughout [Sri Lanka] thereby placing the stamp of inferiority on the Tamils and the Tamil Language.[167]

From the early 1970s, Tamil youths began civil disturbances in the northern parts of Sri Lanka in a move to air their grievances against language use and other issues.[168] These activities entered a new phase with the formation of the Liberation Tigers of Tamil Eelam (LTTE) in the mid-1970s, which had the objective of carrying out an armed struggle for the establishment of the separate State of

164 Vaddukoddai Resolution: The Resolution unanimously adopted at the First National Convention of the Tamil United Liberation Front held at Vaddukoddai on 14 May 1976.
165 Ibid.
166 Ibid.
167 Ibid., (emphasis added).
168 Coperahewa, above n 105, 69, 120.

Tamil Eelam on the Sri Lankan territory.[169] The LTTE became a terrorist group in the years to come. In 1983, it killed 13 soldiers of the Sri Lankan armed forces in Jaffna, following which the Sinhalese in Colombo reacted with ethnic riots against Tamils living in that area. Immediately after this, the Sri Lankan government started to combat the LTTE and the battle continued between the two parties for more than 25 years until the LTTE was officially defeated by the Sri Lankan government in 2009.

Despite the end of the civil war in 2009, the conflict with regard to language use between the Sinhalese and the Tamils remains alive in Sri Lanka. Even the provisions relating to language introduced into the *Constitution 1978* (discussed in the next section) in order to pacify the aspirations of the Tamil people have not been able to effectively solve this issue. Since language remains a very sensitive issue in Sri Lanka, it is unlikely that the use of Tamil and Sinhala languages will be replaced by English, although its importance is strongly felt in modern Sri Lanka.

2.4.1.2. Language rights in the Constitution

The constitutional entrenchment of the right to use Sinhala and Tamil languages is another reason that it is difficult to promote English in Sri Lanka, particularly as a compulsory medium of instruction in government schools.

The present Constitution of Sri Lanka, that is, the *Constitution 1978*, contains certain important provisions with regard to the people's right to use Sinhala and Tamil. These provisions are in chapter 4 of the *Constitution 1978*, which incorporates Articles 18–25A. Article 18(1) of the *Constitution* declares Sinhala the official language of Sri Lanka, while Article 18(2) also declares Tamil to be an official language. Apart from this, Article 18(3) states that 'English shall be the link language'. Further, Article 19 states that '[t]he National Languages of Sri Lanka shall be Sinhala and Tamil'.

Article 21 of the *Constitution 1978* deals with a person's right to receive education in a national language, i.e. Sinhala or Tamil. In particular, it states:

> A person shall be entitled to be educated through the medium of either of the National Languages:
>
> Provided that the provisions of this paragraph shall not apply to an institution of higher education where the medium of instruction is a language other than a National Language.

Thus, a person has the right to receive primary and secondary education in Sinhala or Tamil. This right does not extend to tertiary (higher) education where the language of instruction in the institution providing such education is not Sinhala or Tamil. However, Article 21(2) of the *Constitution 1978* states:

169 Ibid.

> Where one National Language is a medium of instruction for or in any course, department or faculty of any University directly or indirectly financed by the State, the other National Language shall also be made a medium of instruction for or in such course, department or faculty for students who prior to their admission to such university, were educated through the medium of such other National Language:
>
> Provided that compliance with the preceding provisions of this paragraph shall not be obligatory if such other National Language is the medium of instruction for or in any like course, department or faculty either at any other campus or branch of such University or of any other like University.

Given that almost all the universities in Sri Lanka are financed by the State, a person may have a right to receive tertiary education in Sinhala or Tamil in appropriate circumstances which fall under Article 21(2).[170] Apart from this, Article 25 of the *Constitution 1978* requires the State to 'provide adequate facilities for the use of the languages provided for in [chapter 4]'. This means that Sri Lanka has a positive obligation to provide adequate facilities for the use of Sinhala and Tamil in education.

As provided in Article 126 of the *Constitution 1978*, a person can seek redress from the Supreme Court of Sri Lanka in the event the rights declared and recognised by chapter 4 are infringed or about to be infringed by 'executive or administrative action'.[171] The Supreme Court, which is vested with the 'sole and exclusive jurisdiction to hear and determine' such matters,[172] has the power to grant any relief or make any directions 'as it may deem just and equitable'.[173] Therefore, a person can resort to the Supreme Court in a situation where he or she is prevented from receiving education in either Sinhala or Tamil by an action of the government. Given that the government is the main provider of education in Sri Lanka, it has a constitutional obligation to provide education at least at the primary and secondary levels in the mediums of both Sinhala and Tamil.[174] If not, the government can be held liable for breach of language rights declared by chapter 4 of the *Constitution* for which the Supreme Court can impose sanctions.

2.4.1.3. Lack of facilities for the teaching of English

Another factor that affects the promotion of English in Sri Lanka is the lack of facilities for the teaching of English in schools. Although '[t]eachers are the most important resource in the promotion of English language skills among students

170 See Angela W Little and Siri T Hettige, *Globalisation, Employment and Education in Sri Lanka: Opportunity and Division* (Routledge, 2013) 96.
171 *Constitution of the Democratic Socialist Republic of Sri Lanka 1978*, art 126(2).
172 Ibid., art 126(1).
173 Ibid., art 126(4).
174 Aturupane et al., above n 107, 2.

at all grade levels',[175] there is a marked deficiency of quality English teachers in Sri Lanka, especially in the rural areas. There is also a shortage of expertise to train and advise English teachers in Sri Lanka. This not only prevents making education in English compulsory but also affects the teaching of English as a secondary language.

As observed earlier, from the 1980s onwards the government of Sri Lanka has taken a keen interest in promoting English at the school level. In recent years, it has taken certain special steps in this regard. The appointment of a Special Task Force by the President of Sri Lanka to expand and strengthen English language skills is one such example.[176] Despite these efforts, lack of facilities for teaching English, particularly quality teachers, is a severe problem for the promotion of English in Sri Lankan schools. According to a World Bank study, the quality of English teachers is a key constraint for the promotion of English language skills among students in Sri Lankan schools, especially in rural areas.[177] In particular, '[a]bout 35 percent of schools are considered to have a deficit of [English] teachers'.[178] Apart from this, there are serious issues with regard to the quality of the English teachers. As the World Bank study stated:

> The quality of [English] teachers is highly variable. At the upper end of the distribution, there are good, competent and dedicated teachers. However, at the lower end of the distribution, there are serious issues of teacher quality.[179]

The shortage of qualified experts to train and advise English teachers is another serious problem which Sri Lanka is facing in promoting English language skills in schools. In particular, there is 'a shortage of teacher educators and teacher trainers qualified in the Teaching of English as a Second Language (TESL) to provide pre-service teacher education and continuing teacher development for school teachers'.[180] In addition, there is also 'a shortage of English Subject Directors with English teaching/training experience, and of English In-Service Advisors (ISAs) in many locations'.[181]

2.4.2. Constitutional mandate and past government practices

The language rights in the *Constitution 1978* and past practices of the governments of Sri Lanka have identified translation as an important mechanism to promote access to knowledge.

175 Ibid., 73.
176 Ibid., 67.
177 Ibid., 73.
178 Ibid. (citations omitted).
179 Ibid., 73 (citations omitted).
180 Ibid., 74 (citations omitted).
181 Ibid.

The language rights in the *Constitution 1978* indirectly mandate the government of Sri Lanka to facilitate translation. In particular, provision of education in the two national languages requires knowledge products to be made available in both Sinhala and Tamil for educational purposes. Given that Sri Lanka still imports knowledge products, particularly in the field of science and technology, from developed countries, and that knowledge products produced in these countries (and in Sri Lanka) are mostly available in English, Sri Lanka needs to translate them into the Sinhala and Tamil languages for the purpose of provision of education. This need is furthered by the constitutional obligation of the Sri Lankan State to 'provide adequate facilities for the use' of Sinhala and Tamil, and the instructions under the Directive Principles of State Policy to 'assist the development of the cultures and the languages of the People'.[182]

The need for translation, particularly for the provision of education in Sri Lanka, was recognised during the British colonial period. For instance, British Governor Stewart-Mackenzie, who was 'keenly interested in education as well as promotion of Christianity [in Sri Lanka] through the education system' and who believed that 'conversion to Christianity [of Sri Lankans] must be preceded by education, after learning to read in their own language', proposed in 1840 'the encouragement of general elementary instruction in Sinhala and Tamil as a prelude to English education'.[183] For this purpose, he 'suggested the establishment of a Native Normal School to train teachers in the local languages and a Translating Committee to translate the Bible and other books to the local languages'.[184] However, the Colonial Office rejected this proposal, stating that

> [i]t would be unnecessary for the government to direct its attention to devote the funds available for education to instruction in the native languages and that the preferable plan would be to encourage the acquirement of the English language by conveying instruction in that language.[185]

The need for translation was also recognised as part of the education reforms which took place in the mid-twentieth century on the recommendations of the Special Committee on Education. This was because the widespread use of local languages in education meant that educational and learning materials (especially in the field of science and technology) had to be prepared in these languages, which, in turn, necessitated the translation of these works from English into local languages. Baldsing noted:

> With the entry of Sinhala and Tamil as media of instruction in the secondary schools and the increase in enrolments, positive steps had to be taken to

182 *Constitution of the Democratic Socialist Republic of Sri Lanka 1978*, art 27(10).

183 Swarna Jayaweera, 'Language and Colonial Education Policy in Ceylon in the Nineteenth Century' (1971) 2(2) *Modern Ceylon Studies* 153, 157 (citations omitted).

184 Ibid.

185 Ibid.

> procure books in the national languages for higher education. Out of this necessity, the Swabasha Textbook Production Unit was founded in 1955 as a wing of the Official Languages Department [which] addressed itself mainly to preparing glossaries of scientific and technical terms and to compiling and translating science and mathematics books.[186]

The introduction of the *Official Language Act 1956* and the *Tamil Language (Special Provisions) Act 1958* also necessitated translation of knowledge products, particularly in the field of science and technology into Sinhala and Tamil. Prime Minister SWRD Bandaranaike, who identified the need to translate these knowledge products, was of the view that Sri Lanka should have more liberty for translation. Thus, on 20 July 1959 (two months prior to his assassination) he wrote the following to the Swiss Federal Political Department regarding Sri Lanka's membership to the *Berne Convention*:

> [T]he Government of Ceylon, while acceding to the [Berne] Convention reserves for itself the right to enact local legislation for the translation of educational, scientific and technical books into the national language.[187]

However, the purported reservation to the *Berne Convention* regarding Sri Lanka's right to enact local legislation for the translation of educational, scientific and technical books into the national language did not yield any results. Despite that, the government of Sri Lanka was keen to translate knowledge products required for educational purposes until the latter part of twentieth century. In particular, translation of these knowledge products was mainly carried out by certain government departments and units. However, the government has moved away from translating scientific and technical knowledge products, primarily because of the enormous costs and delays involved in translation. Fernando noted:

> Attempts made by the Government of Sri Lanka to undertake the translation of renowned English text-books were abandoned many years ago when it was realized that the exponential growth of scientific knowledge cannot be matched by such costly and expensive endeavours in any satisfactory or pragmatic manner.[188]

2.5. Copyright law and translation in Sri Lanka

The copyright law of Sri Lanka fetters timely and affordable translation of scientific and technical knowledge products produced in developed countries. The

186 LindZay Baldsing, 'Making English the Lynchpin for Globalisation of Education in Sri Lanka: Quality versus Equality' (PhD Thesis, Edith Cowan University, 2013) 61 (citations omitted).

187 'Documents of the Twentieth Session including the Report of the Commission to the General Assembly' [1968] II *Yearbook of the International Law Commission* 1, 15.

188 Fernando, above n 100.

reason for this is the way copyright owners' translation rights are protected in Sri Lankan copyright law.

Copyright law in Sri Lanka does not address Sri Lanka's translation needs. As previously pointed out, Sri Lanka needs to be able to translate scientific and technical books and learning materials to allow access to scientific and technical knowledge. There are three special characteristics relating to Sri Lanka's need for translation. Firstly, (as discussed before) Sri Lanka needs to promptly translate scientific and technical books and learning materials that are mostly produced in developed countries. Secondly, Sri Lanka needs to translate these knowledge products in whole and to reproduce them in large quantities. This is because these knowledge products are required to be used in mass educational programs. Thirdly, Sri Lanka needs to translate these knowledge products and to reproduce the translations at an affordable cost because of the financial resource constraints. However, because Sri Lankan copyright law protects copyright owners' translation rights without providing for adequate exceptions thereto, it is unlikely that Sri Lanka would be able to translate most of these knowledge products and reproduce the translations in large quantities on time and at affordable prices.

2.5.1. An outline of Sri Lanka's copyright law and international copyright obligations

Copyright law in Sri Lanka is a British legacy. Karunaratna observed that 'the norms of copyright entered the domestic legal system [of Sri Lanka] during the British colonial period.'[189] The first domestic copyright legislation in Sri Lanka was enacted in 1908, when Sri Lanka was under British rule. At present, Sri Lanka's copyright law is exclusively governed by the *Intellectual Property Act 2003.*

Sri Lanka is a signatory to a number of international conventions regarding copyright. These include the *Berne Convention*, the *Universal Copyright Convention 1952* (*UCC*)[190] and the *TRIPS Agreement.*[191] Out of these, the *TRIPS Agreement* and the *Berne Convention* are the most influential instruments on copyright law in Sri Lanka since the provisions of the *Intellectual Property Act 2003* are compliant with the *TRIPS Agreement* and the *Berne Convention.*[192] In addition, Sri Lanka has also concluded a bilateral agreement with the United States: *Agreement on the Protection and Enforcement of Intellectual Property Rights between the United States of America and the Democratic Socialist Republic of Sri Lanka*, signed on 20 September 1991 (*US-Sri Lanka IPR Agreement*), which covers copyright protection in the two countries.

189 DM Karunaratna, *An Introduction to the Law of Copyright and Related Rights in Sri Lanka* (Sarvodaya Vishva Lekha, 2006) 5.

190 Sri Lanka acceded to the *Universal Copyright Convention* as revised on 24 July 1971, with Appendix Declaration relating to Article XVII and Resolution concerning Article XI on 25 October 1983.

191 The *TRIPS Agreement 1994* entered into force in Sri Lanka on 1 January 1995.

192 DM Karunaratna, *Elements of the Law of Intellectual Property in Sri Lanka* (Sarasavi Publishers, 2010) 19, n 10.

The objective of Sri Lankan copyright law is to promote public benefit. To this end, it strives to strike a balance between the 'rights of the creators in their literary and artistic creations and the legitimate interests of the users of such creations.'[193] Thus, copyright law of Sri Lanka is essentially a balancing act between the protection of the rights of authors (copyright owners) and the ability of users of copyright protected works to access them. However, with regard to translation of copyright protected works, the "balance" that is struck by the Sri Lankan copyright law (i.e. the *Intellectual Property Act 2003*) between the protection of rights of copyright owners and the ability of the users of copyright protected works to access them in the form of translations is tilted in favour of the copyright owners.

2.5.2. *The Intellectual Property Act*

The *Intellectual Property Act 2003* constrains translation of copyright protected knowledge products in the field of science and technology produced in developed countries. It also constrains the reproduction of the translations in bulk quantities within acceptable time frames and at affordable prices, because it protects copyright owners' translation rights without providing adequate exceptions thereto.

The *Intellectual Property Act 2003* protects original literary and scientific works produced in Sri Lanka as well as in foreign countries with which Sri Lanka has international copyright protection arrangements.[194] For the most part, knowledge products produced in developed countries in the field of science and technology are original literary and scientific works. Because of the *Berne Convention*, *TRIPS Agreement* and the *US-Sri Lanka IPR Agreement*, these knowledge products receive copyright protection in Sri Lanka under the *Intellectual Property Act*. As a result, the copyright owners of scientific and technical knowledge products produced in developed countries receive protection for translation rights in Sri Lanka.

2.5.2.1. *Translation rights under the Intellectual Property Act*

The *Intellectual Property Act 2003* affords extensive protection to translation rights of the owners of original literary and scientific works (copyright protected works) produced in Sri Lanka as well as in foreign countries with which Sri Lanka has international copyright protection arrangements. In particular, Section 9(1) of the *Intellectual Property Act 2003* states:

> [T]he owner of copyright of a work shall have the exclusive right to carry out or authorize the . . . translation of [that] work.

193 Karunaratna, above n 189, 1. See also *Vasantha Obeysekera v Anthony Christopher Alles*, (Unreported) CA No 730/92(F) decided on 22 March 2000 at 10.

194 *Intellectual Property Act No 36 of 2003* (Sri Lanka) s 26(2).

Under the *Intellectual Property Act 2003*, the translation rights of the copyright owners last for the 'lifetime of the author [of the work] and for a further period of seventy years from the date of his death'.[195] It is to be noted that the duration of translation rights under the *Intellectual Property Act* exceeds that under the *Berne Convention* and the *TRIPS Agreement*. In particular, under the *Berne Convention* and the *TRIPS Agreement*, translation rights are only protected for the life of the author and for 50 years after his or her death.[196]

As stated in the previous chapter, copyright owners' translation rights have the potential to prohibit translation of copyright protected works or increase the cost of translation and/or delay the process of translation. As such, protection of translation rights under the *Intellectual Property Act 2003* is inimical for the timely and affordable translation of scientific and technical books and learning materials produced in developed countries and the publication of translations in large quantities.

2.5.2.2. Exceptions to translation rights

The *Intellectual Property Act 2003* recognises certain exceptions to translation rights. However, these exceptions are inadequate to facilitate translation of copyright protected scientific and technical books and learning materials produced in developed countries. They are also inadequate for the publication of translations in large quantities in a timely and affordable manner.

The *Intellectual Property Act 2003* recognises only general exceptions to translation rights. The main general exception to translation rights in the *Intellectual Property Act* is fair use. The *Intellectual Property Act* does not provide for special exceptions to translation rights. Given that Sri Lanka is a developing country that needs to translate copyright protected scientific and technical books and learning materials produced in developed countries in order to promote access to scientific and technical knowledge, the absence of a special exception to translation rights in the *Intellectual Property Act* is rather peculiar. This is particularly so in light of the fact that the Appendix to the *Berne Convention* (*Paris Act 1971*) provides for special exceptions to translation rights in developing countries. Although Sri Lanka did not ratify the Berne Appendix until 2005, and therefore was not able to introduce these exceptions into the *Intellectual Property Act* when it was enacted, Sri Lanka could have subsequently amended the Act to introduce these exceptions.[197] However, this has not yet occurred.

195 Ibid., s 13(1).

196 *Berne Convention* (*Paris Act 1971*) art 7; *TRIPS Agreement*, art 12.

197 Sri Lanka's initial ratification of the *Paris Act 1971* of the *Berne Convention* excluded Articles 1 to 21 and the Appendix. However, in 2005 Sri Lanka ratified Articles 1 to 21 and the Appendix of the *Paris Act*. Also, Sri Lanka availed itself of the faculties provided for in Articles II and III of the Appendix. The relevant declaration which Sri Lanka made on 27 September 2005 was effective until 10 October 2014. WIPO, *Berne Notification No 248:*

2.5.2.2.1. FAIR USE

The fair use defence in the *Intellectual Property Act 2003* is the most important exception to copyright owners' translation rights. However, this defence is inadequate to facilitate timely and affordable translation of copyright protected scientific and technical books and learning materials produced in developed countries—and the publication of translations in large quantities. There are two main reasons for this: the uncertainty attached to the fair use defence and its narrow scope.

Section 11(1) of the *Intellectual Property Act 2003*, which provides for the fair use defence, states:

> Notwithstanding the provisions of subsection (1) of section 9, the fair use of a work, including such use by reproduction in copies or by any other means specified by that section, for the purposes such as criticism, comment, news reporting, teaching (including multiple copies for classroom use), scholarship or research, shall not be an infringement of copyright.

Although not specifically mentioned in Section 11(1), the fair use defence applies to translation rights. It is also clear that the application of fair use extends beyond the purposes listed in Section 11(1).[198] In other words, if translating a copyright protected work can be considered as fair use, the purposes mentioned in Section 11(1) would not really matter. This is because, as Karunaratna observed, '[t]he purposes of fair use referred to in this section are merely a set of examples. They do not constitute an exhaustive list'.[199] As such, fair use in the *Intellectual Property Act* 'is obviously open-ended'.[200] However, the *Act* provides for a set of criteria that the courts should adopt to determine fair use.[201] These are:

(a) The purpose and character of the use, including whether such use is of a commercial nature or is for non-profit educational purposes;
(b) The nature of the copyrighted work;
(c) The amount and substantiality of the portion used in relation to the copyrighted work as a whole; and
(d) The effect of the use upon the potential market for, or value of, the copyrighted work.[202]

The provisions relating to fair use in the *Intellectual Property Act 2003* closely resemble those in the United States *Copyright Act 1976*.[203] However, there are two main

---

Berne Convention for the Protection of Literary Works and Artistic Works <www.wipo.int/treaties/en/notifications/berne/treaty_berne_248.html>.

198 Karunaratna, above n 189, 77.

199 Ibid.

200 Ibid.

201 *Intellectual Property Act No 36 of 2003* (Sri Lanka) s 11(2).

202 Ibid.

203 Cf *Intellectual Property Act No 36 of 2003* (Sri Lanka) s 11 and *Copyright Act 1976* (United States) s 107.

differences between the Sri Lankan *Act* and the United States *Act*. Firstly, the discretion granted to the courts to determine fair use by the Sri Lankan *Act* is more constrained than in the United States *Act*.[204] This is because the factors that a court should consider to determine fair use in the United States *Act* are non-exhaustive, whereas under the Sri Lankan *Act* they are exhaustive.[205] Secondly, the United States *Act* does not distinguish between published and unpublished works in determining fair use.[206] However, the Sri Lankan *Act* is silent on this aspect. As Hemeratne observed, this makes it arguable '[w]hether a work is published or unpublished should be a crucial element to determine the application of fair use under the [Sri Lankan] Act'.[207] Apart from this, the Sri Lankan *Intellectual Property Act* enumerates certain specific 'acts of fair use'.[208] Yet none of these 'acts of fair use' covers translation.

The fair use defence in the *Intellectual Property Act 2003* suffers from two main defects that make it unlikely that the defence would help to facilitate timely and affordable translation of copyright protected scientific and technical books and learning materials, which is a prerequisite for Sri Lanka to promote access to scientific and technical knowledge. Firstly, fair use is an uncertain defence, which makes reliance on it for unauthorised translation of copyright protected works risky. Secondly, the fair use defence appears to be too narrow and limited, in that it is unlikely that the defence would allow the translation of a whole work (as distinct from part of a work) and for a translated work to be published (reproduced) in multiple quantities.[209]

Before discussing the uncertainty surrounding the fair use defence and its narrow scope, it is important to note that there are no authoritative judicial decisions in Sri Lanka which set out the scope and parameters of the defence. Therefore, reference has to be made to the judicial decisions with regard to fair use in the United States while bearing in mind the different ways this defence has been articulated in the Sri Lankan *Intellectual Property Act* and the United States *Copyright Act*. In fact, Karunaratna observed that since 'Section 11(1) [of the Sri Lankan *Intellectual Property Act*] is almost a verbatim reproduction of Section 107 of the US Copyright Act', '[t]he relevant judicial decisions in the US courts would . . . be useful in understanding the doctrine of fair use and its parameters' in Sri Lanka.[210]

Uncertainty of the fair use defence In the United States, the fair use defence has been stated as 'the most troublesome in the whole law of copyright'.[211] This

204 See Karunaratna, above n 189, 80.
205 Ibid.
206 Kate O'Neill, 'Against Dicta: A Legal Method for Rescuing Fair Use from the Right of First Publication' (2001) 89 *California Law Review* 371, 375 n 17.
207 TSK Hemaratne, 'Intellectual Property Law and E-Commerce in Sri Lanka: Towards a Jurisprudence Based on Constitution, Roman-Dutch Law and Buddhist Principle' (PhD Thesis, Queen Mary, University of London, 2005) 213.
208 *Intellectual Property Act No 36 of 2003* (Sri Lanka) ss 11(3), 12.
209 Chamila Talagala and Leanne Wiseman, 'Copyright, Open Access and Translation' (2015) 37(8) *European Intellectual Property Review* 498, 500–501.
210 Karunaratna, above n 189, 77.
211 Eric J Schwartz and David Nimmer, LexisNexis, *International Copyright Law and Practice*, vol 2 (at Release 25) § 8[2][a][i] citing *Deller v Samuel Goldwyn Inc*, 104 F2d 661, 662 (2d Cir1939).

statement would be equally applicable to Sri Lanka owing to the legal uncertainty attached to the defence. In particular, because the *Intellectual Property Act 2003* of Sri Lanka does not define what is meant by a fair use, and thus keeps it open-ended, the liability for copyright infringement of a person who purports to translate a copyright protected work under fair use remains uncertain. Although the Act enumerates a set of criteria (the four factors under Section 11(2) mentioned earlier) which courts should adopt to determine fair use, it tells very little about when this defence would be available. Also, referring to the same set of criteria enumerated in the United States *Copyright Act 1976*, David Nimmer observed that 'reliance on the four statutory factors to reach fair use often seems naught but a fairy tale'.[212]

The uncertainty surrounding the fair use defence acts as a deterrent for carrying out unauthorised translation under fair use. Also, given that deciding whether an unauthorised translation of a copyright protected work is fair use is ultimately left to the courts,[213] the costs involved in litigation deter many people in Sri Lanka who may otherwise embark on unauthorised translation of copyright protected works under fair use.[214] This is because litigation in Sri Lanka is a protracted and a costly affair that many Sri Lankans cannot afford.[215] Also, since copyright owners of most of the scientific and technical books and learning materials are well-established international publishers who are financially powerful, litigation to decide whether the unauthorised translation of these knowledge products is fair use imposes a lesser burden for copyright owners when compared with the defendant translators in Sri Lanka who do not have the financial means to afford the cost of litigation.[216] Moreover, since the burden of proving (in litigation) that translating a copyright protected work is fair use falls on the translator, it becomes easy for the copyright owners to prevent translation of their works by frightening the translators with claims of infringement, even in circumstances in which the fair use defence would likely succeed. In such situations, the translators might refrain from proceeding with translation rather than spending money on litigation.[217] Apart from this, the fact that copyright infringement can entail criminal sanctions, particularly imprisonment, may also effectively deter translators from embarking on unauthorised translation of copyright protected works even in circumstances where the nebulous fair use defence would likely allow such translation.[218]

212 David Nimmer, '"Fairest of Them All" and Other Fairy Tales of Fair Use' (2003) 66 *Law and Contemporary Problems* 263, 287.

213 Eric J Schwartz and David Nimmer, LexisNexis, *International Copyright Law and Practice*, vol 2 (at Release 25) § 8[2][a][i].

214 See Strba, above n 96, 133.

215 See Sahanika Sriyananda, 'Law's Delays—A Major Concern—Justice Ministry Secretary' *Sunday Observer* (online), 29 January 2012 <www.sundayobserver.lk/2012/01/29/fea06.asp>.

216 Strba, above n 96, 133.

217 Ibid.

218 *Intellectual Property Act* No.36 of 2003 (Sri Lanka), s 178(1).

Narrow scope of the fair use defence Because the scope of the fair use defence in the *Intellectual Property Act 2003* is too narrow and limited, it is unlikely that the defence would allow the translation of copyright protected scientific and technical works in whole and the publication of translations in large quantities, which is a prerequisite to the promotion of access to scientific and technical knowledge in Sri Lanka. As mentioned earlier, the scope of the fair use defence in the *Intellectual Property Act* is narrower than that in the United States *Copyright Act 1976*. Even under United States *Copyright Act*, the '[v]erbatim replication of an entire work, or almost an entire work or of the "heart" of the work, threatening to supplant the market for that work, rarely qualifies as fair use', although there is 'no categorical rule [that] may be specified to determine the extent or manner of copying allowable as fair use'.[219]

It is important to note that unauthorised translation of the whole of a copyright protected work and the publication of the translation in multiple quantities are uses that are likely to have an impact on 'the potential market for, or value of, the copyrighted work',[220] which is one of the factors that courts should consider when determining fair use. As the Supreme Court of the United States decided, this 'is undoubtedly the single most important element of fair use.'[221] Also, as Melville Nimmer observed:

> Fair use, when properly applied, is limited to copying by others which does not materially impair the marketability of the work which is copied.[222]

When determining 'effect of the use upon the potential market for, or value of, the copyrighted work', courts in the United States have considered several matters.[223] In particular, in *Harper & Row Publishers Inc v Nation Enterprises*,[224] the Supreme Court of the United States observed that in order 'to negate fair use one need only show that if the challenged use "should become widespread, it would adversely affect the *potential* market for the copyrighted work".'[225] More importantly, the Court stated:

> The inquiry must take account not only of harm to the original but also of harm to the market for derivative works. . . . 'If the defendant's work

219 Eric J Schwartz and David Nimmer, LexisNexis, *International Copyright Law and Practice*, vol 2 (at Release 25) § 8[2][a][i] (citations omitted).
220 *Intellectual Property Act* No.36 of 2003 (Sri Lanka), s 11(2)(d).
221 *Harper & Row Publishers Inc v Nation Enterprises*, 471 US 539, 566 (1985); 105 SCt 2218, 2233 (1985) (citations omitted).
222 Melville B Nimmer, 'Does Copyright Abridge the First Amendment Guarantees of Free Speech and Press?' (1970) 17 *UCLA Law Review* 1180, 1200–1201; see also Melville B Nimmer, Matthew Bender, *Nimmer on Copyright* (at Release 4) § 145.
223 See Karunaratna, above n 189, 83.
224 471 US 539 (1985); 105 SCt 2218 (1985).
225 471 US 539, 566 (1985); 105 SCt 2218, 2234 (1985) (citations omitted).

> adversely affects the value of any of the rights in the copyright work . . . the use is not fair'.[226]

Unauthorised translation of the whole of a copyright protected work into a particular language (for example, Sinhala), and the publication of the translation in multiple quantities, would essentially cause harm to the market for potential translations of that copyright protected work into that particular language (i.e. Sinhala).[227] As such, an unauthorised translation of the whole of a copyright protected work and the publication of the translation in multiple quantities would not qualify as a fair use.

According to Venuti, however, '[a] translation, insofar as it is written in a different language for a different culture, does not limit the potential market for the foreign text in its own language and culture.'[228] Instead, 'the translation of a work into many languages could increase its literary and commercial value at home by demonstrating its value abroad.'[229] How far this argument would be valid in the case of the translation of scientific and technical books and learning materials (which are the ones that are mostly and urgently need to be translated in Sri Lanka) remains doubtful. This is because, even if these works are not translated, there will still be people in Sri Lanka (especially those who are bilingual and have the financial resources) who would buy these works since they are essential for knowledge enhancement. However, if these works are translated and provided at a relatively lower price (to that of the originals), most Sri Lankans, including those few who are bilingual and have financial resources, would prefer to buy the translations rather than the originals. Strba stated:

> Mass copying or bulk access means that fewer people will buy the original book. This inevitably affects the market of that book, and thus causes financial harm to the copyright holder. In such a case, the bulk copying constitutes not only unfair use but also causes unreasonable prejudice to the legitimate interests of the copyright holder.[230]

Sometimes it may be thought that the permission under Section 11(1) of the Sri Lankan *Intellectual Property Act 2003* and Section 107 of the United States *Copyright Act 1976* to make 'multiple copies [of copyright protected works] for classroom use' would allow translation of the whole of copyright protected scientific and technical works and the reproduction of translations in multiple copies for classroom use. However, this thought is misconceived. The reason is that both these sections make the permission to make 'multiple copies for classroom

226 Ibid.
227 See Melville B Nimmer, Matthew Bender, *Nimmer on Copyright* (at Release 4) § 145.
228 Lawrence Venuti, *The Scandals of Translation: Towards an Ethics of Difference* (Routledge, 1999) 64.
229 Ibid.
230 Strba, above n 96, 135.

use' subject to the four factors that courts should consider when determining fair use (which includes effect of such use upon the potential market for, or value of, the copyright protected work). Thus, the permission to make multiple copies of copyright protected works for classroom use under these sections would not allow the translation of the whole of copyright protected scientific and technical works, and the reproduction of translations in multiple copies for classroom use, since that would affect the marketability of the original copyright protected works. Strba further noted:

> [A]ccording to case law, multiple copying for classroom distribution . . . is fair use. This is in line with section 107 of the US Copyright Act, which allows for fair use for teaching (including multiple copying for classroom use). However, this does not mean copying of whole volumes or textbooks. It refers to making many copies of a few pages from a textbook.[231]

Given these reasons, it is hard to believe that the fair use defence in the *Intellectual Property Act 2003* would permit translation of the whole of copyright protected scientific and technical works, and the reproduction of translations in large quantities.

Because there are no meaningful exceptions in the *Intellectual Property Act 2003* which would allow translation of the whole of copyright protected scientific and technical works, and the reproduction of translations in multiple quantities, Sri Lanka would not be able to translate copyright protected scientific and technical books and learning materials produced in developed countries and to reproduce the translations without the consent or authorisation of the copyright owners.

Since translation of copyright protected scientific and technical books and learning materials require authorisation from the copyright owners, the copyright owners can either refuse to grant this authorisation or can charge a license fee for granting the authorisation. In addition, although they grant authorisation for translation, they still can prevent the reproduction of the translations by refusing to grant authorisation to that effect. Alternatively, they can charge an additional license fee for granting authorisation to reproduce translations. Therefore, the need to obtain authorisation from the copyright owners to translate their scientific and technical books and learning materials and to reproduce the translations in multiple quantities could affect Sri Lanka's access to these knowledge products in four ways. Firstly, if the copyright owners do not grant authorisation to translate their knowledge products, this could prevent altogether the translation of these knowledge products. Secondly, if the copyright owners grant authorisation to translate their knowledge products while not allowing the translations to be reproduced in multiple quantities, this could prevent the reproduction of the translations in large quantities, which would make the whole purpose of

231 Ibid., 134–135.

translation futile. Thirdly, if the copyright owners were to charge a license fee for authorising the translation of their knowledge products and the reproduction of the translations, this could impose a huge financial burden on Sri Lanka. Fourthly, obtaining authorisation from the copyright owners in developed countries for translation of their knowledge products and reproduction of the translations could impose administrative burdens and expenses on Sri Lanka. In light of these reasons, the *Intellectual Property Act 2003* (copyright law of Sri Lanka) constrains the translation of copyright protected works required for promoting access to scientific and technical knowledge in Sri Lanka.

2.6. Conclusion

Sri Lanka is dependent on developed countries for scientific and technical knowledge. Scientific and technical knowledge produced in developed countries is disseminated mostly in English. Given that English is not a widely used language in Sri Lanka and that there are many barriers to promoting English, translation of scientific and technical knowledge products produced in developed countries, and the publication of the translations in large quantities, is crucially important if Sri Lanka is to allow and promote access to scientific and technical knowledge. This, in turn, is essential if Sri Lanka is to further economic development and to meet its constitutional and human rights obligations. However, the way in which the present copyright law in Sri Lanka (*Intellectual Property Act 2003*) protects the translation rights of the copyright owners constrains the ability of people to translate scientific and technical knowledge products produced in developed countries and to reproduce these translations in large quantities in a timely and affordable manner.

III The British model of copyright law and translation [1908–1979]

3.1. Introduction

The copyright regimes implemented in Sri Lanka from 1908 to 1979 mark the first stage of the history of Sri Lankan copyright law. These regimes were modelled entirely on British copyright law. The British model of copyright law that was adopted in Sri Lanka in this period was inimical to timely and affordable translation. The purpose of this chapter is to examine the reasons for this and why this copyright law was implemented in Sri Lanka.

As discussed further in this chapter, the British model of copyright law was first incorporated into domestic statute law in Sri Lanka through the *Copyright Ordinance 1908*. The model got entrenched in Sri Lanka with the application of the *Imperial Copyright Act 1911*.[1] The *Imperial Copyright Act* continued to govern the copyright law of Sri Lanka until the introduction of the *Code of Intellectual Property Act 1979* (*IP Code*).

Both the *Copyright Ordinance 1908* and the *Imperial Copyright Act 1911* conferred an exclusive right on copyright owners to translate their works without providing for commensurate exceptions to that right. This restricted timely and affordable translation of copyright protected works required for promoting access to scientific and technical knowledge in Sri Lanka.

The British model of copyright law introduced into Sri Lanka was essentially a direct response to the interests of the key stakeholders in the British publishing industry, namely, the British government, publishers, authors and the reading public. To understand the British model of copyright law in Sri Lanka and why it protected translation rights, it is necessary to understand these interests and the extent to which they influenced the protection of translation rights in British copyright law. Therefore, this chapter will examine how the interests of key stakeholders in the British publishing industry influenced the protection of translation rights in British copyright law throughout its history, that is, from the point of the introduction of printing to Britain in the fifteenth century up to the enactment of the *Imperial Copyright Act* in 1911. The chapter demonstrates

1 See *Copyright Ordinance No 20 of 1912* (Sri Lanka).

that the reason for British copyright law's delay in conferring translation rights to British authors until the twentieth century was that translations were seen as an important aspect of public access to knowledge. However, when literary, artistic and scientific activities and book publishing in Britain blossomed (making it a developed country in the field of literature, arts and science), the prominence attached to translations as an important means of promoting public access to knowledge lost its value. Moreover, the new trade interests that persuaded Britain to expand the scope of copyright protection ultimately resulted in the right to translate being recognised as an important and fully fledged exclusive right of the copyright owner.

3.2. British model of copyright in Sri Lanka

Copyright law was first introduced into Sri Lanka during British rule (1796–1948).[2] The British model of copyright law was one of the means through which British interests were accepted in Sri Lanka. It also signified the right of Britain to use Sri Lanka as part of the British Empire.[3] Surprisingly, even after Sri Lanka's independence in 1948, the country remained a part of Britain as far as copyright law was concerned. This was because Sri Lanka continued with the British model of copyright law until 1979. As Minister Athulathmudali observed, it was only with the passage of the *IP Code* that Sri Lanka began to be liberated from 'restrictive English practices in regard to copyrights'.[4]

The *Copyright Ordinance 1908* was the first domestically enacted copyright statute in Sri Lanka.[5] This Ordinance was repealed and replaced by the *Imperial Copyright Act 1911*, which governed the subject of copyright in Sri Lanka until the *IP Code* was enacted in 1979. The *Copyright Ordinance 1908* and the *Imperial Copyright Act 1911* were hallmarks of British copyright, with their roots in the British Parliament. Although the *Copyright Ordinance 1908* was enacted by the British Governor of Colonial Sri Lanka with the consent of the Ceylon Legislative Council, it was almost a verbatim reproduction of the *Copyright Act 1905* of the Commonwealth of Australia which, in turn, was based on the British Copyright Bill 1900.[6] Likewise, the *Imperial Copyright Act 1911* was an all-embracing copyright statute enacted by the Parliament of Britain. According

2 See especially *Copyright Act 1842*, 5 & 6 Vict, c 45, s 29. See also DM Karunaratna, *An Introduction to the Law of Copyright and Related Rights in Sri Lanka* (Sarvodaya Vishva Lekha, 2006) 5; Harsha Cabral, *Intellectual Property Law in Sri Lanka: The Act No 36 of 2003, the TRIPS Agreement and a Case Digest* (2004) 1.

3 Sri Lanka, *Parliamentary Debates*, 25 May 1979, col 501.

4 Ibid.

5 Karunaratna, above n 2, 5.

6 See Ceylon, *Council Debates*, Ceylon Legislature, 9 September 1908, 60–61; Copyright Law Review Committee, *Report of the Committee Appointed by the Attorney General of the Commonwealth to Consider What Alterations Are Desirable in the Copyright Law of the Commonwealth* (1959) 9.

to Sherman and Bently, with the passage of the *Imperial Copyright Act* Britain formally completed at a statutory level the process of 'domestic embodiment of the model of copyright which was institutionalised in the international copyright agreements' entered into by that country.[7] The *Imperial Copyright Act 1911* became applicable in Sri Lanka by direct extension, as in many other countries of the British Empire.[8]

For these reasons the *Copyright Ordinance 1908* and the *Imperial Copyright Act 1911* can hardly be described as Sri Lankan copyright legislation in the true sense of that term. As Minister Athulathmudali stated when he moved the second reading of the Code of Intellectual Property Bill 1979 in the Sri Lankan Parliament:

> Our country [Sri Lanka] has never had a copyrights ordinance until this Bill was introduced. Until now it was 99 per cent based on English law—without even a parliamentary statute. This English law of 1911 applied to Sri Lanka and we have carried on with that. That is, their interests were accepted here—all their English copyrights and their right to use this country as part of England as far as the copyrights law in England was concerned.[9]

3.2.1. *The Copyright Ordinance 1908 and translation*

The *Copyright Ordinance 1908* was inimical to the timely and affordable translation of copyright protected scientific and technical works. The reason for this was the stringent and unbalanced way in which the *Copyright Ordinance* protected copyright owners' translation rights.

The aim of the *Copyright Ordinance 1908* was to secure the right of property in literary and artistic works. While securing this right, the Ordinance also granted an exclusive right to translate copyright protected books to authors (copyright owners) for a term of 42 years or for the author's life and seven years.[10] However, the Ordinance also recognised certain exceptions to this right. In particular, it provided that the translation right of the copyright owner did not extend to the following situations: where a book was translated for a person's private use, where translation was with regard to fair extracts from a book or where the making of the translation constituted a fair dealing with the contents of a book 'for the purpose of a new work, or for the purposes of criticism, review, or refutation, or in the ordinary course of reporting scientific information'.[11] Further, the Ordinance

7 Brad Sherman and Lionel Bently, *The Making of Modern Intellectual Property Law: The British Experience, 1760–1911* (Cambridge University Press, first published 1999, 2003 ed) 127–128.

8 *Copyright Act 1911*, 1 & 2 Geo 5, c 46, s 25.

9 Sri Lanka, above n 2, col 501.

10 *Copyright Ordinance No 12 1908* (Sri Lanka) ss 9(1)(c), 12(1).

11 Ibid., s 23.

also provided for a compulsory licensing system in the event that a copyright owner of a book failed to make a translation thereof into a 'particular language' within a period of ten years from the date of the publication of that book.[12]

Although the aim of the exceptions to copyright owners' translation rights, as recognised under the *Copyright Ordinance 1908*, was to limit the rigour of translation rights and their adverse impact on translation, nonetheless these exceptions are unlikely to have facilitated timely and affordable translation. This is because the exceptions were narrowly defined. In particular, the translation of books in the absence of their copyright owners was only permitted for certain specified purposes. Also, they did not allow translation of a whole book to be reproduced in multiple copies. The compulsory licensing system provided for in the Ordinance is also unlikely to have facilitated the translation of copyright protected books in Sri Lanka because the time period a person had to wait to make an application to translate a copyright protected book was excessive. Thus it is not implausible to assume that the *Copyright Ordinance 1908* would have impeded free translation of the copyright protected scientific and technical works required for promoting access to scientific and technical knowledge in Sri Lanka during the short period in which the Ordinance was in force.

3.2.2. The Imperial Copyright Act 1911 and translation

Like the *Copyright Ordinance 1908*, the *Imperial Copyright Act 1911* also protected copyright owners' translation rights stringently. It was also inimical to the timely and affordable translation of copyright protected scientific and technical works.

The *Imperial Copyright Act 1911* was the first British copyright statute to protect the translation rights of domestic (British) authors. In particular, this *Act* granted an exclusive right to 'produce, reproduce, perform, or publish any translation of [a] work' to its author (copyright owner) throughout his or her life and a further period of 50 years after death.[13] The main exception to this exclusive right was the fair dealing defence. While the *Imperial Copyright Act* did not define what fair dealing meant, it nevertheless allowed translation of a copyright protected work without the consent of its copyright owner for the purpose of private study, research, criticism, review, or newspaper summary, provided such translation constituted fair dealing with regard to the work.[14]

The fair dealing defence in the *Imperial Copyright Act 1911* was too narrow to facilitate timely and affordable translation of copyright protected works. This was because translation of copyright protected works under fair dealing was only

12 Ibid., s 25.

13 *Copyright Act 1911*, 1 & 2 Geo 5, c 46, ss 1(2)(a), 3; Walter Arthur Copinger and JM Easton, *The Law of Copyright* (Stevens and Haynes, 5th ed, 1915) 163.

14 *Copyright Act 1911*, 1 & 2 Geo 5, c 46, s 2(1).

permitted for certain specified purposes. In particular, there was a great deal of uncertainty about whether or not this defence would help to facilitate the translation of copyright protected works in whole and the reproduction of the translations in large quantities without the consent of copyright owners. Also, the defence only became applicable once infringement had been established. Thus the *Imperial Copyright Act* posed a severe obstacle to the timely and affordable translation of copyright protected scientific and technical works that Sri Lanka needed to promote access to scientific and technical knowledge. The *Imperial Copyright Act* also created severe hardships among literary circles and translators in Sri Lanka. As Jayathilaka stated, the provisions relating to translation rights in the *Imperial Copyright Act* were the most unfair provisions for Sri Lankans.[15] Also, as identified at the Conference on Sinhala Translation Literature held in 1965, the *Act* suffered from a number of deficiencies, imposing many hardships on Sri Lankan translators and publishers.[16]

3.3. British copyright and translation

As noted earlier, both the *Copyright Act 1908* and the *Imperial Copyright Act 1911* were instruments developed in Britain. Therefore, in order to identify the reasons why these statutes protected copyright owners' translation rights in a manner that was inimical to the timely and affordable translation of copyright protected works, we need to examine the prehistory of these statutes.

The formulation of a holistic copyright law in Britain (*Imperial Copyright Act 1911*), which recognised a fully fledged translation right for authors, was a result of the government's responses to the various developments that took place within the printing and book industry since the introduction of printing into that country. Although British copyright law recognised the translation rights of certain foreign authors in a limited form during the period between 1852 and 1911, prior to 1852 these rights were virtually unknown in the law of Britain.[17] Thus, up until the mid-nineteenth century, the copyright law of Britain did not constrain translation. One reason for this was that until this period, translations were considered to be an important means for Britain to promote public access

15 K Jayathilaka, 'Pitapath Aithiwasikam Panatha' [Copyright Act], *Dina Sangarawa* (Ceylon), 25 October 1956, 2–3.

16 Department of Cultural Affairs, 'Sinhala Parivarthana Sahithya' [Sinhala Translation Literature] (Report and Proceedings of the Conference on Sinhala Translation, Colombo, 16–25 February 1965).

17 For the first time, the international copyright regime of Britain conferred a limited translation right (for a duration of five years) on certain foreign authors through the *International Copyright Act 1852*. Subsequently, the *International Copyright Act 1886* also conferred a limited translation right (for a duration of ten years) on certain foreign authors. Finally, the *Imperial Copyright Act 1911* conferred a fully fledged translation right on certain foreign authors as well as domestic authors for the full term of copyright protection. *International Copyright Act 1852*, 15 & 16 Vict, c 12, s II; *International Copyright Act 1886*, 49 & 50 Vict, c 33, s 5; *Copyright Act 1911*, 1 & 2 Geo 5, c 46, ss 1(2)(a), 29.

to knowledge. This was particularly the case during the early period of British printing.

3.3.1. Translations in the early period of British printing

During the early period of printing in Britain (between the fifteenth and the end of the eighteenth centuries), translations played an important role in furthering the interests of printers, translators and the reading public in the ultimate direction of promoting public access to knowledge.

3.3.1.1. Printers

Translations were very important to early printers in Britain. This is perhaps reflected by the fact that the first English language book ever printed in Britain—*The History of Troy*—was a translation.[18] Several factors influenced early British printers to be heavily reliant on translations. Firstly, printing translations was partly a means of exercising caution in a market full of risks.[19] Secondly, because of the dominance of certain scholarly languages in literary fields, such as Latin and French, English books were very limited. Thus, this gap had to be filled with English translations. Thirdly, translations were an effective means of bridging the knowledge gap that existed between people who were conversant in scholarly languages and those who were only conversant in English. Thus, early British printers' reliance on translations can primarily be described as their inclination to identify the attributes of the British book market with the objective of maximising their interests.

The introduction of the printing press in Britain by William Caxton (1415–1492) in 1477 made the process of book publishing easier than ever before. However, it also posed many new risks and challenges for British printers. Feather noted that 'printing led to fundamental changes in the economics of book production.'[20] Printers had to make a significantly increased capital investment in the process of book production. In particular, they had to invest in a press, skilled labour and a stock of consumables such as ink and paper.[21] However, the return of this investment was 'necessarily slow'.[22] These problems were exacerbated by the

18 John A Wagner, *Encyclopaedia of the Wars of the Roses* (ABC-CLICO, 2001) 50. This book was both translated and printed by William Caxton, who introduced the printing press into Britain. He also printed many other translations, of which a considerable number were his own translations.

19 HS Bennett, *English Books & Readers 1475 to 1557: Being a Study in the History of the Book Trade from Caxton to the Incorporation of the Stationers' Company* (Cambridge University Press, 2nd ed, 1969) 153.

20 John Feather, *Publishing, Piracy and Politics: A Historical Study of Copyright in Britain* (Mansell, 1994)10.

21 Ibid. See also William St Clair, *The Reading Nation in the Romantic Period* (Cambridge University Press, 2004) 43–44.

22 Feather, above n 20, 10.

fact that the book trade became one of the highly competitive trades in Britain pursuant to the introduction of printing. As such, printers had to look for suitable means of protecting their investments,[23] and printing translations of books that had an already established demand (especially in foreign markets) answered this call. In particular, whenever printers saw that certain books were in high demand (especially in foreign markets), and they were convinced that those were works upon which a fair risk could be taken, they translated those books into other languages for publication.[24] In other words, translations of well-received books were commodities on which printers could make a better prediction of success.[25]

When Caxton introduced printing to Britain, English was neither a scholarly language nor a standardised language in Britain.[26] In particular, it had no 'recognised common usage' and 'varied considerably from one part of the country to another, causing practical difficulties of everyday communication'.[27] This was largely a result of the overwhelming influence of Greek and Latin languages in the European continent, especially during the Middle Ages. Harris and Taylor observed that '[t]hroughout the Middle Ages, linguistic thought in Europe was moulded by the intellectual predominance' of Greek and Latin.[28] Latin, in particular, 'was the international working language of European education and administration; it was the language of law, of government, of the universities and of the Church.'[29] Notably, Latin was the *lingua franca* up until the late sixteenth century. As such, it was the most effective language through which writers or scientists could secure a wide international audience for their scholarly works during this period. For instance, great scientists like Nicholas Copernicus (1473–1543), Francis Bacon (1561–1626), Galileo Galilei (1564–1642) and Isaac Newton (1642–1727) frequently wrote in Latin. Moreover, for many scholarly writers, English was not a viable alternative to writing in Latin. Indeed, as Harris and Taylor observed, '[h]alf a century after Caxton, English writers were still apologizing for writing in English.'[30] Especially with regard to books on science subjects, such as medicine, this trend continued even up into the eighteenth century, despite strong claims that English should be increasingly used.[31]

23 Ibid.
24 Many of the translations which were printed during this period were produced at the command or exhortation of the printers. Bennett, above n 19, 153.
25 Bennett, above n 19, 152–153.
26 As Dom Henry Wansbrough noted, 'the cultural loss to the English language consequent on the Norman Conquest had delayed its development for several centuries.' Dom Henry Wansbrough, 'The Bible in the Renaissance—William Tyndale' <http://users.ox.ac.uk/~sben0056/Tyndale.London.htm>.
27 Roy Harris and Talbot J Taylor, *Landmarks in Linguistic Thought I: The Western Tradition from Socrates to Saussure* (Routledge, 2nd ed, 1997) 89.
28 Ibid., 87–88.
29 Ibid., 88.
30 Ibid.
31 HS Bennett, *English Books & Readers 1603 to 1640: Being a Study in the History of the Book Trade in the Reigns of James I and Charles I* (Cambridge University Press, 1970) 140.

The dominance of scholarly languages (especially Latin and Greek) in the literary and scientific fields during the first few centuries of printing in Britain had two important consequences. From the point of view of printers, it meant that the English books available for printing were limited. This was particularly so because 'English print culture was [still] germinating in the sixteenth and early seventeenth centuries', and Britain 'produced comparatively few original works'.[32] Also, from the perspective of people who could only read English, this meant that they were deprived of the wealth of knowledge contained in scholarly works in other languages. Against this background and to address both of these concerns, early printers strategically started printing translations of scholarly books. In fact, as Bennett noted, '[t]ranslations formed a large part of booksellers' stock',[33] most of which were produced 'at the command or exhortation of the printer'.[34]

3.3.1.2. Readers

Translations were very important for readers who could only understand English (English-only readership) in the early period of printing in Britain. While translating was partly a commercial pursuit for printers, for the English-only readership (and the translators) it was a scholarly pursuit that benefited 'society and which chimed well with the Enlightenment's pursuit of knowledge'.[35] In particular, translations had the aim of informing people who were only able to read English.[36] In other words, translations were an effective means of providing the English-only readership with access to knowledge, which had formerly been confined to the affluent classes in Britain and foreigners who were conversant in scholarly languages.

However, to claim that translations exclusively catered to the English-only readership who were often deprived of scholarly knowledge would be overstating the actual situation. This is because during this time, translations played an important role even within communities of scholars such as the Royal Society of Science and its fellowship. In particular, Henderson stated that 'translations formed part of a set of knowledge-making processes at meetings' of the Royal Society in the period from 1660 to around 1700.[37] Thus, translation benefited both the scholarly community and the public alike. Nonetheless, as far as the

32 Patrick R Goold, 'The Statute of Anne and Translations' (Unpublished Paper, Selected Works of Patrick R Goold, March 2013) <http://works.bepress.com/patrick_goold/1>. Also see Edward Arber, *A Transcript of the Registers of the Company of Stationers of London: 1554–1640 AD* (1894) vol 5, xxxiii–xxxv.

33 HS Bennett, *English Books & Readers 1558 to 1603: Being a Study in the History of the Book Trade in the Reign of Elizabeth I* (Cambridge University Press, 1965) 93.

34 Bennett, above n 19, 153.

35 Goold, above n 32.

36 Bennett, above n 19, 154.

37 Felicity Henderson, 'Faithful Interpreters? Translation Theory and Practice at the Early Royal Society' (2013) 67 *Notes and Records of the Royal Society* 101.

London book trade was concerned, the main beneficiary of translations was the English-only readership. In fact, the printers catered for much of the religious, informative and literary interest of the English-only readership through translations.[38] More often than not, the early translators were motivated by a moral duty to support these 'less-gifted brethren' by making knowledge available to them in English, or at least raised this point to justify the unauthorised use of the literary and scientific works of others in the course of translation.[39]

3.3.1.3. Translators

During the early period of British printing, translators in Britain were seen as people acting with a moral duty who were 'truly adding something important to society'.[40] This was partly due to the characteristics of the profession of translators and to the nature of the task of translating at this time. Translating was not a particularly profitable profession during the early years of printing. Translators, who were usually men of education, were paid very little for their work. As a result, translation became more or less a part-time occupation, and many translators during this period had other means of livelihood. Thus, as Bennett remarked, it is safe to assume that 'to make a living by translating alone was a precarious and not often practiced occupation'.[41] Moreover, translation at this time was a tedious task which could be distinctively separated from a mere mechanical process, such as machine translation in the modern context. More specifically, translation involved a massive amount of mental labour, skill and judgement on the part of the translator. As a result, it was often seen as an art comparable to original composition or writing.[42] Apart from this, 'translation was a tricky business' as well as 'a painful office'.[43] In these circumstances, translators were more often seen as performing a benevolent service to the society.[44] Although, this was not always the case,[45] translators at least often made that claim in situations where they were confronted with unauthorised use of works of others or with the quality of their translations. For instance, many translators emphasised that translation was a means for making knowledge common and that their translations were for the 'simple' or the 'unlearned and ignorant' Englishmen who were not expert in the scholarly languages.[46] Importantly, these justifications appeared to be sufficient to condone their transgressions—especially the ransacking of works of both ancient and modern writers in making cheap translations of those works available

38 Bennett, above n 19, 154.
39 Bennett, above n 33, 93.
40 Goold, above n 32.
41 Bennett, above n 19, 159.
42 Goold, above n 32.
43 Bennett, above n 31, 67–68.
44 Bennett, above n 33, 98.
45 Ibid.
46 Ibid., 87 (emphasis added).

for the use of British public.[47] In short, it was believed (as Bennett did) that 'for the most part men who were making the translation[s]' did so 'for the good of the commonwealth'.[48]

3.3.1.4. Opposition to translation

Translation had many enemies during the early days of printing.[49] Translation was opposed on three main grounds. Firstly, those who were publishing translations were accused of making knowledge common. Secondly, it was claimed that translators were reaping what they had not sown. Thirdly, translations were also considered contemptible on the basis that erroneous (inaccurate or distorted) translations abused the original works as well as their authors. On that basis, translations were seen to be 'enemies to all good learning'.[50]

The first argument in opposition to translation, namely, that translation was making knowledge common, had two bases of reasoning. Firstly, the noble and the elite community of scholars, who were well versed (and already practising) in the fields of science, art and literature, maintained that the mysteries of their fields (especially medicine and science) should remain within their bounds and not reach the common people, who were unlearned and ignorant. For instance, Andrew Boorde (1490–1549), a British physician and the author of *The Fyrst Boke of the Introduction of Knowledge*, thought that 'a great detriment' will be caused to the 'noble science of physics' when ignorant people will 'enterprise to meddle' with it.[51] According to Bennett, many others were of the same view as Boorde or believed that the 'secrets of physics' should not be shared among the common men but be known only by the 'professors of the art'.[52] Secondly, it was also claimed by certain segments of the elite community of Britain that making knowledge on certain matters common among ordinary people in the country would not serve these people any meaningful way. In particular, it was contended that 'certain philosophical or religious matters were not things that the untrained could discuss with any profit.'[53] Moreover, it was also believed that what such discussions could least do was to cause injury on those sacred matters. For instance, it was believed that 'Christian morality . . . might be undermined by making classical stories and the tales of some Italian or French writers easy to come by.'[54]

Translators and those others who propagated translation used moral arguments to counter the proposition that translation was undesirable because it

47 Bennett, above n 19, 156.
48 Ibid., 171.
49 Bennett, above n 33, 93–111.
50 A Brucioli, *A Commentary upon the Canticle of Canticles* (1598), cited in Bennett, above n 33, 95.
51 Bennett, above n 33, 180.
52 Ibid.
53 Ibid., 93 (citations omitted).
54 Ibid.

made knowledge common. Specifically, they claimed that there was a moral duty imposed on the 'learned to help their less-gifted brethren'.[55] Translators like Thomas Hoby (1530–1566) also argued that translations of the works of Latin or Greek authors did not 'hinder learning' by any means. Instead, such translations furthered learning because they helped common people to fill their minds with virtues and their bodies with civil conditions.[56] John Florio (1553–1625) gave new life to these sentiments when he forthrightly declared that 'learning cannot be too common, and the commoner the better'.[57]

The second argument that translators had to contend with was that they were reaping the fruits sown by others, namely the authors of original works that were translated. Translators countered this argument in two ways. Firstly, they maintained that the task of translation was a laborious and painful task which was justified. Secondly, they also justified benefiting from the work of others on the basis of the public good achieved; that is, they were making knowledge common among the British public and expanding their horizons of learning. In particular, it was stated that the 'English Nation also should be no longer deprived of what others have already [e]njoyed, to their great profit', and that English 'should not be deprived of the treasures of other tongues'.[58]

The third argument against translation was a more pragmatic one. This was that the translations corrupted original works and misinterpreted their authors. As a result, it was claimed that translations (as well as the translators) were 'enemies unto the common wealth [and] enemies to all good learning'.[59]

The contention that translations were undesirable because they could misinterpret or sometimes even corrupt the ideas expressed in original works was the strongest argument that translators and those others who propagated translation at this time had to contend with.[60] This was also because translation into English during this time ran a high risk of misinterpretation of the original work, particularly owing to the belief that there were defects in the English language, and to the perception of the English language at the time as being in an underdeveloped state. Some claimed that English was an uncivilised language, lacking the capacity to communicate scholarly thoughts. Moreover, English had no recognised common usage and had conflicting dialects even within the four corners of Britain. As Harris and Taylor observed, it 'varied considerably from one part of the country to another, causing practical difficulties of everyday communication'.[61] This posed a serious challenge for the translators (as well as the printers), who needed to produce translations that were both readable by a broader British public and also faithful to the original works. In view of these matters, it was contended that 'translation into English was

55 Ibid.
56 Ibid., 93–94.
57 Ibid., 94.
58 Bennett, above n 31, 68.
59 Bennett, above n 33, 95.
60 Ibid., 94.
61 Harris and Taylor, above n 27, 89.

foolish, since they affected to despise English as an uncouth language.'[62] However, this contention was countered by many translators. In particular, translators claimed that if English was uncouth, translations into English could enrich it and make it civilised. In fact, George Pettie (1548–1589) made this clear when he said that translation 'is indeed the ready way to enrich our tongue, and make it copious, and it is the way which all tongues have taken to enrich themselves.'[63]

In theory as well as in practice, Pettie's claim was fruitful. As he correctly envisaged, translations played a significant contribution to the development of the English language in early modern Britain. Though this was a collective effort of all the translators at this time, the contributions of William Caxton (1415–1492) and William Tyndale (1494–1536) were especially profound and significant. In particular, Caxton printed translations, many of which were his own. By doing so, Caxton also standardised the English language, particularly through homogenising regional dialects. This played a vital role in helping not only to establish English as the language of literary Britain[64] but also to establish it as the national language of the country.[65]

Tyndale's translation of the Bible also provided a great impetus for the development of the English language. In the course of his translation, he introduced many new words into the English language (some of which were later disapproved of and held against him by the Roman Catholic Church).[66] As Bragg observed, Tyndale (through his translation) was not just bringing the work of God to people; he was also 'bringing in words which carried ideas, described feelings, gave voice to emotions, expanded the way we could describe how we lived.'[67] According to Gary, Tyndale's work 'gave English rhythm, range, richness and resonance'.[68] Moreover, they also 'gave continuity to the "English language" and, in the process, consolidated it'.[69] In short, '[t]he development of the [English] language is thus greatly indebted to Tyndale's translation of the Bible.'[70]

3.3.2. *Translation and the early law in Britain*

Whether the common law of Britain protected the literary works of authors in the same manner as property is a vexatious question into which this book does not

62 Bennett, above n 33, 95.
63 Ibid., 96 (citations omitted).
64 Jennifer Bowers and Peggy Keeran, *Literary Research and the British Renaissance and Early Modern Period: Strategies and Sources* (Scarecrow Press, 2010) 252.
65 See Ambreen Safder Kharbe, *English Language and Literary Criticism* (Discovery Publishing House, 2009) 52.
66 See Ray L Huntington and W Jeffrey Marsh, 'Revisiting William Tyndale, Father of the English Bible' (2011) 12(2) *Religious Educator* 12, 15.
67 Melvyn Bragg, *The Adventure of English 500AD to 2000: The Biography of a Language* (Sceptre, first published 2003, 2004 ed) 110.
68 Gary Day, *Literary Criticism: A New History* (Edinburgh University Press, 2008) 115–116.
69 Ibid., 115.
70 Ibid.

intend to delve. Instead, the ensuing discussion examines how the laws relating to printing impacted upon translations during the first few centuries of printing in Britain until the enactment of the famous *Statute of Anne 1710*.

Between the fifteenth and the end of the eighteenth centuries, the laws to regulate printing (laws of printing) in Britain were partly a means utilised to protect the interests of the printers and occasionally the authors of literary and scientific works. This was the same in many other countries in Europe.[71] Before the introduction of the *Statute of Anne 1710*, the primary laws of printing in Britain that affected literary and scientific works (and their translations) were (1) printing patents and monopolies granted by the Crown in the exercise of its prerogative (hereinafter collectively referred to as printing patents) and (2) printing privileges conferred on the Stationers. As Deazley stated, these two systems provided the first two proprietary models for protecting literary works which prefigured the provisions of the *Statute of Anne*.[72] More importantly, they also affected translation.

The printing patents and the privileges conferred on the Stationers between the fifteenth and the end of the eighteenth centuries in Britain were predominantly an outcome of the Crown's reaction to the impact of the then new technology of printing. With the introduction of the technology of printing, the British Crown and the Church had to face a new set of challenges. Of particular concern was the impact of this technology on the production and distribution of literary and scientific works that severely questioned the established ideology of both institutions. This was primarily because printing enabled these types of works to be produced and distributed in large quantities with ease. As Harvey has observed:

> In addition to the wide dissemination of multiple copies, those who received the books and pamphlets were able to read them for themselves and pass them on to friends in far greater numbers than had been the case in the scribal culture.'[73]

Printing also compelled the British Crown to protect the trade interests of various stakeholders in the print industry for the ultimate purpose of maintaining a sound economic order in the Kingdom. The main reason for the need for government support for the print industry was the substantial capital investment that had to be made in the process of printing books and other works using the new

71 See *An Enquiry into the Nature and Origin of Literary Property* (1762), L Bently and M Kretschmer (eds), *Primary Sources on Copyright (1450–1900)* 31–33 <www.copyrighthistory.org>.

72 Ronan Deazley, 'Commentary on Early Tudor Printing Privileges' in L Bently and M Kretschmer (eds), *Primary Sources on Copyright* (2008) <www.copyrighthistory.org>.

73 David Harvey, 'Law and the Regulation of Communications Technologies: The Printing Press and the Law 1475–1641' (2005) *Australian and New Zealand Law & History Society E Journal* 160, 166–167 <www.anzlhsejournal.auckland.ac.nz/otherpapers/otherpapers_2005/Harvey.pdf>.

technology. Added to this was the competitiveness in the industry.[74] The result of all these factors was the necessity for the Crown to intervene in the regulation of printing. To this end, the Crown introduced various regulations concerning the printing press and the book trade. Of these, the most important (for the purposes of our discussion) were the printing patents and privileges conferred on the Stationers.

3.3.2.1. Printing patents

Printing patents were 'discretionary privilege grants . . . [i]ssued under the Crown's prerogative power [which] bestowed upon a specified printer or publisher the exclusive right of printing and selling a particular book or category of books, usually for a limited time.'[75] Some printing patents granted between the fifteenth and the end of the eighteenth centuries, particularly during the reign of William III (1650–1702) and Queen Anne (1665–1714), expressly conferred the privilege of printing translations on their grantees.[76] However, as Deazley rightly observed, '[t]his type of privilege was not typical of its kind' since the majority of royal privileges granted between the Restoration and the end of the seventeenth century simply prohibited 'printing, selling, and importing the work in question'.[77] In particular, of the total patents granted by Queen Anne, only three appear to have conferred the privilege of printing translations.[78] Thus, it can be observed that printing patents that conferred a privilege of printing translations on their grantees were the exception rather than the norm.

Because certain printing patents granted between the fifteenth and the end of the eighteenth centuries conferred an exclusive privilege of printing translations on their grantees, this might lead a person to think that the laws of printing in Britain during this period recognised an exclusive right of the authors of literary and scientific works to translate their works. However, such a thought is incorrect. One reason for this is that printing patents never established a general or abstract concept of an exclusive right of translation (conferred on authors of literary and scientific works) which would be akin to the concept of translation rights in modern copyright law. In addition to this, the main aim of printing patents was to safeguard the interests of printers and the Crown (including the Church), whereas the main aim of the concept of translation rights in modern copyright law is to secure and promote the interests of the author. Finally, in certain instances,

74 Feather, above n 20, 10.

75 Oren Bracha, 'The Adventures of the Statute of Anne in the Land of Unlimited Possibilities: The Life of a Legal Transplant' (2010) 25 *Berkeley Technology Law Journal* 1427, 1432 (citations omitted).

76 Ronan Deazley, 'What Is New About the Statute of Anne? *Or* Six Observations in Search of an Act' in L Bently, Uma Suthersanen and Paul Torremans (eds), *Global Copyright: Three Hundred Years Since the Statute of Anne, from 1709 to Cyberspace* (Edward Elgar, 2010) 26, 36–37.

77 Ibid., 36.

78 Ibid.

the exclusive privilege of printing translations granted through printing patents was in direct conflict with the modern notion of translation rights, since this privilege was granted to the translators and printers of translations rather than to the authors of literary and scientific works.

3.3.2.1.1. NO GENERAL RIGHT OF TRANSLATION

Although printing patents were an important means of regulating printing and protecting literary and scientific works, it was hardly a solid or a comprehensive system. This was mainly because of the inconsistent and ad hoc nature of the grant of these patents.[79] In addition, the number of patents granted was very limited. As Feather observed, the works in respect of which these patents were granted constituted a minority of literary and scientific works produced in this period.[80] In contrast, for the majority of the literary and scientific works 'there was no legal mechanism at hand to protect their creators and producers'.[81] Therefore, printing patents 'certainly did not constitute a general system for protecting rights in [literary and scientific works]', as it benefited only a handful of people.[82] Moreover, even in relation to this limited number of patents, exclusive privilege to translate or print translations was the exception rather than the norm. As such, the system of printing patents did not create a general concept of translation rights as understood in modern copyright law.

3.3.2.1.2. PRINTING PATENTS AS A DEVICE TO SECURE THE INTERESTS OF PRINTERS

A vast majority of printing patents granted by the British Crown benefited the printers, the Crown, and the Church, rather than the authors of literary and scientific works. As Feather observed, '[m]ost of the privileges granted by patent to particular texts were not granted to authors at all, but to publishers.'[83] Commenting on the purpose of granting patents for individual titles, he also noted that 'if a living author were the beneficiary of such grants, that was a purely coincidental consequence'.[84]

The fact that printing patents were primarily a device to secure the interests of the printers, the Crown, and the Church suggests that the objective of restraining translations through these patents was quite different to the objective of protection of translation rights in modern copyright law. This is because in modern copyright law translation rights are granted to authors primarily with the objective of protecting their interests. This distinction can be observed more clearly when the key aims of granting printing patents are considered.

79 Feather, above n 20, 13.
80 Ibid., 14.
81 Ibid.
82 Ibid.
83 Ibid., 13.
84 Ibid., 14.

Printing patents were granted for various reasons by the Crown.[85] However, in securing the interests of printers by granting privileges, the Crown had two important aims. One of these related to the concern of the Crown to maintain a 'sound economic order' in the Kingdom. The other related to its concern over press censorship.

One of the most important aims of the British Crown in granting printing patents was regulating the economy of Britain. In particular, it was part of extending government support for a budding industry in the country. The printing patents conferred 'a valuable economic protection' to printers, which was necessary for them to survive in their trade and recoup the substantial investment made in the process of printing literary and scientific works.[86] Importantly, this involved (where required) a prohibition against making and printing of translations by others—a means to protect the translation rights of the printers.

Another important aim of the British Crown in granting printing patents was press censorship. Although printing patents ultimately proved to be an ineffective means of censorship, initially (especially during the first few centuries of the introduction of printing), the Crown believed that these patents would be important in ensuring the secure and accurate communication of ideologies and doctrines advocated by the Crown and the Church to the public. More specifically, the Crown thought that they would be able to use printing patents to limit the ability of people to print and distribute certain important works, such as the Bible, and ecclesiastical and legal texts. By only granting these patents to selected persons who were faithful to the Crown and the Church, the Crown also thought that it would be possible to ensure that these people would print and distribute these works while preserving the ideologies and doctrines advocated by these institutions with accuracy.[87] Essentially, prohibitions on translation played an important role in this connection because translation, particularly into English, ran a high risk of misinterpretation or abuse of the original work, as was initially claimed in the case of Tyndale's Bible translation.[88]

3.3.2.1.3. PRIVILEGE TO PRINT TRANSLATIONS AS A RIGHT OF THE TRANSLATORS AND PRINTERS

For the most part, the recipients of printing patents that conferred an exclusive privilege to translate works (and print translations) were translators and printers.[89] This was particularly so when the work for which the printing patent was

85 John Feather, *A History of British Publishing* (Routledge, 2nd ed, 2006) 26.

86 Deazley, above n 72.

87 See Feather, above n 20, 11–12.

88 See Dorothy Auchter, *Dictionary of Literary and Dramatic Censorship in Tudor and Stuart England* (Greenwood Press, 2001) 246; AW Ward, GW Prothero and Stanley Leathes (eds), *The Cambridge Modern History* (Palgrave Macmillan, 1907) vol 2, 465.

89 The three recipients of patents from Queen Anne that prohibited the printing of translations were printers and translators. See S Mendyk, 'Blome, Richard (bap. 1635?, d 1705)' in *Oxford Dictionary of National Biography* (Oxford University Press, 2004) <www.oxforddnb.

granted was itself a translation. An early example of such a grant was the privilege conferred on Ludovick Lloyd in 1573 with regard to his English translation of Plutarch's work, *Lives*. In particular, this grant carried the 'important rider that no other translation was to be published' during the period specified in the grant.[90] Certainly, these kinds of exclusive privileges are contrary to the concept of translation rights in modern copyright law. This is also because such privileges had prohibited even the original authors of literary and scientific works from translating their works into certain languages.[91]

3.3.2.2. Privileges conferred on the stationers

Feather said, '[t]he "stationers" were the freemen of the Company of Stationers of London, the trade guild, or livery company, to which members of the book trade belonged.'[92] The British Crown conferred certain privileges on the Stationers with regard to the printing of books. These privileges constituted an important part of the laws of printing that were in force prior to *Statute of Anne 1710*. Obviously, the privileges conferred on the Stationers addressed the interests of the Stationers and the Crown. In contrast, they hardly dealt with the rights and interests of the authors of books. Therefore, although book translation and the right to print those translations played an important part in the business of the Stationers, the privileges conferred on them by the Crown did not create an exclusive author's right to translate their books.

The primary purpose of granting privileges to the Stationers by the Crown was twofold, namely, safeguarding the interests of the Crown itself and performing the Crown obligations to the citizenry. The first related to the need of the Crown to prevent the printing and distribution of books that were considered heretical and treasonous, and the second related to the need to maintain sound economic order in the Kingdom.[93]

From the early fifteenth century onwards, the Stationers were seen by the Crown (and the Church) as 'a reputable organisation which could be entrusted

---

com/view/article/2662>; Paul Chamberlen, *An Impartial History of the Life and Reign of Our Late Most Gracious Sovereign Queen Anne* (1738) 460; Reavley Gair, 'Chamberlayne, John (1668/9–1723)' in *Oxford Dictionary of National Biography* (Oxford University Press, online ed, 2009) <www.oxforddnb.com/view/article/5060>; Leslie Stephen (ed), *Dictionary of National Biography* (Palgrave Macmillan, 1887) vol 10, 9, 8.

90 Feather, above n 20, 13.

91 The privilege conferred on Ludovick Lloyd appears to have prohibited even the author of the source work from publishing a translation. See Lionel Bently, 'Copyright and Translations in the English Speaking World' (1993) 12(4) *Translatio: FIT Newsletter* 491, 523; William Briggs, *The Law of International Copyright* (Stevens & Haynes, 1906) 359–360.

92 Feather, above n 20, 15.

93 In other words, it was believed at this time that dissemination of heretical and treasonous information can best be suppressed through regulation of printing. Apart from this, regulation of printing was also essential for the Crown to protect the interests of various stakeholders in the printing and book trade for the ultimate purpose of maintaining a sound economic order in the Kingdom.

with the task of ensuring that error free and approved copies [of books] were made available for public consumption.'[94] With the introduction of printing, the Crown began to rely more on the Stationers and received their assistance extensively in preventing the printing and distribution of books that were considered seditious, heretical and treasonous. Partly because of this, the Stationers received a Royal Charter from Queen Mary (1516–1558) in 1557.[95] The Charter granted the Stationers' Company 'a virtual monopoly over printing and bookselling both in London and throughout the kingdom'[96] and the power to make ordinances, provisions and statutes for their 'good and sound rule and, government'.[97] In addition, the Master, Keepers or Wardens of the Stationers' Company were granted the powers to search for books that had been printed contrary to the statutes, acts, or proclamations and to 'seize, take hold, burn' those books or turn them to the proper use of the Company.[98] The subsequent Star Chamber Decrees extended these powers.[99]

Obviously, the virtual monopoly granted by the Royal Charter over printing and bookselling enabled the Stationers' Company to promote its primary interest, that is, 'securing to its members the exclusive control over their published works'.[100] The Company's power to make 'ordinances, provisions and statutes' for its internal governance further assisted this. In particular, the Stationers' Company established a prepublication licensing system, which required members 'to obtain from the Wardens of the Company a license to print any particular work, and enter that license in the company's register' before printing and publishing that work.[101] The power to make internal regulation under the Charter also enabled the Stationers' Company to set up a body called 'Court of Assistants',[102] which could impose financial penalties upon persons who printed a work against the license of the company. The result of this was that the prepublication licensing system secured members of the Company an exclusive privilege to print the works entered in the Company's Register under their names. The subsequent Star Chamber Decrees further expanded and strengthened this privilege.[103] Despite the abolition of the Star Chamber in 1640,[104] the Stationers' Company continued to exercise this licensing system and many of its other

94 Harvey, above n 73, 160, 164.
95 Ronan Deazley, 'Commentary on the Stationers' Royal Charter 1557' in L Bently and M Kretschmer (eds), *Primary Sources on Copyright (1450–1900)* (2008) <www.copyrighthistory.org>.
96 Feather, above n 20, 15.
97 *Royal Charter of the Company of Stationers 1557.*
98 Ibid.
99 *Star Chamber Decree 1566*; *Star Chamber Decree 1586*; *Star Chamber Decree 1637.*
100 Deazley, above n 95.
101 Ibid.
102 Feather, above n 20, 16.
103 Ronan Deazley, 'Commentary on Star Chamber Decree 1566' in L Bently and M Kretschmer (eds), *Primary Sources on Copyright (1450–1900)* (2008) <www.copyrighthistory.org>.
104 Feather, above n 20, 41.

related powers through the *Licensing Act 1662*,[105] until the House of Commons refused to renew the Act in 1695.[106]

3.3.2.2.1. EXCLUSIVE PRIVILEGE TO PRINT TRANSLATIONS

The prepublication licensing system was a primary means used by the members of the Stationers' Company to secure an exclusive privilege to print translations. This is demonstrated by notes appended to the entries in the Stationers' Register which state: 'To be translated into English when he hath gotten sufficient authority for it.'[107] However, there is an important issue which arises when we closely examine these notes. That is, what was exactly meant by the term 'sufficient authority'? More specifically, did it mean that a stationer who wanted to print a translation of a literary or scientific work had to obtain consent from the author of that work to translate and print it?

Inevitably, seeking an answer to this question leads us to the perennial controversy over literary property, that is, whether the common law granted authors property rights in their literary works. Although this is a matter outside the scope of this book, it is necessary to understand that there was no hard and fast rule requiring printers or translators to obtain consent from the authors for translation of their works. The available evidence relating to the practice of translation between the fifteenth and the end of the eighteenth centuries also seems to support this position. As was pointed out earlier, despite the objections that translators were reaping what they had not sown and that translations abused the authors of their source works, translation was continued as a lucrative enterprise during this period. Also, as Bennett noted, '[a]uthorities, ancient and modern, were ransacked, and often ruthlessly adapted [by printers] to provide a cheap handbook on astronomy, dietary or popular medicine.'[108] Moreover, as Attorney General Thurlow said:

> Lord Bacon and several of the old learned writers, always gave their thoughts in Latin; surely if they had a right to their own ideas, it would have been very hard for a translator to have published an English edition as soon as possible after their appearance in Latin.[109]

Arguably, these factors indicate that neither the translators who translated literary and scientific works nor the printers who printed translations of these works were necessarily required to obtain the consent or approval from their authors.

105 See, e.g., Cyprian Blagden, *The Stationers' Company: A History, 1403–1959* (Stanford University Press, 1977) 148, where referring to the introduction of the *Licensing Act 1662*, it is observed that '[t]he clock was put firmly back to 1637.' Cf Feather, above n 20, 44.

106 Ronan Deazley, *On the Origin of the Right to Copy: Charting the Movement of Copyright Law in Eighteenth-Century Britain (1695–1775)* (Hart Publishing, 2004) 1–2.

107 Bennett, above n 31, 75.

108 Bennett, above n 19, 156.

109 United Kingdom, *Cobbett's Parliamentary History of England*, 1774, vol 17, cols 969–970.

Apart from this, it is unsafe to rely on the entries in the register of the Stationers' Company to determine whether a stationer who wanted to print a translation of a literary or scientific work had to obtain consent from the author of that work to translate and print it. This is because the original purpose behind the entries in the Stationers' Company's Register was keeping a record. As Feather noted, these entries were 'a record of the fact that, in the opinion of the Master and Wardens, the book had been properly licensed, or that it could be printed without giving offence'.[110] Although these entries later took 'a very different and more extensive meaning' so as to prevent 'printing another man's copy',[111] nothing in the written law of Britain nor the rules of the Stationer's Company prevented a person from printing a translation without the consent of the original author. However, in contrast to this, Greg and Boswell argued that a decision of the Court of Assistants, handed down on 18 June 1578 laid down the general rule that a translation must be printed by its owner as 'assignee of the holder of the original copyright'.[112]

This decision to which Greg and Boswell refer is related to the Welsh translation of the book *The Least Catechism*.[113] This book was authored by Alexander Nowell (1507–1602), while John Day (1522–1584) had a license properly recorded in the Stationers' Register to print it. However, at the same time, Richard Jones (1564–1613) had a license from the Stationers' Company to print a translation of this book in Welsh, although a copy of the translation was not entered in the Stationers' Register. When the dispute was referred to the Court of Assistants, it decided that Jones should print the translation in the name of John Day. In addition, the court also pronounced that the translation should properly belong to Jones and not to Day.[114]

Commenting on this decision, Greg and Boswell suggested that '[g]eneralised this means that a translation could be registered as an independent work but must be printed by the owner as assignee of the holder of the original copyright'.[115] However, this contention appears to be misconceived. This is partly because, as Blagden observed, the basis of the Court of Assistants' decision in this dispute was a compromise entered into between Jones and Day.[116] As such, it is implausible to assume (as Greg and Boswell appear to have done) that the Court of Assistants set a general rule that a translated work must be printed by the owner as assignee of the holder of the original copyright. Moreover, inferring such a general rule contradicts the very clear pronouncement of the court that the translation should properly belong to Jones and not to Day. In these

110 Feather, above n 20, 17.
111 Ibid., 17–18.
112 WW Greg and E Boswell (eds), *Records of the Court of the Stationers' Company (1576 to 1602—From Register B)* (Bibliographical Society, 1930) lxxiv.
113 Ibid., lxxiii.
114 Greg and Boswell (eds), above n 112, lxxiv.
115 Ibid.
116 Blagden, above n 105, 55.

circumstances, it is more plausible to assume that the prepublication licensing system exercised by the Stationer's Company did not create or acknowledge an author's (or copyright owner's) exclusive right to translate their literary and scientific works. Instead, what it provided was an exclusive privilege on Stationers to print translations.

3.3.3. *The* Statute of Anne *and translation*

The *Statute of Anne 1710* is a landmark in the history of British copyright law and in the history of the British book trade.[117] In fact, it was the first legislation in Britain to ever confer an exclusive right on the authors to 'print and reprint' their books. In particular, this Act provided:

> That from and after the tenth day of April, one thousand seven hundred and ten, the author of any book or books already printed, who hath not transferred to any other the copy or copies of such book or books, share or shares thereof, or the bookseller or booksellers, printer or printers, or other person or persons, who hath or have purchased or acquired the copy or copies of any book or books, in order to print or reprint the same, shall have the sole right and liberty of printing such book and books for the term of one and twenty years, to commence from the said tenth day of April, and no longer; and That the author of any book or books already composed, and not printed and published, or that shall hereafter be composed, and his assignee or assigns, shall have the sole liberty of printing and reprinting such book and books for the term of fourteen years.[118]

Importantly, the *Statute of Anne* was silent on whether it conferred an exclusive right on authors to translate their books. However, this silence was neither a mistake nor a lapse on the part of the British Parliament. There are four factors that support this position, namely, (i) the purpose which was meant to be served by the *Statute of Anne*; (ii) the attitude of the courts during the period when the statute was in force; (iii) legislative practices during this period; and (iv) the matters discussed in the course of the literary property debate.

3.3.3.1. *Purpose of the* Statute of Anne

Academic views on the precise objective and the effect of the *Statute of Anne 1710* are unsettled.[119] For instance, Patterson believed that the *Statute of Anne* was simply 'a trade-regulation statute directed to the problem of monopoly in various

117 Feather, above n 20, 64.
118 *Statute of Anne 1710*, 8 Anne, c 19.
119 See Catherine Seville, 'The Statute of Anne: Rhetoric and Reception in the Nineteenth Century' (2010–2011) 47 *Houston Law Review* 819, 873.

forms'.[120] According to him, this legislation 'was an attack on the traditional stationers' monopoly'.[121] Saunders concurred with Patterson when he stated that the purpose of the *Statute of Anne* was 'to break the [Stationers'] Company's 150-year-old monopoly on the publishing of books in England'.[122] However, in Feather's account, the *Statute of Anne* was by and large a restoration of much of the traditional powers of Stationers, because:

> For the [book] trade, the 1710 Act represented a simple continuation of legal and commercial practices which had developed since the middle of the sixteenth century, but which had been under challenge in the absence of any statutory authority since 1695.[123]

In contrast to these views, Deazley stated that the *Statute of Anne* was not 'primarily concerned with securing the position of the booksellers, nor with guarding against their monopolistic control of the press, although it provided an opportunity for addressing both of these issues'.[124] According to him, this statute was 'primarily concerned with the continued production of books'.[125]

When observed from different angles, the views of all these scholars are accurate. In any case, all these views are compatible with the contention of this book, namely, that the reason for the silence on translation rights in the *Statute of Anne 1710* was that the purpose (and effect) of this statute was not to overexpand the rights of proprietors of books—whether these be the authors or the printers—by granting them copyright. In effect, this contention is similar to Bently's observation that the rights conferred by the *Statute* were 'rights to "print and reprint" books, not "copyright"'.[126]

As Birrell claimed, the *Statute of Anne 1710* was 'set in motion not by an irate populace clamouring for cheap books (as a generation later they were to clamour for cheap gin), but by authors and their proprietors, the booksellers.'[127] However, the booksellers' real intention of employing the authors for this purpose was only as a conduit to further their own interests rather than those of the authors.[128] This becomes clearly evident from the legislative background of the *Statute of Anne.*

120 LR Patterson, *Copyright in Historical Perspective* (Vanderbilt University, 1968) 150.

121 Oren Bracha, 'Owning Ideas: A History of Anglo-American Intellectual Property' (JSD Thesis, Harvard Law School, 2005) 177.

122 David Saunders, *Authorship and Copyright* (Routledge, 1992) 26.

123 Feather, above n 20, 63.

124 Deazley, above n 106, 46.

125 Ronan Deazley, 'Commentary on the *Statute of Anne* 1710' in L Bently and M Kretschmer (eds), *Primary Sources on Copyright (1450–1900) (2008)* <www.copyrighthistory.org>.

126 Lionel Bently, 'Introduction to Part I: The History of Copyright' in Lionel Bently, Uma Suthersanen and Paul Torremans (eds), *Global Copyright: Three Hundred Years Since the Statute of Anne, from 1709 to Cyberspace* (Edward Elgar, 2010) 7, 9.

127 Augustine Birrell, *Seven Lectures on the Law and History of Copyright in Books* (Cassell, 1899) 22.

128 Mark Rose, *Authors and Owners: The Invention of Copyright* (Harvard University Press, 1994) 34–37.

Sherman and Bently observed:

> With the lapse of the Licensing Acts in 1695 . . . the Stationers began to lose the control that they had long exercised over the book trade [and in] response to this, they began a campaign to have their monopoly powers restored.[129]

The early reactions of Stationers to this situation was rather traditional, namely, 'lobbying for new legislation regulating printing and vesting the company with broad powers' under the guise of the need for press censorship.[130] However, these old arguments hardly bore any fruits, as there was strong ideological opposition to press censorship by this time.[131] Of the various arguments for and against press censorship during this period, the argument put forward by Daniel Defoe (1660–1731) in his *Essay on the Regulation of the Press* (1704) was both unique and influential. In particular, Defoe did not deny altogether the importance of press regulation but criticised the prepublication censorship of books that had existed under the *Licensing Act 1662*.[132] In his *Essay*, Defoe also highlighted the value of public access to knowledge and emphasised how it could be directly restricted by a system of prepublication censorship of books. As an alternative to a system of prepublication censorship, he suggested a system of post-publication censorship which gave authors of books a more prominent place. More specifically, Defoe identified that the only reason for preferring prepublication censorship of books to post-publication censorship was the difficultly in ascertaining the true authors of those books. To overcome this, he suggested a means of post-publication censorship that could identify the authors with their books. Essentially, this system of post-publication censorship required authors to be given a property right in their books.[133] Defoe also justified the conferring of property rights on the basis that it 'would also put a Stop to a certain sort of Thieving which [was] in full practice in England, and which no Law extende[d] to punish, viz. some Printers and Booksellers printing Copies none of their own'.[134]

Defoe's arguments provided the Stationers with a new strategy for lobbying Parliament.[135] Stern stated that 'during the fifteen-year struggle for legislation recognizing an exclusive right to print, the booksellers shifted from censorship-oriented regulatory rationales of the kind that had been persuasive in the seventeenth century, to arguments emphasising authors' interests'.[136] The result of this was the *Statute of Anne 1710*, which recognised an author's exclusive right to 'print and reprint' their books.

129 Sherman and Bently, above n 7, 11–12 (emphasis added).
130 Bracha, above n 121, 178.
131 See Deazley, above n 106, 1–29.
132 Daniel Defoe, *An Essay on the Regulation of the Press* (1704), Bently and Kretschmer (eds), above n 71.
133 Ibid.
134 Ibid., 25.
135 Rose, above n 128, 35.
136 Simon Stern, 'From Author's Right to Property Right' (2012) 62 *University of Toronto Law Journal* 29, 42.

Although the *Statute of Anne 1710* was enacted in response to the agitation of the Stationers, it is important to note that it did not restore the privileges that Stationers had enjoyed prior to the lapse of the *Licensing Act 1662*. Also, it did not empower authors with extensive rights.

As Feather stated, the *Statute of Anne* 'was an unintended consequence of the actions taken by those who had promoted the legislation'.[137] This was because the *Statute* did not address the interests of Stationers to the extent they wished. Nor did it address the interests of authors in any material way. In view of this, Feather observed that the *Statute of Anne* 'wholly ignored the authors of books, and certainly was not intended to confer any additional rights upon them'.[138] Similarly, Birrell observed that the *Statute of Anne* 'spoilt all [and] gave away the whole case of the British author'.[139]

Evidently there was an important reason for the *Statute of Anne 1710* to pay less attention to authors and curtail the interests of Stationers. That reason was, above all, that the *Statute of Anne* was an 'Act to Encourage Learning',[140] which had the primary objective of promoting knowledge and thus public benefit.[141] As such, the *Statute* conferred rights on the authors or Stationers only to the extent that there was public benefit, particularly with respect to the encouragement of learning or access to knowledge. To that end, while the *Statute of Anne* recognised some of the interests of Stationers, it 'also responded to the concerns regarding monopolistic practices [of Stationers] by placing certain limits on the rights granted to them'.[142] In fact, as Patterson noted, the introduction of 'author' in the *Statute of Anne* was a technique used to place these limits with justification.[143]

The *Statute of Anne 1710* did not intend to overexpand the rights of the author by introduction of the author as a figure in the *Act*.[144] Thus, the *Act* did not protect authors' translation rights, as it would have not only overexpanded the rights of the author but also would have been detrimental to public benefit, particularly to the encouragement of learning.

3.3.3.2. Attitude of courts

As Bently noted, '[t]ranslating was neither printing, nor was the printing of a translation the printing of the same book.'[145] The attitude of the British courts towards translating and printing translations of books during the period in which

137 Feather, above n 20, 64.
138 Ibid.
139 Birrell, above n 139, 22.
140 *An Act for the Encouragement of Learning, by Vesting the Copies of Printed Books in the Authors or Purchasers of such Copies, During the Times therein mentioned 1710*, 8 Anne, c 19.
141 Bently, above n 91, 491, 492.
142 Isabella Alexander, *Copyright and the Public Interest in the Nineteenth Century* (Hart Publishing, 2010) 24.
143 Patterson, above n 120, 147.
144 Ibid.
145 Bently, above n 91, 491, 496.

Statute of Anne 1710 was in force was that this *Act* clearly did not prohibit translation and printing of translations. In other words, the British courts were of the view that the *Statute of Anne* did not protect translation rights. Although there is no direct authority for this proposition, the judicial pronouncements in several cases have clearly demonstrated this view.

The case of *Burnet v Chetwood*[146] was the earliest instance in which a British court considered whether the *Statute of Anne 1710* protected translation rights.[147] In this case, the plaintiff, as executor of Burnett, the author of the book *Archaelogia Sacra*, brought a bill against the defendant for an injunction to stay the printing and publishing of a translation of that book. The bill suggested that the printing and publishing was an injury to the executor, in whom the property of the book was vested by the *Statute of Anne*. The defendant argued against this, stating that the *Statute of Anne* 'intended only to restrain the mechanical art of printing' books and therefore 'a translation of a book was not within the intent' of it.[148] In addition, the defendant also argued that a translation 'in some respects may be called a different book, and the translator may be said to be the author [of the translation], in as much as some skill in language' is expended by him in the process of translation, which is 'not barely a mechanic art, as in the case of reprinting [a book] in the same language'.[149] In response to the arguments of the defendant, the Lord Chancellor conceded that 'a translation might not be the same with the reprinting [of] the original, on account that the translator has bestowed his care and pains on it', and therefore 'not within the prohibition of the [*Statute of Anne*]'.[150] However, he granted the injunction in favour of the plaintiff on the ground that the book 'contained strange notions, intended by the author to be concealed from the vulgar in the Latin language, in which language it could not do much hurt, the learned being better able to judge of it'.[151]

Apparently, *Burnet v Chetwood*[152] is the only recorded case where the British courts had to decide whether the *Statute of Anne 1710* protected translation rights.[153] Nonetheless, discussions have ensued on the position of translation rights under the *Statute of Anne* in the course of subsequent cases, namely, *Millar*

146 (1721) 2 Mer 441; 35 ER 1008.
147 Deazley, above n 106, 56.
148 (1721) 2 MER 441; 35 ER 1008, 1008–1009.
149 (1721) 2 MER 441; 35 ER 1008, 1009.
150 Ibid.
151 (1721) 2 Mer 441; 35 ER 1008, 1009.
152 (1721) 2 Mer 441; 35 ER 1008.
153 However, see Dennis WK Khong, 'The Historical Law and Economics of the First Copyright Act' (2006) 2(1) *Erasmus Law and Economics Review* 35, 49, where it is contended that:

> Burnett v Chetwood is not a definitive statement of . . . [translation rights] for two reasons. First, the court which heard this case was the Court of Chancery, which was not a common law court. . . . Secondly, the statement about a translation as not prohibited by the Act was made as an *obiter dictum*, as decision contrary to the statement was in fact made.

v Taylor[154] and *Donaldson v Beckett*.[155] In *Millar v Taylor*, where one of the main issues was whether authors' rights under the common law subsisted despite the provisions of the *Statute of Anne*, Justice Willes, who lined up with the majority decision holding that the common law right of an author to copies of their works was not taken away by the *Statute*,[156] observed that translations may be considered as new works (and not copies).[157] Similarly, Justice Aston (who also aligned with the majority decision) acknowledged that it is lawful for a purchaser of a book to translate it.[158] Apart from this, when the House of Lords deliberated over the case of *Donaldson v Beckett*,[159] Lord Chief Justice De Grey noted that (unauthorised) translations were permissible under the *Statute of Anne* despite the fact that they 'effectually deprive the original author of the fruits of his labours, as direct particular copies'.[160]

3.3.3.3. Legislative practices: the Booksellers' Bill 1737

The fact that the British Parliament did not intend to protect translation rights in the *Statute of Anne 1710* is further supported by the provisions in the Booksellers' Bill 1737.[161] This Bill was the first instance in which the British Parliament attempted to confer a translation right on authors.[162] However, the translation right recognised in this Bill was a limited right when compared with the right of 'printing and reprinting' recognised in the *Statue of Anne*.[163] This is mainly because the translation right recognised in the Bill only survived for three years,

154 (1769) 4 Burrow 2303; 98 ER 201, reversed in *Donaldson v Becket* (1774) II Brown 129: 1 ER 837.
155 (1774) II Brown 129: 1 ER 837.
156 (1769) 4 Burrow 2303, 2411; 98 ER 201, 259.
157 (1769) 4 Burrow 2303, 2310; 98 ER 201, 205.
158 (1769) 4 Burrow 2303, 2249; 98 ER 201, 226.
159 (1774) II Brown 129: 1 ER 837.
160 United Kingdom, *Cobbett's Parliamentary History of England*, 1774, vol 17, col 990.
161 A Bill for the better Encouragement of Learning, by the More Effectual Securing the Copies of Printed Books to the Authors or Purchasers of Such Copies, during the Times Therein to be Mentioned 1737; Draft Act for the Encouragement of Learning, by the More Effectual Securing the Sole Right of Printing Books to the Authors Thereof, Their Executors, Administrators, or Assigns, during the Times Therein Mentioned 1737; An Act for the Encouragement of Learning (Draft). London (1737), Bently and Kretschmer (eds), above n 71.
162 Ronan Deazley, 'Commentary on the Booksellers' Bill (1737)' in L Bently and M Kretschmer (eds), *Primary Sources on Copyright (1450–1900)* (2008) <www.copyrighthistory.org>; Draft Act for the Encouragement of Learning, by the More Effectual Securing the Sole Right of Printing Books to the Authors Thereof, Their Executors, Administrators, or Assigns, during the Times Therein Mentioned 1737; An Act for the Encouragement of Learning (Draft). London (1737), Bently and Kretschmer (eds), above n 71.
163 The Bill conferred the 'Sole Right and Liberty of printing and reprinting' for the lifetime of the authors whereas the translation rights which it conferred lasted only for three years. See specifically, Draft Act for the Encouragement of Learning, by the More Effectual Securing the Sole Right of Printing Books to the Authors Thereof, Their Executors, Administrators, or Assigns, during the Times Therein Mentioned 1737; An Act for the Encouragement of Learning (Draft). London (1737), Bently and Kretschmer (eds), above n 71.

whereas the right of 'printing and reprinting' under the Bill survived for the lifetime of the author. Also under the *Statute of Anne*, this right lasted for 21 years with respect to old books already published by 1710 and 14 years with respect to new books.[164] Therefore, the Booksellers' Bill 1737 also supports the view that, even in 1737, the British Parliament was not willing to protect authors' translation rights in the same manner in which it was willing to protect their right of 'printing and reprinting'. Instead, the objective of the British Parliament in recognising translation rights in the Bill was to remedy the specific mischief of 'hasty and incorrect translations' by which authors were 'often greatly injured', in a generalised form of prohibition on all translations.[165]

As Deazley observed, the Booksellers' Bill 1737 marks the 'first occasion on which the British legislature proposed to confer upon authors a lifetime interest in their literary works . . . as well as limited rights of translation and abridgement'.[166] As one of the clauses of the Bill stated:

> AND whereas the Authors and Proprietors, of Works composed with great Labour and long Study, are often greatly injured by such hasty and incorrect Abridgements or Translations of the same, as not only lessen the Sale, but also frequently sink the Reputation of the original Composition; be it further enacted, That if any Person or Persons shall, within Three Years after the Publication of any Book, print, publish, import, or sell any Abridgement of the same, or any Translation thereof, into any other Language, without the Consent of the Author or Proprietor first obtained . . . then such Offender shall forfeit such Abridgement or Translation . . . to the Proprietor or Proprietors of the original Book, who shall damask or make waste Paper thereof; and every such Offender shall likewise forfeit the Sum of Five Shillings for every Sheet thereof to the Proprietor or the Proprietors of the original Book so abridged or translated.[167]

This provision clearly suggests that British Parliament did not intend to protect authors' translation rights through the *Statute of Anne*. As Sag stated:

> The fact that booksellers found it necessary to make their monopoly over . . . translations explicit suggests that this right was not perceived as part of the original grant contained in the Statute of Anne. This suggestion becomes

164 William Cornish, 'The Statute of Anne 1709–10: Its Historical Setting' in Lionel Bently, Uma Suthersanen and Paul Torremans (eds), *Global Copyright: Three Hundred Years Since the Statute of Anne, from 1709 to Cyberspace* (Edward Elgar, 2010) 14, 23.

165 Draft Act for the Encouragement of Learning, by the More Effectual Securing the Sole Right of Printing Books to the Authors Thereof, Their Executors, Administrators, or Assigns, during the Times Therein Mentioned 1737; An Act for the Encouragement of Learning (Draft). London (1737), Bently and Kretschmer (eds), above n 71.

166 Deazley, above n 106, xxiv–xxv.

167 Draft Act for the Encouragement of Learning, by the More Effectual Securing the Sole Right of Printing Books to the Authors Thereof, Their Executors, Administrators, or Assigns, during the Times Therein Mentioned 1737; An Act for the Encouragement of Learning (Draft). London (1737), Bently and Kretschmer (eds), above n 71.

even stronger when considering that this 'new' right was only granted for a period of three years.[168]

As such, the Booksellers' Bill 1737 forms clear evidence not only that the *Statute of Anne 1710* did not protect translation rights but also that the intent of the British Parliament during this period was not to equate translation rights with the main right of protection granted to the authors, namely, the right of 'printing and reprinting'.

The Booksellers' Bill 1737 was the culmination of a legislative process instigated by London Booksellers to safeguard their interests in reaction to the deficiencies of the *Statute of Anne 1710*. On account of this, Alexander argued that the primary objective of protecting translation rights in the Bill was to protect these booksellers. In particular, she stated:

> The leading booksellers [in London] were clearly concerned with the prospect of free-riding activity that abridgements and partial copying made possible. In the 1730s these booksellers included clauses seeking to address the issues of partial taking, abridgements, and translations while lobbying for new legislation to extend the term of the rights given under the Statute of Anne. The resulting Bill of 1737 [Booksellers' Bill 1737] addressed both partial copying and altered copying problems.[169]

However, this view is implausible for two main reasons. Firstly, while it is true that the booksellers once again used authors as a conduit for furthering their interests when lobbying for a new legislation in 1730s, their claims put forward in connection to this suggest that translation rights were not a pressing need. Secondly, even if it is assumed that translation rights were a pressing need of the booksellers' (and, in fact, they did lobby the legislature for these rights), the way these rights were purported to be protected in the Booksellers' Bill 1737 suggests that the Parliament did so in order to promote the interests of the authors rather than those of the booksellers.

The fact that translation rights were not presented by booksellers as a pressing need to the Parliament can be seen in the petition they submitted to the House of Commons on 3 March 1735.[170] In particular, this petition did not make any ref-

168 Matthew Sag, 'The Prehistory of Fair Use' (2011) 76(4) *Brooklyn Law Review* 1371, 1381–1382 (citations omitted).

169 Isabella Alexander, 'All Change for the Digital Economy: Copyright and Business Models in the Early Eighteenth Century' (2010) 25 *Berkeley Technology Law Journal* 1351, 1366.

170 The Humble Petition of Several Proprietors of Copies of Books whose Names are Hereunto Subscribed on behalf as well as of the Authors and Compilers of such Books as of Themselves and a Great Number of Others Concerned in the Manufactury of Printing (1735), Private and Local Bills and Acts: Petition, Harper Collection of Private Bills 1695–1814, 11 February 1732 to 27 March 1735, British Library.

erence to translation rights.[171] The situation is the same with regard to the majority of bookseller pamphlets produced in connection with lobbying Parliament for more protection. Be that as it may, even if the booksellers had agitated for translation rights, the response of the Parliament (in both Houses) was clearly against it.[172] Two pieces of evidence demonstrate this. Firstly, the Booksellers' Bill 1735, which preceded the Booksellers' Bill 1737 (and which was the initial response of the Parliament to the booksellers' agitations in 1730s over the deficiencies of the *Statute of Anne*), did not make any reference to translation rights. Secondly, the Booksellers' Bill 1737 recognised only a narrow right of translation.

The reason for the (limited) protection set forth for translation rights in the Booksellers' Bill 1737 was to protect authors from the injury caused by hasty and inaccurate translations. While this was explicitly stated in the Bill, a shorter term of protection for translation rights was largely sufficient for this purpose.[173]

The Booksellers' Bill 1737 was, in part, a legislative attempt to empower the figure of author.[174] As, Deazley stated, this Bill 'for the first time, introduced the authorial figure as a significant third party.'[175] Moreover, according to its preamble, the Bill was:

> [F]or more effectual vesting in Authors, their Executors, Administrators, and Assigns, the Property of their own Writings, and thereby encouraging learned Men to write, compile, translate, and compose useful Books.[176]

In fact, the way in which translation rights were proposed to be protected in the Booksellers' Bill 1737 was in line with this aim. More specifically, this Bill proposed that translation rights should be protected not to discourage translations altogether but to prohibit printing, publishing, importing or selling translations for a period of three years in order to prevent 'hasty and incorrect' translations.[177] This was because these kinds of translations were a severe threat to the 'reputation of the original composition' of books as well as their authors. In addition,

171 Ibid.

172 This is because both the House of Commons and House of Lords did not intend to protect translation rights for the full term of the authors' 'right of printing and reprinting'. According to Deazley, it was the Commons that introduced the provision addressing the translations (and abridgements) of an author's work during the Bill's passage through the House. Deazley, above n 106, 107, n 92.

173 See Deazley, above n 106, 106.

174 Deazley, above n 162.

175 Ibid.

176 A Bill for the better Encouragement of Learning, by the More Effectual Securing the Copies of Printed Books to the Authors or Purchasers of Such Copies, during the Times Therein to be Mentioned 1737; Draft Act for the Encouragement of Learning, by the More Effectual Securing the Sole Right of Printing Books to the Authors Thereof, Their Executors, Administrators, or Assigns, during the Times Therein Mentioned 1737.

177 Deazley, above n 106, 108.

hasty and inaccurate translations also had the potential to compete unfairly with their source works.[178] As Stern noted:

> [T]he prohibition was restricted to a three-year window, justified by language suggesting that the primary concern involved the author's right to control the integrity of the text following its initial publication. Three years, evidently, was thought to be enough time to allow the author's message to circulate without contamination; after that, the revisers and paraphrasers would be free to ply their trade, even if their efforts might reduce the sales of a book published so recently.[179]

The inference that can be drawn from all these factors is that the paramount objective of protecting translation rights in the Booksellers' Bill 1737 was to protect the authors from the evils of inaccurate translation.[180] Yet the failure of this Bill in the House of Lords shows that the Parliament was not willing to protect the translation rights of the author even to remove this evil, primarily because it was thought that such protection would run counter to the encouragement of learning.[181]

3.3.3.4. Translation rights in the literary property debate

The proposition that the silence of the *Statute of Anne 1710* on translation rights was not a mistake or a lapse on the part of the British Parliament is further strengthened by the debate over literary property which took place in Britain in the second half of the eighteenth century. The central theme of this debate was whether the common law of Britain protected literary works as property and granted authors perpetual rights over their literary works. Sherman and Bently observed:

> [T]he debate was prompted by the fact that the Stationers' Company, whose power and control over the publication of books was being undermined, argued that, whatever the Statutes of the day may have said, at common law authors (and their assigns) enjoyed perpetual rights over their creations.[182]

As Deazley noted, booksellers who failed in their strategies to persuade Parliament to bring legislation which furthered their interests 'turn[ed] instead to the courts

178 See Deazley, above n 162.

179 Stern, above n 136, 29, 88.

180 It is apparent that the aim of the protection of translation rights in the Booksellers' Bill was not to promote the interests of booksellers. Indeed, '[f]rom the booksellers' point of view, the proposed Bill was anathema'. Deazley, above n 162.

181 According to Alexander Pope, the House of Commons 'added Some Clauses [to the Bill] that were prejudicial . . . to the True Intention of Encouraging Learning' to which the House of Lords 'objected'. George Sherburn (ed), *The Correspondence of Alexander Pope* (Clarendon Press, 1956) vol 4, 69.

182 Sherman and Bently, above n 7, 9.

to try to shore up their commercial interests'.[183] In fact, the decision in *Baller v Watson*,[184] which 'provided the plaintiff with both a "perpetual injunction", as well as an account of the profits which the defendant had made in selling the plaintiff's work', encouraged the booksellers to pursue this new course of action.[185]

The question of whether the property rights in literary and scientific works extended to the translation of those works was explored in the course of the literary property debate by both proponents and opponents of literary property. These discussions indicate that translation rights were not initially considered part of property rights in literary and scientific works and that the *Statute of Anne 1710* did not protect these rights. In particular (as discussed in detail in the sections that follow), both the opponents and early proponents of literary property were of the view that the translation of literary and scientific works without the consent of their authors or proprietors was permissible. However, when these opponents used the exclusion of translation rights from the scope of property rights in literary property (as expounded by the early proponents of literary property) to challenge the rationality of the claims in favour of this new property (by distinguishing it from real property), the proponents had to accept that the scope of the property rights in literary property should extend to cover translation rights as well.

The early proponents of literary property viewed translation as creating a new form of literary property (the translated work) which did not affect the property rights in the original work. Therefore, they believed that it should be lawful for any person to translate a work without the consent of its author (or owner). In particular, it was said in the influential anonymous pamphlet, *A Vindication of the Exclusive Right of Authors to Their Own Works* (1762),[186] that literary works such as books consisted of a combination of a 'doctrinal composition' and a 'mechanical composition'.[187] The doctrinal composition was construed as the 'end' and the mechanical composition was construed the 'means' of promulgating that end.[188] More specifically, the mechanical composition in a book meant the 'writing or printing' which promulgated the 'doctrinal composition' of the author in that book.[189] Further, this pamphlet also claimed that this doctrinal composition (in respect to which the authors have their property rights) need not necessarily be original. Instead, what was required was that the author produce a 'different composition' or establish a 'different doctrine'.[190] More

183 Deazley, above n 162.
184 Baller v Watson: Entry from the Court's Book of Orders, London (1737), Bently and Kretschmer (eds), above n 71.
185 Deazley, above n 162.
186 A Vindication of the Rights of Authors, London (1762), Bently and Kretschmer (eds), above n 71.
187 Ibid., 9.
188 Ibid., 11.
189 Ibid.
190 Ibid., 9.

importantly, a change of language was viewed as sufficient to produce a different composition. Thus, it was stated that 'being the author of the language only, is a good ground for maintaining an exclusive right in a copy, though the ideas belong to another.'[191] In short, it was accepted that 'a translator may claim [an exclusive] right, being, in respect of those who are not skilled in the original, the parent of a new doctrine.'[192] Since promulgating a new doctrine by appropriating ideas contained in another doctrinal composition did not impinge on the property in it, translation was not seen as an infringement of the property rights in the original work.[193]

The dominant argument of the opponents of literary property was regarding the adverse impact that literary property would have on the public interest (for instance, promotion of science and knowledge).[194] However, opponents also drew on the idea put forward by early proponents of literary property that unauthorised translation did not amount to an invasion of property rights in the original works, in order to attack the appositeness of equating literary works with (real) property. More specifically, opponents of literary property claimed that literary works could not be construed as a form of property because, in the case of real property, any unauthorised use of a right which derives from it (a derivative right) would 'diminish or subtract' the right in the original. For instance, in *An Enquiry into the Nature and Origin of Literary Property* (1762), it was argued:

> We may derive a Property from the Ideas of others, not only by improving and adding to them, but merely by employing more Labour on them. Thus the Translator gains an Interest in the Ideas of an original Author, perhaps contrary to the Will of that Author; whereas in real Property the latter Right must flow from the Act of the first Proprietor. Whence arises this notable Difference? From hence, if I mistake not, in ideal Property the derivative right neither diminishes nor subtracts from the original one, therefore there is no Injury done. It is otherwise in real Property, where the former Right diminishes in Proportion as the latter increases. Hence the Consent of the first Proprietor is necessary.[195]

The argument of the opponents of literary property was that if literary works were to be construed as a form of property, why should an unauthorised translation not be construed as an infringement of those property rights? Chief Justice

191 Ibid.
192 Ibid.
193 Ibid., 13–14.
194 It is interesting to note that certain proponents of literary property construed (unauthorised) translations as permissible in terms of the law on the basis that they were beneficial for the general public. See Information for Messrs John Hinton et al., Edinburgh (1773), Bently and Kretschmer (eds), above n 71.
195 An Enquiry into Literary Property, London (1762), Bently and Kretschmer (eds), above n 71.

De Grey explicitly made this claim in the course of the proceedings of the House of Lords in *Donaldson v Beckett*[196] when he observed:

> Nor is it possible to support the Respondents' claim upon this principle, and not allow its operation in a variety of other cases, where, it is confessed on all hands, it cannot be allowed. Abridgments of books, translations, notes, as effectually deprive the original author of the fruit of his labours, as direct particular copies, yet they are allowable.[197]

Notably, this claim severely weakened the position of the proponents of literary property. To overcome this, they had to accept that the scope of the literary property right 'should extend beyond the surface of the text'[198] to cover translations and other kinds of derivative uses. However, this course of action encountered two main problems. Firstly, once it was acknowledged that property rights 'should extend beyond literal copying (that is, beyond the surface of the text) print no longer provided 'the manner and facility for tracing the difference between one literary work and another'.[199] Secondly, the notion of literary property, construed with its new extended scope, came to be attacked by the opponents on the basis that it was detrimental to the public benefit (in particular for promotion of science and knowledge) since it sternly restricted the development of new works, including translations and abridgements. Lord Camden, for instance, proclaimed:

> This perpetuity now contended for is as odious and as selfish as any other, it deserves as much reprobation, and will become as intolerable. Knowledge and science are not things to be bound in such cobweb chains; when once the bird is out of the cage—*volat irrevocabile*—Ireland, Scotland, America, will afford her shelter, and what, then, becomes of your action?[200]

3.3.4. Modern copyright law and translation

The approach in Britain toward authors' or copyright owners' right to translate their literary and scientific works started to change with the emergence of modern copyright law in the mid-nineteenth century. While the modern copyright law initially recognised the right to translate in a rudimentary form, by 1911 this right came to be protected as one of the fully fledged exclusive rights of the copyright owner. The main reasons for this change of approach included the new way

196 (1774) II Brown 129: 1 ER 837.

197 United Kingdom, *Cobbett's Parliamentary History of England*, 1774, vol 17, col 990.

198 Sherman and Bently, above n 7, 32.

199 Ibid., citing Francis Hargrave, *An Argument in Defence of Literary Property* (1774), Bently and Kretschmer (eds), above n 71.

200 United Kingdom, *Cobbett's Parliamentary History of England*, 1774, vol 17, cols 1000–1001.

in which protection of literary property was conceptualised under modern copyright law and the changed socio-economic and political background in Britain. In fact, the changed socio-economic and political conditions in Britain not only influenced this new conceptualisation of protection of literary property but also called for a comprehensive law protecting literary property which was premised on that conceptualisation. The result of this was the *Imperial Copyright Act 1911.*

3.3.4.1. New conceptual basis of copyright protection

The modernisation of copyright in the 19th century changed the conceptual basis of copyright protection. The recognition of authors' translation rights was partly an outcome of this change.

As Sherman and Bently observed, modern copyright law was an outcome of 'an important transformation [which] took place in the law which granted property rights in mental labour'.[201] Prior to the mid-nineteenth century, the law that granted property rights in mental labour was not organised in a consistent and meaningful way. Thus, there was no clear idea of what was meant by copyright law, although the term 'copyright' was used frequently. However, by the 1850s or thereabouts, copyright law 'emerged as a separate and distinct area of law replete with its own logic and grammar'.[202] In other words, by this time 'there was a much clearer idea of what copyright law was and how it differed from the other areas of law which provided protection for mental labour'.[203] Still, to enact a fully fledged legislation which codified all the concepts of modern copyright law, Britain had to wait until 1911.

The modernisation of copyright brought significant changes to the conceptual basis of copyright law. One notable change related to the role of mental labour as a justification for copyright protection. Prior to the mid-nineteenth century, the mental labour of the creator was the central factor which justified protection for literary and scientific works. However, with the modernisation of copyright, the central position afforded to mental labour began to fade away. Sherman and Bently observed:

> [A]s the law took on its modern guise it shifted its attention away from the labour that was embodied in the protected subject matter to concentrate more on the object in its own right. That is, instead of focusing, for example, on the labour that was embodied in a book, on what was considered to be the essence of intangible property, modern [copyright] law was more concerned with the object as a closed and unitary entity; with the impact that the book had on the reading public, the economy and so on.[204]

201 Sherman and Bently, above n 7, 2–3.
202 Ibid.
203 Brad Sherman, 'Remembering and Forgetting: The Birth of Modern Copyright Law' (1995) 10 *Intellectual Property Journal* 1, 5.
204 Sherman and Bently, above n 7, 4.

This shift of copyright law's attention away from mental labour had a significant impact on extending copyright protection to translation rights. More specifically, under premodern copyright law, the mental labour and skill extended by the translators (in translating works) were weighed against granting an exclusive right to the authors to translate their works. In other words, translating was not seen to infringe on the authors' rights because (or in recognition) of the mental labour extended by the translator in translating the work. However, when the emphasis placed on mental labour for granting exclusive rights began to fade, the old justification for refusing protection for translation rights was no longer watertight. Yet, at its emergence in the mid-nineteenth century, the modern copyright law was not fully prepared to easily discard the merits of the translators' contribution. As such, modern copyright law still grappled with a range of issues, such as whether only translation of works of domestic authors should be construed as infringement of copyright (as opposed to the works of foreign authors); whether all types of translation (both colourable and meritorious) should be construed as infringements; or whether only colourable translation should be construed as infringement. In fact, this uncertain status of the law becomes clearly discernible in the writings of the leading copyright scholars in the second half of the nineteenth century.

Curtis was among the first few scholars in the mid-nineteenth century to address the conceptual basis of protection of translations under copyright law. He said that a translation is considered a new literary work because of the 'new labour' spent in the translation.[205] The policy of copyright law was to encourage the creation of new works. Therefore, encouraging translations was within the objectives of copyright law.[206]

Having said that, however, Curtis raised an important question as to whether the rule that a translation is a new work would only apply to translations of original works first published in a foreign country. This was because original works first published in foreign countries did not receive copyright protection in the domestic country. Thus, any person could translate an original work first published in a foreign country and publish that translation in the domestic country without infringing upon the rights of the original author.[207] In contrast, when the original work was first published in the domestic country, its author received copyright protection for that work within the domestic country. The question here was whether any person could translate that original work and publish the translation in the domestic country without infringing upon the rights of the author. In other words, the question was whether the 'new labour' spent in the translation was 'sufficient to override the exclusive right of the original author in the matter itself'.[208]

205 George Ticknor Curtis, *A Treatise on the Law of Copyright* (A Maxwell & Son, 1847) 186–187.
206 Ibid., 187.
207 Ibid., 187–188.
208 Ibid., 188.

Although the issue still remained uncertain under English law, Curtis believed that the new labour added by the translator was not always sufficient to override the exclusive rights of the original author.[209] In particular, he said:

> Where the adoption and use of the matter of an original author, whose work is under the protection of copyright, is direct and palpable, and nothing new is added but form or dress, or an immaterial change of arrangement, the law will treat the alteration as merely colourable, and will stamp it with the character of piracy. Whether the change of form, or dress, produced by a close translation, in cases where the original work is under the protection of copyright, can have any greater effect than belongs to a change of form or dress, in other cases, is an interesting question, not determined, as it seems to me, by the general principle of the law of England, which treats translations as original works. This general principle was established only with reference to translations of foreign works, not under the protection of copyright.[210]

At the same time, Curtis was also of the view that the adoption of a general principle that the exclusive right of the original author would always override the new labour added by the translator would be incongruous, particularly in the case of scientific works.[211] More specifically, he said that 'in the case of a scientific work written, for instance, in Latin, intended for the Learned, and intended to convey a new discovery, or other information peculiarly original' it is possible to argue that translations give 'the work a new dress, in which the matter of it would be brought within the reach of far greater number of persons.'[212] Further, it could be contended that these types of translations were 'not only meritorious, but [were] a result of new labour of a purely intellectual kind'.[213] Yet even in such a case, 'the principle which allows the character of originality to the product of new labour upon old materials, would . . . encounter the exclusive right of the original author in the matter of the work itself'.[214]

The imprecise conceptual basis of modern copyright law with regard to the right of authors to translate their works continued well into the last decades of the nineteenth century. This becomes particularly evident in the writings of Scrutton and Birrell. In particular, writing in 1896, Scrutton stated that on principle a translation was clearly an infringement of copyright in the original work.[215]

209 Ibid., 291.
210 Ibid., 188–189.
211 Curtis said that '[n]otwithstanding the general principles of the English law in relation to translations, this question, I apprehend, would be not easy of solution, in the case of scientific work written.' Curtis, above n 205, 188.
212 Curtis, above n 205, 188.
213 Ibid., (emphasis added).
214 Ibid.
215 Thomas Edward Scrutton, *The Law of Copyright* (William Clowes & Sons, 3rd ed, 1896) 134. In support of this proposition, Scrutton cited *Murray v Bogue* (1852) 1 Drewry 353: 61 ER 487.

Yet courts 'would draw a distinction between translations of poetry or prose having a literary merit and style, and translations merely mechanical, as of educational or scientific works.'[216] Similarly, writing in 1899, Birrell stated, '[i]f the original book is entitled to protection, it would seem unreasonable to permit it to be translated without the consent of the owner of copyright.'[217] Yet in the case of certain types of translations, Birrell said that 'it might be argued that the translator had expended more care in the production of his translation than ever did the author on his so-called original work.'[218]

In contrast to this, the dawn of the twentieth century witnessed the emergence of a clearer view of how modern copyright law should approach the question of translation rights. In fact, many scholars at this time were prepared to concede that all types of translation infringed copyright. The reason for this was perhaps best explained by MacGillivray, who said:

> A translation takes everything in a book but the actual words; it takes the selection of material and its arrangement, and is certainly a very material taking of the work and labours of another. The Translator is making a profit from the author's work by using it in a manner in which the author might have himself used it and made similar profit. The only real answer which the translator has is that he has expended a great deal of skilled labour in putting the author's book into another form. This might have been a defence fifty years ago, but I do not think it is a good defence now.[219]

3.3.4.2. New socio-economic and political conditions in Britain

The socio-economic and political conditions in Britain dramatically changed in the nineteenth and early twentieth centuries. The new socio-economic and political conditions not only influenced modern copyright law to shift 'its attention away from the labour that was embodied in the protected subject matter to concentrate more on the object in its own right'[220] but also facilitated, stimulated and even compelled Britain to fully implement this new formulation of the conceptual basis of copyright protection, which was in favour of a fully fledged exclusive right of authors to translate their literary and scientific works. In other words, as Sherman and Bently stated, modern copyright law 'was more concerned with the object as a closed and unitary entity; with the impact that the book had on the reading public, the economy and so on.'[221] Therefore, in protecting authors' translation rights under the copyright law of Britain, what was most important was the impact the protection of authors' translation rights had on the

216 Scrutton, above n 215, 134.
217 Birrell, above n 139, 154.
218 Ibid., 154–155.
219 EJ MacGillivray, *A Treatise Upon the Law of Copyright* (John Murray, 1902) 117.
220 Sherman and Bently, above n 7, 4.
221 Ibid.

socio-economic and political context in Britain or vice versa, rather the question of mental labour per se.[222]

3.3.4.2.1. POWER OF BRITAIN IN THE 19TH CENTURY

In the nineteenth century, Britain became a developed nation in terms of both economic status and literary, artistic and scientific activities. Against this background, none of the justifying factors for promoting translation that existed in Britain between the fifteenth and the end of the eighteenth centuries remained pertinent at the end of the nineteenth century.[223]

As Feather observed, when printing was first introduced in the fifteenth century:

> England, brought low by external defeat and sapped by civil war, lay at the edge of the world, isolated both by the surrounding sea and her obscure and virtually unknown language. Even her great university at Oxford, once equal of Paris or Bologna, had fallen into provincial obscurity, while the Englishmen who had absorbed something of the intellectual ferment which was brewing in Italy were few indeed. It was not very promising ground in which to plant a printing press.[224]

By the mid-nineteenth century, however, the situation in Britain was the complete opposite. As Baugh and Cable observed by this time:

> The success of the British on the sea in the course of Napoleonic Wars, culminating in Nelson's famous victory at Trafalgar in 1805, left England in a position of undisputed naval supremacy and gave it control over most of the world's commerce.[225]

In addition, during the period of 1700–1860, Britain led the world in the process of industrialisation.[226] By the 1860s, Britain was the wealthiest country in

222 See Willem Grosheide, 'General Introduction' in Willem Grosheide (ed), *Intellectual Property and Human Rights: A Paradox* (Edward Elgar, 2010) 3, 8; Bently, above n 91, 491, 500.

223 As noted before, the main factors which justified translation during the early period of printing in Britain were: translation promoted access to knowledge of the common man (made knowledge common), printing translations was a means of safeguarding the business interests of printers and lack of English books for printing necessitated printers to resort to translations.

224 Feather, above n 85, 6–7.

225 Albert C Baugh and Thomas Cable, *A History of the English Language* (Routledge, 5th ed, 2002) 279.

226 Nicholas Crafts, 'Long-run Growth' in Roderick Floud and Paul Johnson (eds), *The Cambridge Economic History of Modern Britain: Economic Maturity, 1860–1939* (Cambridge University Press, 2004) vol 2, 1, 2.

Europe.[227] Moreover, by the 1870s Britain appeared to dominate the international economy.[228] Apart from this, by the mid-nineteenth century the English language had already started to gain global momentum, especially in view of Britain's economic power and the expansion of the Empire to more than a quarter of the earth's surface.[229] More importantly, by this time the country was already witnessing a flourishing book trade with great potential for overseas expansion.

3.3.4.2.2. BRITISH BOOK TRADE IN THE NINETEENTH AND EARLY TWENTIETH CENTURIES

At the beginning of the twentieth century, Britain had a well-developed book trade with a large readership base for English books both at home and overseas. This meant that Britain no longer needed to rely on translations in order to allow access to knowledge, as it had done before. It also meant that Britain was now more concerned about the rights and interests of the main stakeholders of the book trade, namely, the authors and publishers.

A notable feature of the British book trade during the nineteenth century was the massive growth of book production. As Barnes et al. observed, 'by the mid-nineteenth century the British book trade was transformed from a cottage trade into a mass manufacturing industry.'[230] The 'advances in industrial manufacture of paper, printing and binding' immensely contributed to this transformation.[231]

Another notable feature of the British book trade during the nineteenth century was that markets expanded both at home and overseas. Market expansion at home was integral in the transformation of the British book trade from a cottage trade into a mass manufacturing industry. As Britain began to produce books on a mass scale as never before, it had the potential to export ever more books to overseas markets.

The market for books during the first two centuries after the introduction of printing in Britain was very small. From the eighteenth century onwards, however, there was an unprecedented growth in the demand for books. As Feather noted, the eighteenth century showed 'the beginnings of the final stages of the transformation of Britain into a print-dependent society'.[232] By the twentieth century, the process was almost complete.

227 George R Boyer, 'Living Standards' in Roderick Floud and Paul Johnson (eds), *The Cambridge Economic History of Modern Britain: Economic Maturity, 1860–1939* (Cambridge University Press, 2004) vol 2, 280, 282.

228 C Knick Harley, 'Trade, 1870–1979: From Globalisation to Fragmentation' in Roderick Floud and Paul Johnson (eds), *The Cambridge Economic History of Modern Britain: Economic Maturity, 1860–1939* (Cambridge University Press, 2004) vol 2, 161, 161.

229 Baugh and Cable, above n 225, 273.

230 John Barnes et al., 'A Place in the World' in David McKitterick (ed), *The Cambridge History of the Book in Britain 1830–1914* (Cambridge University Press, 2009) vol 6, 595, 595.

231 Ibid.

232 Feather, above n 85, 85.

The expansion of the market for British books was the cumulative result of a number of factors. The most important of these were the growth of a literate population, the trade strategies used by publishers and the reception of English books overseas.

One of the main contributing factors to the growth of the market for books in nineteenth-century Britain was the country's population growth. In particular, the second half of the nineteenth century was a time of unprecedented population growth in Britain. Between 1841 and 1901, the population of England and Wales more than doubled.[233] This meant there were many more potential readers of English books (provided that they were sufficiently literate in English).

At the same time that Britain was witnessing unprecedented population growth, there was also a remarkable growth in the levels of literacy. As Mitch observed, '[i]n 1840, two-thirds of all grooms and half of all brides in England and Wales were able to sign their names at marriage; in 1900, 97 percent of each group was able to do so.'[234] Also, according to Sanderson:

> In the period from 1870 to 1913 Britain achieved virtual total literacy in the workforce. As measured by the capacity to sign one's name literacy rose from 80 percent in 1870 to 97 per cent by 1900. Even among criminal classes only 19.3 per cent were still illiterate by 1898. In Scotland literacy rose from 90 per cent in 1870 to 98 per cent in 1900 for men and from 80 per cent to 97 per cent for women over the same period.[235]

Another factor that contributed towards growth of the market for books in nineteenth-century Britain was trade strategies employed by publishers. Trade practices in the book trade in the nineteenth century Britain were highly influenced by the laissez-faire concept, which was the dominant economic theory at that time. As such, the marketplace for books became more prominent, and competition among publishers grew even further. As Feather said, 'The marketplace was the master, and the successful publishers were those who recognised how the market was developing.'[236]

More importantly, free trade also compelled publishers to find new markets for their books, some of which were newly created and others hitherto unexploited to the full. The best example of the first category was the market for educational books created by the expansion of education in the second half of the nineteenth century. In particular, the *Elementary Education Act 1870* 'suddenly created a vast new market for elementary textbooks for the newly established

233 JA Banks, 'Population Change and the Victorian City' (1968) 11(3) *Victorian Studies* 277, 277.

234 David Mitch, 'The Spread of Literacy in Nineteenth-Century England' (1983) 43(1) *Journal of Economic History* 287, 287.

235 Michael Sanderson, *Education and Economic Decline in Britain, 1870 to the 1990s* (Cambridge University Press, 1999) 3.

236 Feather, above n 85, 104.

Board Schools'.[237] This effect was particularly pronounced given the fact that 'the number of elementary schools increased by 50 percent in the first four years after the passage of the *Act*, and the number of attendances rose by half a million'.[238]

Groups of low-income readers in Britain and overseas English readers still remained unexploited markets for the British book trade in the nineteenth century. A notable characteristic of the low-income groups was that although there existed a considerable demand in this market for books and other printed matter, that demand was severely restricted by the purchasing power of these groups. In other words, cheap prices were a prerequisite for the demand for books and other printed matter in the market of those with low incomes. Thus, if the publishers were able to exploit this market, they had to provide books and other printed matter at cheaper prices. However, one important obstacle that publishers encountered in this regard was the cost of paper, which was kept artificially high by the continued imposition of government duties and taxes. By the second half of the nineteenth century, however, the publishers were fortunate to overcome this obstacle when the tax on paper was abolished in 1861 (as was the tax on newspapers in 1855).[239] By switching to cheaper methods of book production and distribution, publishers were also able to provide books and other printed matter at a lower price. As Feather observed, this provided publishers with the means 'to sell books in far greater numbers than at any previous time in the history of the trade'.[240]

Increased demand for English books overseas was another factor that led to the expansion of the British book trade in the nineteenth century. During this period, there was a significant growth in the number of books exported to markets in continental Europe, the United States, Australasia, India, Canada and British possessions elsewhere.

Increased demand for English books overseas in the nineteenth century was an outcome of the development of the English language and the emergence of English-speaking colonies and settlements. As English became a developed and widely spoken language, English books began to be well received in Britain's long-standing overseas markets in continental Europe. At the same time, the British Empire (particularly English-speaking colonies) and the United States provided a large readership base for English books.

Although the flow of books from Britain to continental Europe was nothing new, prior to the nineteenth century, language was a factor affecting the reception of English books in continental Europe. As Fabian and Spieckermann noted, English was not a familiar language in many parts of the Continent well into the nineteenth century.[241] They wrote: 'In 1700, English was, in nearly every respect,

237 Ibid 107.
238 Ibid., 116 (citations omitted).
239 Ibid., 112–113.
240 Ibid., 105.
241 Bernhard Fabian and Marie-Luise Spieckermann, 'The English Book on the Continent' in Michael F Suarez and Michael L Turner (eds), *The Cambridge History of the Book in Britain 1695–1830* (Cambridge University Press, 2009) vol 5, 523, 523.

a foreign language of which only merchants doing business with England and, perhaps, some polymathic scholars or men of letters had a more than rudimentary knowledge.'[242] They added: 'By 1800, a heterogeneous cultural elite had acquired not only an uncommon command of the language, but also an impressive familiarity with English culture.'[243] Thus, from the early nineteenth century onwards, there were more continental readers who could read English books than ever before. As a result, the continental market for English books expanded, and there was an acceleration of the flow of books from Britain to this market.[244]

While the continental market remained important for the British book trade, by the second half of the nineteenth century, the United States and colonial markets such as Australasia, East Indies, South Africa and North America became key overseas destinations for British books. In particular, in the United States and English-speaking colonies, there was a large readership for English books.[245]

Although the United States was an extremely important export market for Britain,[246] it was the most volatile owing largely to its postcolonial status.[247] Australasia was another lucrative market in which a steep increase in sales was clearly visible. In 1875, the Australasian market outstripped the United States to become the prime overseas destination for British books, a position that it retained for the rest of the nineteenth century.[248] In addition, India was the third most remunerative overseas market overall.[249] In fact, that country was by far the largest export market for British books during the first half of the nineteenth century.[250]

3.3.4.2.3. THE RISE OF AUTHORSHIP

An important outcome of the growth and expansion of the British book trade was the increase in power of the key stakeholders in the trade, namely, authors and publishers of books.[251] The fact that Britain became a major producer and exporter of books meant that the rights and interests of authors and publishers had to be protected at home as well as overseas as never before. From the

242 Ibid.
243 Ibid., 523–524.
244 Ibid., 523, 541.
245 See Caroline Davis, *Creating Postcolonial Literature: African Writers and British Publishers* (Palgrave Macmillan, 2013) 17; Alexis Weedon, *Victorian Publishing: The Economics of Book Production for a Mass Market, 1836–1916* (Ashgate, 2003) 38.
246 Weedon, above n 245, 39.
247 Barnes et al., above n 230, vol 6, 595, 597.
248 Ibid., 598.
249 Ibid.
250 Lionel Bently, 'Copyright, Translations, and Relations between Britain and India in the Nineteenth and Early Twentieth Centuries' (2007) 82(3) *Chicago-Kent Law Review* 1181, 1196.
251 See Catherine Seville, *Literary Copyright Reform in Early Victorian England: The Framing of the 1842 Copyright Act* (Cambridge University Press, first published 1999, 2003 ed) 5.

mid-nineteenth century there was more pressure on the British government to protect the interests of authors and publishers, because they emerged as a powerful collective group. The rise of authorship in nineteenth-century Britain was a reflection of this. As a result, the British Parliament ultimately had to recognise authors' translation rights in order to safeguard the interests of authors and publishers.

Although the latter part of the eighteenth century saw the emergence of the author as a noticeable figure in the field of law protecting literary and scientific works,[252] it was not until the latter part of the nineteenth and early twentieth centuries that authors became an established profession. Leary and Nash observed: 'Only in the Victorian Britain . . . do we find a significant number of authors themselves claiming the mantle of professional status.'[253] However, the result of this was the emergence of the author as an influential figure who could independently raise their voices and agitate for rights more firmly than before.

The emergence of the author as a professional and a dominant figure in the field of copyright in nineteenth-century Britain was largely a result of the expansion of the book trade and individual success stories of certain renowned British authors of the period. In particular, owing to the expansion of markets and advanced technology, book production in Britain increased fourfold between 1846 and 1916.[254] At the same time, book prices were reduced by half.[255] The amount of other printed material, such as magazines and newspapers, grew at an even more astounding rate.[256] As such, literary activities in Britain expanded at a rapid rate, which meant that there were more opportunities created for authors than ever before.[257] Thus, by the second half of the nineteenth century there was 'a growing sense that literature had become a profession'.[258] As Alexander Shand commented in 1878:

> [I]n the last twenty years or so there have been changes in the world of literature that almost amounted to a revolution. Literature has taken its place among the professions; and its most magnificent pecuniary prizes are not what they once were, at all events the numbers of those who get a living by it have multiplied almost indefinitely.[259]

252 See Bracha, above n 121, 230.
253 Patrick Leary and Andrew Nash, 'Authorship' in David McKitterick (ed), *The Cambridge History of the Book in Britain 1830–1914* (Cambridge University Press, 2009) vol 6, 172, 172.
254 Ibid.
255 Ibid.
256 Ibid.
257 See Seville, above n 251, 26.
258 Patrick Leary and Andrew Nash, 'Authorship' in David McKitterick (ed), *The Cambridge History of the Book in Britain 1830–1914* (Cambridge University Press, 2009) vol 6, 172, 194.
259 Ibid.

The glory and the success achieved by individual authors like Charles Dickens were also important reasons for the increased number of entrants to the field of authorship in the nineteenth and early twentieth centuries. More specifically, successful novelists like Dickens could reap substantial rewards for their works. Dickens's career, in particular, came to be seen as a powerful influence on authorship in Victorian Britain. As Leary and Nash observed:

> The sheer scale of his success—the huge world-wide sales that continued unbroken for year after year, the ubiquity of his novels' characters in the print culture and the theatre of the time, the charismatic celebrity that brought crowds to his readings, the unprecedented (for a literary man) personal fortune—was itself a powerful influence on early Victorian society's attitude towards literary life.[260]

Agitation for authors' rights Until the nineteenth century, authors' rights were more or less a conduit created and used by book publishers in Britain to substantiate and achieve their own interests. However, when the author emerged as a dominant figure and started to air his/her own voice in the nineteenth century, it became difficult for the publishers to continue with their old strategy. In other words, authors on their own started to advocate authors' rights to their benefit, rather than for the benefit of the publishers. However, this did not mean that authors had to always be at loggerheads with publishers in advocating their rights. Quite to the contrary, the experience relating to the *Copyright Act 1842* (which was essentially a product of agitation by authors)[261] showed authors that if they were to improve their position, 'it would have to be done in relation to the existing structure of the publishing industry' in which the publishers had an inevitable stake.[262] In short, this meant that both parties had to work together in securing each other's rights and interests. Thus, much of the agitation starting from the second half of the nineteenth century surrounding protection of authors' rights (copyright) in Britain were the collective efforts of both the authors and publishers.

The agitation of book publishers in Britain for protection of their interests was long-standing. As observed before, booksellers increasingly used authorship as a conduit for this purpose in the eighteenth century. However, from the nineteenth century, authors became a separate interest group that agitated for the protection of their interests hand in hand with publishers. Moreover, rapid expansion of the book trade and its markets in the nineteenth century meant that publishers and authors alike had to agitate for further protection of their interests. Because these agitations were from key stakeholders in a trade that formed an important part of

260 Ibid 176.
261 Feather, above n 85, 134.
262 Ibid., 137.

the much larger picture of the economy of Britain, the British government could not keep them supressed for a long time.

From the first half of the nineteenth century, international copyright protection became a very important means for British publishers and authors to protect their interests. In particular, British publishers and authors saw international copyright protection as a plausible mechanism to safeguard their rights and interests in two ways: firstly, to prevent cheap reprints of their books from the domestic market and secondly, to protect their rights in overseas markets.

As observed earlier, by the mid-nineteenth century there was considerable growth in the reception of English books in countries of the European continent. The negative impact of this on the British book trade was that publishers in these countries reprinted books at cheap prices, which ultimately resulted in these books being present in the domestic market of Britain at lower prices than the prices of their original prints.[263] Notably, such reprinting often happened in France.[264] Bulwer Lytton said in Parliament in 1837, '[a]s soon as a book was published the press of France reprinted it at one-fifth the original price, and the country thus became deluged with foreign piracies.'[265] Thus, he claimed that 'the Government ought to take steps to prevent such occurrences'.[266]

Although the *International Copyright Act 1838* and the *International Copyright Act 1844* were introduced by the British government with the aim of resolving this issue, both these statutes proved to be counterproductive in concluding any copyright protection arrangement with France. This was mainly because the protection offered through these two statutes to authors in France was considerably less than what British authors were to receive in return.[267] In particular, both these statutes expressly excluded translation rights of authors from copyright protection,[268]which was of much importance for the French.[269] Seville observed that this was a 'matter of such irritation to the French that it became an obstacle to an agreement which offered potentially enormous benefits to British authors and publishers.'[270] As such, recognition of authors' translation rights under international copyright law became inevitable if Britain were to conclude any international copyright protection arrangement with France. Thus, the *Convention*

263 See Catherine Seville, *The Internationalisation of Copyright Law: Books, Buccaneers and the Black Flag in the Nineteenth Century* (Cambridge University Press, 2006) 22–23, 41–45.
264 Ronan Deazley, 'Commentary on the *International Copyright Act* 1838' in L Bently and M Kretschmer (eds), *Primary Sources on Copyright (1450–1900)* (2008) <www.copyrighthistory.org>.
265 United Kingdom, *Hansard*, House of Commons, 14 December 1837, vol 39, col 1092.
266 Ibid.
267 Sherman and Bently, above n 7, 114.
268 *International Copyright Act 1838*, 1 & 2 Vict, c 59, s 13; *International Copyright Act 1844*, 7 & 8 Vict, c 12, s 18.
269 Ronan Deazley, 'Commentary on the *International Copyright Act* 1852' in L Bently and M Kretschmer (eds), *Primary Sources on Copyright (1450–1900)* (2008) <www.copyrighthistory.org>.
270 Seville, above n 263, 51.

between Her Majesty and the French Republic for the Establishment of International Copyright signed in 1851 (commonly referred to as the *Anglo-French Copyright Treaty 1851*) made some provisions for the protection of translation rights of French authors in Britain for a period of five years, subject to certain procedural requirements.[271] Notably, this required fresh authority from the British Parliament. The result of this was the *International Copyright Act 1852*, which gave authority of the Parliament to Her Majesty to accede to the *Convention* and carry out its copyright obligations.

The protection of authors' translation rights in the *International Copyright Act 1852* was a compromise for Britain. Lord Cranworth said that the rationale behind protection of translation rights in the *Act* was that if '[Britain] should gain something, [it] should also lose something'.[272] Also, when protecting translation rights in this *Act*, Britain did not fully accede to the proposal of the French Government.[273] This was because the protection of translation rights was necessary for Britain to create copyright relations with France in order 'to prevent the piracy practiced on British authors'.[274] On the other hand, however, translation rights were considered adverse to the interests of Britain. Lord Beaumont said in the House of Lords that these rights were 'very injurious to literature and to the progress of science.'[275] In addition, it was hardly believed at this time that translation rights were essential to promote the interests of British authors.[276] This meant that the scheme of protection of translation rights in the *International Copyright Act 1852* was very restrictive.[277] In particular, the duration of the translation rights under this *Act* was limited to five years. Also, these rights were only given to certain foreign authors.[278] Moreover, those foreign authors had to publicly reserve their right of translating the works and, within the first three months of publishing the original works, had to register the work with the Stationers' Company and to deposit a copy of the same with the British Museum, in accordance with the *International Copyright Act 1844*. In addition, foreign authors had to publish a translation of at least part of their work, either in the country of origin or within the British Dominions no later than one year after registration and deposit of the original, and register and deposit a copy of the work in translation.[279]

271 *Convention Between Her Majesty and the French Republic for the Establishment of International Copyright* signed at Paris on 3 November 1851, art III.
272 United Kingdom, *Hansard*, House of Lords, 30 April 1852, vol 121, col 4.
273 See United Kingdom, *Hansard*, House of Commons, 13 February 1852, vol 119, cols 498–502.
274 United Kingdom, *Hansard*, House of Lords, 30 April 1852, vol 121, col 4.
275 Ibid.
276 This was primarily because the main consumers in the markets (both domestic and foreign) for the works of British authors were 'English readers'. See Lionel Bently and Brad Sherman, 'Great Britain and the Signing of the *Berne Convention* in 1886' (2000–2001) 48 *Journal of the Copyright Society of the USA* 311, 317.
277 *International Copyright Act 1852*, 15 & 16 Vict, c 12, ss 2–8.
278 Ibid., ss 2, 11.
279 Ibid., s 8.

Agitation for translation rights For most of the nineteenth century, translation rights were not a pressing need for publishers and authors in Britain. However, the expansion of the British book trade to India in the latter part of the nineteenth century changed this position. This was because in the Indian market, where there was great potential demand for translations of English language works, translation rights became important for the British publishers and authors to further their interests. In view of this, publishers and authors in Britain started to agitate for translation rights in the latter part of the nineteenth century. The result of this was a series of Copyright Bills that proposed to protect translation rights of British authors. The Copyright Bill 1900 on which both the Australian *Copyright Act 1905* and the Sri Lankan *Copyright Ordinance 1908* were based was one of them.

For a nineteenth-century British author, translation rights in Britain were not worth anything.[280] Also, '[t]he question of Translations as infringements of copyright . . . rarely [arose] in England apart from the International question.'[281] The reason for this was that there was 'no market in England for the translation into a foreign tongue of an English work.'[282] Because of this, the protection of translation rights under domestic copyright law was not a major concern of publishers and authors in Britain. As such, they did not agitate a great deal for recognition of translation rights. Partly because of this, the *Royal Commission on Copyright* (1878), which was Britain's 'first major governmental review of the national, colonial, and international copyright regime[s]',[283] did not recommend the protection of translation rights in the national copyright regime of Britain, although it recommended that abridgement rights (the exclusive right of authors to abridge their works) should be so protected.[284] However, despite the silence of the Royal Commission's Report on translation rights, the Copyright (No2) Bill 1879 introduced by Lord Manners, which was largely based on the Report's recommendations, proposed to prohibit unauthorised printing of translations in

280 While giving evidence before the Select Committee of the House of Lords on the Copyright Bill and the Copyright (Artistic) Bill [HL] in 1899, Scrutton said:

> I do not think an English author's rights of translation in the United Kingdom are worth anything.
>
> Select Committee, House of Lords, *Report from the Select Committee of the House of Lords on the Copyright Bill and the Copyright (Artistic) Bill [HL]* (1899) 7 [76].

281 Scrutton, above n 215, 134.

282 Ibid.

283 Ronan Deazley, 'Commentary on the Royal Commission's Report on Copyright (1878)' in L Bently and M Kretschmer (eds), *Primary Sources on Copyright (1450–1900)* (2008) <www.copyrighthistory.org>.

284 United Kingdom, Royal Commission to Make Inquiry with regard to the Laws and Regulations relating to Home, Colonial, and International Copyright, *Report of the Commissioners* (C 2036, 1878) xv [69]. In particular, the Commission said:

> [W]e recommend, that no abridgements of copyright works should be allowed during the term of copyright, without the consent of the owner of the copyright.

Britain.[285] Yet, the purpose of this Bill was only to facilitate discussion among the various stakeholders on suitable copyright legislation for Britain and the Empire rather than to pass it in the Parliament.[286] Apart from this, the Copyright Bill 1881, initiated by a committee of the Law Amendment Society under the umbrella of the Social Science Association,[287] did not propose to confer translation rights on domestic authors, although it did propose to confer limited translation rights on certain foreign authors.[288]

During the last decade of the 19th century, there was increased agitation by publishers in Britain to protect translation rights in the domestic copyright law. This was particularly because of the Indian market for translations of English books.

As already observed, India constituted one of the major overseas markets for the British book trade throughout the nineteenth century.[289] An important characteristic of Britain's major overseas markets for books during much of the 19th century was that they were primarily concerned with English language works.[290] This was even so in India, where a multiplicity of languages was in existence.[291] However, as Bently pointed out, at least from the mid-19th century onwards there was an increasing demand in India for translations of English books.[292] This in fact created a lucrative market in India for translations of British books. Because of this, the protection of translation rights of British authors in India became important for British publishers.

In the late nineteenth century, 'India, like many British colonies, was the beneficiary of three copyright regimes.'[293] These were the 'imperial regime' embodied in the British *Copyright Act 1842*, the 'national regime' incorporated in the Indian *Copyright Act 1847*, and the 'international copyright regime' incorporated in the British International Copyright Acts.[294] However, none of these copyright regimes protected the translation rights of British authors. In particular, two decisions of the Indian courts, namely *Munshi Shaik Abdurruhma'n v Mirza' Mahomed Shira'zi*[295] and *Macmillan v Shamsul Ulma M Zaka*,[296] clearly held that translation rights were not protected under the *Copyright Act 1842*. Since the Indian *Copyright Act 1847* tracked the British *Copyright Act 1842*,[297] it too did

285 A Bill to Consolidate and Amend the Law relating to Copyright 1879 (265) s 8(c).
286 United Kingdom, *Hansard*, House of Commons, 12 June 1879, vol 246, col 1706; United Kingdom, *Hansard*, House of Commons, 29 July 1879, vol 248, cols 1628–1629.
287 Seville, above n 263, 37, 277.
288 A Bill to Consolidate and Amend the Law relating to Copyright 1881, ss 84–88.
289 See Barnes et al., above n 230, vol 6, 595, 598 (emphasis added).
290 Bently and Sherman, above n 276, 311, 317.
291 Bently, above n 250, 1181, 1196–1197.
292 Ibid., 1191–1192.
293 Ibid., 1183.
294 Ibid., 1183–1184.
295 (1890) 14 ILR (Bombay) 586.
296 (1895) 19 ILR (Bombay) 557.
297 Bently, above n 250, 1181, 1185.

not protect translation rights. Moreover, since India was a dominion of Britain, its international copyright legislation could not be applied to protect the translation rights of British authors in India.[298]

The initial response of British publishers to this situation was to lobby the Government of India for legislation to protect translation rights. Failing that, they started lobbying British Parliament for an imperial copyright regime in India that would have protected translation rights. To this end, Copyright Bills were introduced in the British Parliament in 1897, 1898, 1899 and 1900 that proposed to protect translation rights of British authors.[299] However, because of a number of practical issues, such as insufficient time for both houses in the Parliament to go through the provisions in the Bills and cumbersome attempts at consolidation of copyright, all of these Bills failed.[300] As Britain got engaged with the South African war by 1901 and had 'more pressing concerns', all the efforts of the British publishers seeking protection of translation rights in the domestic copyright law of Britain came to a standstill.[301]

3.3.4.2.4. BRITAIN'S ACCESSION TO THE *BERNE CONVENTION*

While British publishers and authors remained desirous of securing a legislation that would protect authors' translation rights in Britain, ultimately it was the *Berne Convention* that enabled this to happen. Although the original version of the *Berne Convention* required Member Countries to protect translation rights (of authors in other Member Countries) in their copyright laws for a period of ten years, the Berlin revision of 1908 (*Berlin Act 1908*) required Member Countries to extend protection for these rights for the entire duration of copyright protection.[302] In the course of implementing the provisions of the *Berlin Act 1908* (including that which required extended protection for translation rights) into copyright law of Britain through the *Imperial Copyright Act 1911*, Britain also protected translation rights of the British (domestic) authors for the first time in the history of the country. Thus, the *Berne Convention* was a blessing for authors and publishers who sought protection of authors' translation rights in the domestic copyright law of Britain. Nonetheless, Britain's accession to this *Convention* was purely a result of the need to protect the rights and interests of British authors and publishers overseas.

The single most important reason that persuaded Britain to actively get involved in the negotiation process leading to the *Berne Convention* was the expectation that the interests of British publishers and authors would be protected in the

298 See United Kingdom, *Hansard*, House of Lords, 19 July 1897, vol 51, cols 387–389.
299 Copyright (Amendment) Bill 1897 [HL]; Copyright (Amendment) Bill 1898 [HL]; Copyright Bill 1899 [HL]; Copyright Bill 1900 [HL] [295].
300 Bently, above n 250, 1181, 1211–1213.
301 Ibid., 1213.
302 *Berlin Act 1908* of the *Berne Convention*, art 8.

United States.[303] The reason for this was the unprecedented level of piracy of British books in the United States. In fact, creating an international copyright arrangement with the United States, one that could prevent such piracies, was one of the main aspirations of Britain during the nineteenth century.[304] The Board of Trade acknowledged in 1875 that '[f]or England . . . by far the most important International question is that of an arrangement with the United States and perhaps the next most important question is that of Copyright in English and English-speaking Colonies'.[305] Thus, the decision of the United States government to send a delegate to the 1885 Pre-Berne Conference was a compelling reason for Britain to participate actively in the *Berne* negotiation process. As Sherman and Bently noted, the presence of the United States delegate at *Berne* negotiations reassured the British that 'even if the US did not sign the *Convention* (which Adams and Bergne thought it would), the British ratification would not prejudice potential Anglo-American relations'.[306]

Another important reason persuading Britain to actively participate in the negotiation process leading to the *Berne Convention* was the need to maintain the existing levels of international copyright protection which it had secured in Europe. In particular, the British government thought that once the *Berne Convention* came into operation the existing bilateral arrangements into which Britain had entered with other countries in Europe would come to an end.[307] Thus, the need to maintain the existing levels of international copyright protection in Europe required Britain to take a more affirmative approach towards acceding to the *Berne Convention*.[308]

Britain ultimately acceded to the *Berne Convention* in 1887,[309] which required Member Countries to protect translation rights in their copyright laws for a period of ten years. To enable 'Her Majesty to accede to the convention' and to allow Britain to carry into effect the provisions of the convention, the British Parliament enacted the *International Copyright Act 1886*.[310] In essence, this *Act* accorded translation rights the 'same status as the basic right of reproduction', subject to the exception that if a translation had not been produced in the English language after ten years from the date of publication of a work, the translation rights in that work were forfeited.[311] Yet this *Act* (similar to the *International Copyright Act 1852*) only applied to certain foreign authors and thus, translation rights of the British (domestic) authors remained unprotected.[312]

303 Bently and Sherman, above n 276, 311, 334–335.
304 Seville, above n 263, 3.
305 Ibid., 65.
306 Bently and Sherman, above n 276, 311, 335 (emphasis added).
307 Ibid., 333–334.
308 Seville, above n 263, 41.
309 Great Britain signed the *Berne Convention* on 9 September 1886 and ratified it on 5 September 1887. The convention entered into force in Great Britain on 5 December 1887.
310 *International Copyright Act 1886*, 49 & 50 Vict, c 33, Preamble.
311 Ibid., s 5.
312 Ibid.

The revision of the *Berne Convention* in 1908 saw a substantial extension of the scope of protection of translation rights. In particular, Article 8 of the *Berlin Act 1908* provided for the protection of translation rights for the full term of copyright protection. Apart from this, the *Berlin Act* required many other substantial changes to be made to the domestic copyright law of Britain if it were to accede to and comply with the revised *Berne Convention*. Accordingly, the Board of Trade in 1909 appointed a departmental Committee chaired by Lord Gorell to advise on the legislative changes necessary to give effect to the revised *Convention*. The report of this Committee, popularly referred to as the Gorell Report,[313] 'recommended strongly that [British] copyright law should be made "intelligible and systematic" and brought into line with that of other nations as far as was practicable.'[314] According to Seville, '[o]n almost all issues the Committee recommended that the *Convention*'s approach should be adopted'.[315] With regard to Article 8 of the *Berlin Act*, the Committee said:

> There is no conclusive authority *qua* British domestic law as to exclusive translating right in the author.
> It is to be observed that as regards copyright in books the rights of translation constitute its chief value to authors in countries other than their own.
> The Article should be adopted, and legislation will be required both in respect of domestic law and also in respect of that law as applied to international relations. This will involve a provision to the effect that every author shall enjoy during the whole term of right over the original work, the exclusive right of making or authorising a translation of that work.[316]

Britain also held an Imperial Copyright Conference in 1910 to consider whether or not to ratify the *Berlin Act 1908*. This Conference, which 'proved extremely constructive', recommended that the *Berlin Act* 'should be ratified by the Imperial government on behalf of the various parts of the Empire and that reservations should be kept at minimum'.[317] The upshot of this was the *Imperial Copyright Act 1911*, which came into force on 1 July 1912, that is, pursuant to Britain's ratification of the *Berlin Act* of the *Berne Convention* on 4 June 1912.[318]

313 Law of Copyright Committee, *Report of the Committee on the Law of Copyright 1909* (Cd 4976, 1910).
314 Seville, above n 263, 38.
315 Catherine Seville, 'Copyright' in David McKitterick (ed), *The Cambridge History of the Book in Britain 1830–1914* (Cambridge University Press, 2009) vol 6, 214, 236.
316 Law of Copyright Committee, above n 313, 19–20.
317 Seville above n 315, vol 6, 214, 236.
318 Ibid., 237.

3.4. Conclusion

The British model of copyright law that was introduced into Sri Lanka when Sri Lanka was a colony of Britain was inimical to the timely and affordable translation of copyright protected works. This was because it recognised copyright owners' translation rights without commensurate exceptions. The British model of copyright law introduced into Sri Lanka was a mechanism that was designed to address the needs and interests of the book trade and the public in Britain. The British model of copyright law did not recognise the right to translate as a fully fledged exclusive right of the copyright owners until the twentieth century, largely because liberty to translate literary and scientific works was seen as important to allow and to promote access to knowledge. However, when Britain became a developed country in the field of literature, arts and science, and an exporter of copyright protected works, it became necessary for the British model of copyright law to recognise the right to translate as a fully fledged exclusive right of the copyright owners. Since Sri Lanka was, and continues to be, a developing country that is dependent on copyright protected scientific and technical books and learning materials produced in developed countries, the British model of copyright law did not suit the needs and interests of Sri Lanka.

IV WIPO model of copyright law and translation [1979–2003]

4.1. Introduction

The copyright regime implemented from 1979 to 2003 marks the second stage of the history of Sri Lankan copyright. During this period, Sri Lankan copyright law was exclusively determined by the *Code of Intellectual Property Act 1979* (*IP Code*). The *IP Code* was an all-embracing intellectual property statute which provided for a copyright regime. Although the *IP Code* was passed by the Sri Lankan Parliament, it was prepared under the guidance of the World Intellectual Property Organisation (WIPO). As a result, the copyright regime in the *IP Code* closely followed the *WIPO Model Law on Copyright for Developing Countries*.[1] Thus, the copyright regime that was enforced in Sri Lanka from 1979 to 2003 can be called a 'WIPO model of copyright law'.

This chapter will examine how the way in which the WIPO model of copyright law protected copyright owners' translation rights affected the translation of scientific and technical books and learning materials in Sri Lanka. It will also examine the reason for the way in which the WIPO model of copyright law protected copyright owner's translation rights.

As demonstrated in this chapter, the way the WIPO model of copyright law protected copyright owners' translation rights restricted Sri Lanka's ability to translate scientific and technical books and learning materials and to reproduce the translations in large quantities in a timely and affordable manner. The WIPO model of copyright law, therefore, did not facilitate access to scientific and technical knowledge in Sri Lanka. The main reason for the way in which the WIPO model of copyright law protected copyright owners' translation rights was Sri Lanka's membership to the *Berne Convention* and the adherence of the WIPO model of copyright law to the *WIPO Model Law on Copyright for Developing Countries* which, in turn, was based on the provisions of the *Berne Convention*.

The way in which the *Berne Convention* requires Member Countries to protect copyright owners' translation rights is inimical to timely and affordable

1 The *WIPO Model Law on Copyright for Developing Countries* is also referred to as the *Tunis Model Law on Copyright for Developing Countries*.

translation in developing countries like Sri Lanka. This is because the balance which is struck in the *Berne Convention* between copyright owners' translation rights and the users' ability to access translations of copyright protected works is tilted in favour of the copyright owners.[2] Since developing countries mostly represent the interests of the users of copyright protected works, the *Berne Convention* is unsuitable for developing countries. The reason for this is that the *Berne Convention* is inherently an instrument that has been initiated and developed to advocate the interests of the copyright exporting developed countries in Europe such as France, Germany and Britain.[3] This is evident from the history of the way in which protection of translation rights has evolved in the *Berne Convention.* Therefore, this chapter also traces the evolution of the protection of translation rights in the *Berne Convention* from its inception up to the present.

4.2. Background to the WIPO model of copyright law

The copyright law contained in the *IP Code* (WIPO model of copyright law) was the first homemade copyright regime in independent Sri Lanka.[4] By repealing the application of the *Imperial Copyright Act 1911*, it replaced the British model of copyright law enforced in Sri Lanka for more than seven decades.[5]

The WIPO model of copyright law came about as a direct result of the free market economic policy introduced to Sri Lanka in 1977, which had the objective of stimulating rapid economic development.[6] This free market economic policy placed a great deal of emphasis on encouraging innovation, creativity, foreign investment and private entrepreneurship. However, the set of commercial laws that was in operation in Sri Lanka at that time was not conducive to the free market economic policy. The main reason was that by the 1970s most commercial laws, which had been formulated during the British rule (1796–1948), were outdated and obsolete. In fact, while moving the second reading of the Bill that became the *IP Code* in Parliament, Minister Athulathmudali said:

> There is no point in . . . talking about improving [the Sri Lankan] economy, having more exports and imports, if [the country's] legal structure is as ancient as the hills and does not keep up with modern development.[7]

2 See Salah Basalamah, 'Compulsory Licensing for Translation: An Instrument of Development?' (2000) 40(4) *IDEA: The Journal of Law and Technology* 503, 504.

3 See Lionel Bently, 'Copyright, Translations, and Relations between Britain and India in the Nineteenth and Early Twentieth Centuries' (2007) 82(3) *Chicago-Kent Law Review* 1181, 1240.

4 Sri Lanka, *Parliamentary Debates*, 25 May 1979, col 501; DM Karunaratna, *An Introduction to the Law of Copyright and Related Rights in Sri Lanka* (Sarvodaya Vishva Lekha Publication, 2006) 7.

5 *Code of Intellectual Property Act No 52 of 1979* (Sri Lanka) s 187.

6 See Sri Lanka, *Parliamentary Debates*, 25 May 1979, cols 501–502.

7 Ibid., col 500.

The position was the same in relation to copyright law in Sri Lanka. The copyright law that was in force in Sri Lanka in 1977 was the *Imperial Copyright Act 1911* which was not only outdated by this time but also advocated the British interests rather than the Sri Lankan interests.

By the 1970s, the *Imperial Copyright Act 1911* was outdated because it remained virtually in the form in which it was originally enacted in Britain. In contrast, Britain had revised and substituted provisions of the *Imperial Copyright Act* through the *Copyright Act 1956* to cope with new technological advances and changed circumstances in that country.[8]

As was observed in the previous chapter, the *Imperial Copyright Act 1911* was a statute which predominantly catered to the interests of the key stakeholders in the British publishing industry. Such a statute was not in the best interests of Sri Lanka, particularly in view of the differential approach to copyright protection by a developed country like Britain and a developing country like Sri Lanka.[9] In fact, as Minister Athulathmudali said, one of the main objectives of the *IP Code* was to liberate Sri Lanka '[f]rom restrictive English practices in regard to copyrights' in a manner that would promote the interests of Sri Lanka.[10]

4.3. Translation under the WIPO model of copyright law

The way in which the WIPO model of copyright law in the *IP Code* protected copyright owners' translation rights restricted the timely and affordable translation of copyright protected scientific and technical books and learning materials produced in developed countries. As with the British model of copyright law, the WIPO model also recognised the exclusive right of authors to translate their literary and scientific works for the full term of copyright protection. The general exceptions to this right recognised in the WIPO model of copyright law, however, were narrow and limited. Although this copyright law contained a special exception which enabled a person to translate literary and scientific works freely into Sinhala and Tamil in the event these works had not been published in those languages within a period of 10 years from their first publication, that was inadequate to facilitate the timely translation of copyright protected scientific and technical books and learning materials.

The WIPO model of copyright law protected translation rights of the copyright owners for the full term of copyright protection.[11] In particular, Section 10(b) of the *IP Code* stated that the author of a copyright protected work shall have the

8 Intellectual Property Office, *Copyright Act 1956* <www.ipo.gov.uk/types/copy/c-about/c-history/c-history-1956.htm>. See also Leanne Gaye Wiseman, 'Making Copies: The Impact of Photocopying on Copyright Law in Australia' (PhD Thesis, University of Queensland, 2009) 89.

9 See Paul Goldstein and Bernt Hugenholtz, *International Copyright: Principles, Law, and Practice* (Oxford University Press, 2013) 402.

10 Sri Lanka, *Parliamentary Debates*, 25 May 1979, col 501.

11 *Code of Intellectual Property Act No 52 of 1979* (Sri Lanka) ss 10, 19, 22.

exclusive right to make a translation. This exclusive right lasted 'during the life of the author and for fifty years after his death'.[12]

The *IP Code* enumerated certain exceptions to translation rights under the provisions relating to fair use in Section 13. However, the fair use provisions in the *IP Code* only allowed translation in limited circumstances. More specifically, they allowed translation of a copyright protected work without the author's consent for limited purposes, such as, user's own personal and private use, quotations (that were compatible with fair practice), and illustrations for teaching (to the extent justified by the purpose). Thus, in no event did the fair use provisions in the *IP Code* allow translations of literary and scientific works to be published (or reproduced) in bulk quantities.[13]

Be that as it may, the *IP Code* contained a specific exception to copyright owners' translation rights in Section 15. This allowed a person to translate literary and scientific works without the consent of their copyright owners and publish the translations in multiple quantities subject to certain conditions. In particular, this provision stated:

> Where any work has not been published in Sinhala or Tamil within ten years from its having been published for the first time in its original language, it shall be lawful to translate the said work into Sinhala or Tamil, as the case may be, and to publish such translation, even without the authorization of, and without any payment to, the owner of the copyright of the work.[14]

The legislative intent behind this exception is not very clear. Even the parliamentary debates on the *IP Code* do not give any clue with regard to why this exception was created.[15] In these circumstances, perhaps, one could assume that certain provisions in the then newly promulgated Constitution of the country—the *Constitution of the Democratic Socialist Republic of Sri Lanka 1978* (*Constitution 1978*), may have had an impact on giving effect to this specific exception in the *IP Code*. For instance (as was noted in chapter 2), the *Constitution 1978* declares the national languages of Sri Lanka to be Sinhala and Tamil.[16] More importantly, it also recognises the right of education as a fundamental human

12 Ibid., s 19(1).

13 As observed in chapter 2 of this book, from the mid-twentieth century onwards (at least) Sri Lanka needed to translate scientific and technical books and learning materials produced in developed countries and to publish (or reproduce) them in large quantities in a timely and affordable manner to promote access to scientific and technical knowledge. Because the fair use provisions in the *IP Code* only applied to special situations and did not permit translation of copyright protected works in whole and the publication of translations in large quantities, it is hard to believe that these provisions facilitated Sri Lanka's needs.

14 However, this was without prejudice to the moral rights of the author of the original work. *Code of Intellectual Property Act No 52 of 1979* (Sri Lanka) s 15.

15 See Sri Lanka, *Parliamentary Debates*, 25 May 1979, cols 500–509.

16 Ibid., art 19.

right[17] and grants an entitlement to every person in the country to be educated through the medium of either of the national languages.[18] Moreover, the *Constitution 1978* imposes an obligation on the State financed higher educational institutions in the country to offer their courses in both national languages.[19] Since the implementation of these provisions demands freedom to translate educational materials produced in developed countries (which are often copyright protected) into Sinhala and Tamil, it would be logical to assume that the specific exception to translation rights in Section 15 of the *IP Code* may have been created to support the implementation of these constitutional provisions.

Be that as it may, it is hard to believe that the specific exception to copyright owners' translation rights in Section 15 of the *IP Code* was able to facilitate timely and affordable translation in Sri Lanka to effectively meet the requirements mandated by the constitutional provisions or to promote access to scientific and technical knowledge in the country. This is because under Section 15, a person had to wait at least ten years to commence translation of a copyright protected work into Sinhala and Tamil. This was far too long, particularly with regard to scientific and technical books and learning materials. Unlike fiction, these types of knowledge products are often outdated a few years from publication. As such, a ten-year waiting period to commence translation essentially meant that by the time translations of these types of (copyright protected) knowledge products could be published, they would have been outdated. However, as observed in chapter 2 of this book, these types of knowledge products urgently need to be translated in Sri Lanka for use in educational and vocational training programmes.

4.4. Reason for the way in which the WIPO model of copyright law protected translation rights

The *Berne Convention* and the *WIPO Model Law on Copyright for Developing Countries* had a profound impact on the way in which the WIPO model of copyright law protected copyright owners' translation rights. Since Sri Lanka remained a member to the *Berne Convention* when it enacted the WIPO model of copyright law, this copyright law had to comply with the obligations of the *Berne Convention*. Because Sri Lanka sought assistance from the WIPO when drafting the provisions of this copyright law, WIPO offered the *WIPO Model Law on Copyright for Developing Countries* to Sri Lanka as a guide to draft the copyright provisions. Accordingly, Sri Lanka drafted the WIPO model of copyright law based on the *WIPO Model Law on Copyright for Developing Countries*.

17 See *Kavirathne and Others v Commissioner General of Examinations and Others* (2012) BLR 139.

18 *Constitution of the Democratic Socialist Republic of Sri Lanka 1978*, art 21(1).

19 Ibid., art 21(2).

4.4.1. The Berne Convention

The way in which the *Berne Convention* obliges Member Countries to protect copyright owners' translation rights is hostile to the timely and affordable translation that is required to promote access to scientific and technical knowledge in developing countries like Sri Lanka. In particular, it restricts the ability of developing countries to translate copyright protected scientific and technical books and learning materials produced in developed countries and to reproduce the translations in large quantities in a timely and affordable manner. The reason for this is that the *Berne Convention* requires copyright owners' translation rights to be protected without providing for commensurate exceptions thereto. In other words, the balance which is struck in the *Berne Convention* between copyright owners' translation rights and users' ability to access translations of copyright protected works is tilted in favour of copyright owners.

Although the *Berne Convention* was revised in 1967 (at Stockholm) and in 1971 (at Paris) with the objective of addressing the needs and interests of developing countries, the *Convention* still fails to facilitate the timely and affordable translation of copyright protected scientific and technical books and learning materials produced in developed countries and the reproduction of translations in large quantities. The primary reason for this is the inherent nature of the *Berne Convention*. Having been initiated and developed by a group of economically well-advanced copyright exporting countries in the West, with a 'set of international norms well-suited to their own cultural and moral values (particularly romantic authorship and natural law)' to meet 'the demands of their own cultural industries, particularly those of established and reputable book publishers',[20] the *Berne Convention* is essentially biased towards the interests of copyright owners. This becomes clearly evident when we examine the history of the way in which protection of translation rights has evolved in the *Berne Convention*.

4.4.1.1. Translation rights and the Berne Convention

The *Berne Convention* was an initiative of a Eurocentric group of stakeholders and countries that advocated for the interests of authors and publishers (copyright owners).[21] The main objective that these stakeholders and countries tried to achieve through the *Convention* was the protection of the rights of copyright owners in foreign countries.[22] Thus, it is not surprising that translation rights came to be one of the key rights that was sought to be protected under the *Berne Convention*.[23] This was because translation rights 'were the most important rights

20 Bently, above n 3, 1240.

21 Ibid.

22 YiJun Tian, *Re-Thinking Intellectual Property: The Political Economy of Copyright Protection in the Digital Era* (Routledge-Cavendish, 2009) 22.

23 See Eva Hemmungs Wirten, *Cosmopolitan Copyright: Law and Language in the Translation Zone* (Uppsala Universitet, 2011) 18; Eva Hemmungs Wirten, *No Trespassing: Authorship,*

for authors seeking protection for their works in foreign countries'.[24] Indeed, protection of translation rights was '*la question internationale par excellence*', as 'translation was really the only international means of reproduction in the case of books'.[25] As a result, protection of translation rights turned into an issue which attracted a lot of attention in the nineteenth century and became 'the subject of an increasing number of bilateral agreements between states'.[26] In fact, as Ricketson said, translation rights were 'probably the most important factor which drew states into international copyright agreements in the late nineteenth century.'[27] Yet the majority of the conventions which existed before *Berne* 'placed significant restrictions on the way in which [translation] rights were to be exercised.'[28]

Although the authors' right to translate their literary and scientific works was the first right recognised at the inception of the *Berne Convention* in 1886,[29] the *Convention* did not accord translation rights the same status which it accorded to the right of reproduction.[30] This was because of the intense opposition to translation rights by certain prospective members to the *Berne Convention* who belonged to the category of 'developing countries' at that time.[31] In particular, although developed countries like France that were well advanced in literary and scientific traditions pushed for translation rights to be accorded the same status as the right of reproduction, countries like Norway and Sweden (that were less developed and therefore wanted to have ready access to works in these fields produced in foreign countries) were opposed to this.[32] Sweden contended that 'readily available translations were of great importance to the Scandinavian countries in view of their small, dispersed populations and educational needs'.[33]

To understand the opposition of these Scandinavian countries to granting translation rights the same status as the right of reproduction under the *Berne Convention*, it is important to recall that there is a difference in the perception of copyright between developed and developing countries. Because developing countries mostly represent the interests of the users of copyright protected works, extending copyright protection for translation rights or according translation rights

---

Intellectual Property Rights, and Boundaries of Globalisation (University of Toronto Press, 2004) 39.

24 See Sam Ricketson and Jane Ginsburg, *International Copyright and Neighbouring Rights: The Berne Convention and Beyond* (Oxford University Press, 2nd ed, 2006) vol 1, 35.

25 Sam Ricketson, *The Berne Convention for the Protection of Literary and Artistic Works: 1886–1986* (Kluwer, 1987) 384.

26 Ricketson and Ginsburg, above n 24, vol 1, 14.

27 Ricketson, above n 25, 384.

28 Ricketson and Ginsburg, above n 24, vol 1, 35.

29 Ricketson, above n 25, 384; Goldstein and Hugenholtz, above n 9, 321.

30 Although the *Berne Convention* did not explicitly mention the right of reproduction until the *Stockholm Act 1967*, being 'the most basic author's right', it was implicitly recognised from the inception of the *Convention*. Ricketson and Ginsburg, above n 24, vol 1, 127.

31 See Eva Hemmungs Wirten, above n 23, 33.

32 Ricketson and Ginsburg, above n 24, vol 1, 67.

33 Ibid., (citations omitted).

the same status as the right of reproduction can be hostile to the interests of these countries. This is especially true for those countries that would need to translate copyright protected works produced in developed countries to promote access to knowledge. The reason for this is that copyright owners in developed countries can exercise their translation rights and refuse to allow their copyright protected works to be translated. Alternatively, they can also charge a license fee for permitting the translation of their works which can increase the cost of translations to the users.[34] Indeed, the Swedish Supreme Court made these considerations explicit in 1876 when it advised 'against granting translation rights too liberally' in what was later to become the 'first Swedish copyright law'.[35] As the Swedish Supreme Court said:

> [Protection for translation rights] received its importance solely through agreements with foreign nations, and such agreements would provide the main advantages to the foreigner, while all of the disadvantages would fall on the Swedish public.[36]

This was because '[f]or a people whose language is so small and geographically limited as the Swedish, any restriction on freedom of translation could not but have a negative impact on the dissemination of knowledge and education.'[37] For such a people, the need 'to complete its own literature by translations of the better works from abroad is infinitely greater than what it is for people with a widespread language and considerably richer literature than the Swedish.'[38] As a result of foreign authors asking for exorbitant fees to permit their works to be translated into Swedish, the domestic literature would 'lack access to many valuable foreign works'.[39] At the same time, according to Wirten, 'foreign publishers would generally not extend to Swedish authors the same remuneration for the rights to translate Swedish works.'[40]

As a result, countries like Norway and Sweden were only prepared to accept a shorter term of protection for translation rights in the *Berne Convention*.[41] As Ricketson and Ginsburg said, this situation aptly demonstrates that even at the inception of the *Berne Convention* 'there were considerable gulfs between what may be called the "producing nations"—that is, those [developed] nations, such as French, that were net exporters of literary and artistic products—and those [developing] nations, such as Scandinavians, which were "users"—that is, importers—of these products.'[42]

34 Lionel Bently, 'Copyright and Translations in the English Speaking World' (1993) 12(4) *Translatio: FIT Newsletter* 491, 496.
35 Eva Hemmungs Wirten, above n 23, 22.
36 Ibid., quoting Hogsta domstolens protokoll, 22 November 1876.
37 Ibid.
38 Ibid.
39 Ibid.
40 Ibid.
41 See, e.g., ibid., 30–31.
42 Ricketson and Ginsburg, above n 24, vol 1, 67.

Given that certain prospective members to the *Berne Convention* who belonged to the category of importers/users of copyright protected works were only prepared to protect translation rights for a limited period, there were two choices available to the initiators of the *Berne Convention*. The first option was to have a convention protecting translation rights for the full term of the right of reproduction that excluded copyright importing countries, such as Norway and Sweden, from the convention. The other option was to adopt a less rigorous convention affording a shorter term of protection for translation rights to which as many countries as possible would be able to adhere.[43] Eventually, the initiators of the *Berne Convention* preferred the second option. In fact, this was a pragmatic choice advocated by Britain. In particular, by recognising translation rights in a limited form, it was possible for the *Berne Convention* to get the adherence of the greatest number of countries.[44] Accordingly, Article 5 of the original text of the *Berne Convention* provided:

> Authors who are subjects or citizens of any of the countries of the Union, or their lawful representatives, shall enjoy in the other countries the exclusive right of making or authorising the translation of their works until the expiration of ten years from the publication of the original work in one of the countries of the Union.

In essence, this provision granted copyright owners a translation right limited to a period of ten years. However, this limitation was only a temporary setback for developed countries like France who stridently insisted on affording translation rights the same status as the right of reproduction.[45] In fact, these countries earmarked stronger initiatives towards extensive protection of translation rights for the future.[46]

The two subsequent revisions of the *Berne Convention* at Paris in 1896 and at Berlin in 1908 saw the gradual extension of protection of translation rights. In particular, the *Paris Additional Act 1896* provided that translation rights in a particular copyright protected work should be protected during the full term of copyright subject to the exception that these rights ceased to exist if a translation had not been published during a period of ten years from the first publication of

43 'Minutes of the Second Meeting of the Conference for the Protection of Authors Rights' *Records of the International Conference for the Protection of Authors' Rights Convened in Berne* (8–9 September 1884) in Ricketson and Ginsburg, above n 24, vol 2, Appendix, 68; 'Minutes of the Third Meeting of the Conference for the Protection of Literary and Artistic Works' *Records of the Second International Conference for the Protection of Literary and Artistic Works Convened in Berne* (7–18 September 1885) in Ricketson and Ginsburg, above n 24, vol 2, Appendix, 109.

44 See Ricketson and Ginsburg, above n 24, vol 1, 67, 80–95.

45 See 'Report Presented to the Conference on behalf of its Committee' *Records of Conference Convened in Berlin* (14 October–14 November 1908) in Ricketson and Ginsburg, above n 24, vol 2, Appendix, 195.

46 See Ricketson and Ginsburg, above n 24, vol 1, 67, 80–95.

that work in the language for which protection was to be claimed.[47] The *Berlin Act 1908* provided for complete protection of translation rights for the full term of copyright protection similar to the right of reproduction.[48] In particular, Article 8 of the *Berlin Act 1908* said:

> The authors of unpublished works, being subjects or citizens of one of the countries of the Union, and the authors of works first published in one of those countries shall enjoy, in the other countries of the Union, during the whole term of the right in the original work, the exclusive right of making or authorising a translation of their works.[49]

Thus, Article 8 of the *Berlin Act* protected translation rights of the copyright owners for a term of 'the life of the author and fifty years after his death'.[50] However, there were still countries who feared this provision. For instance, the Netherlands said:

> [T]oo strict a rule on translation might be an obstacle to the Netherlands joining the Union; the reasons of justice indicated in favour of the author's copyright were fully recognized, but the transition needed to be carefully contrived.[51]

The Russian Empire expressed a similar view.[52] Rather peculiarly, Japan (which was a developing country at that time) proposed that '[t]he translation into Japanese of a work written in a European language and vice versa [should] be completely free.'[53] The rationale behind this was to engender mutual understanding between the Japanese and the Europeans. More specifically, Japan said that owing to the difference 'between the customs, practices, religion and traditions of the Japanese, on the one side, and the European and American peoples, on the other,' there was a 'difficulty of becoming acquainted, of understanding one another, which could create misunderstandings'.[54] A viable solution for this was the 'reciprocal freedom to translate'.[55] As Japan claimed, its proposal for free translation

47 *Paris Additional Act 1896* of the *Berne Convention*, art III.
48 See *Berlin Act 1908* of the *Berne Convention*, art 8.
49 This right was protected for 'the life of the author and fifty years after his death'. *Berlin Act 1908* of the *Berne Convention*, art 7.
50 *Berlin Act 1908* of the *Berne Convention*, art 7.
51 'Report Presented to the Conference on behalf of its Committee' *Records of Conference Convened in Berlin*, (14 October–14 November 1908) in Ricketson and Ginsburg, above n 24, vol 2, Appendix, 197.
52 Ricketson and Ginsburg, above n 24, vol 1, 98.
53 Report Presented to the Conference on behalf of its Committee' *Records of Conference Convened in Berlin*, (14 October–14 November 1908) in Ricketson and Ginsburg, above n 24, vol 2, Appendix, 197.
54 Ibid.
55 Ibid.

was not harmful to the Western authors (copyright owners), but rather was beneficial to them since by making Western works known in Japan (through translation into Japanese) the desire among the Japanese to read the original (Western) works could be inspired, 'thus facilitating the sale of original editions'.[56] As Ricketson and Ginsburg observed, although this Japanese proposal was rejected, the attitude of Japan as a 'rapidly developing country' reflected at an early stage the desire of these types of countries 'to gain ready access to European technical and other literature' which turned into a more radical issue in the second half of the twentieth century.[57]

4.4.1.2. Translation rights and newly independent developing countries

From about the 1950s to the early 1970s, there was pressure from newly independent developing countries to revise the way the *Berne Convention* protected copyright owners' translation rights. This was because of the growing need of these countries to translate knowledge products produced in developed countries in order to promote access to scientific and technical knowledge. Although in response to the pressure from developing countries, the way in which translation rights were protected in the *Berne Convention* was revised in 1967 and 1971, these revisions provided minimal benefit to these countries.

In the aftermath of World War II, many developing countries gained political independence. Drahos and Braithwaite observed, '[t]he achievement of sovereignty by developing states left them with many responsibilities, including that of educating their populations.'[58] To fulfil these responsibilities, these countries tried 'to put a priority on mass education, literacy and economic development.'[59] Fundamental to this was access to knowledge products, particularly in the field of science and technology, in large quantities and at affordable prices.[60] However, developing countries faced a massive shortage of these types of works, as the production of these types of works in developing countries was very low.[61] Therefore, they had to look to developed countries that produced these types of works on a mass scale and for export. At the same time, the developing countries also needed to translate these works into local languages. However, Article 8, which was created

56 Ibid.

57 Ricketson and Ginsburg, above n 24, vol 1, 98.

58 Peter Drahos and John Braithwaite, *Information Feudalism* (EARTHSCAN, 2002) 74.

59 Alan Story, 'Don't Ignore Copyright, the "Sleeping Giant" on the TRIPS and International Educational Agenda' in Peter Drahos and Ruth Mayne (eds), *Global Intellectual Property Rights: Knowledge, Access and Development* (Palgrave Macmillan, 2002) 125, 137; Alpana Roy, 'Copyright: A Colonial Doctrine in Postcolonial Age' (2008) 26(4) *Copyright Reporter* 112, 121.

60 See Frederick M Abbott, 'Protecting First World Assets in the Third World: Intellectual Property Negotiation in the GATT Multilateral Framework (1989) 22(4) *Vanderbilt Journal of Transnational Law* 689, 695.

61 Drahos and Braithwaite, above n 58, 74.

by the *Berlin Act 1908* and carried forward in successive versions of the *Berne Convention*, was inimical to this.[62] More specifically, Article 8 severely impeded the ability of developing countries to freely translate copyright protected scientific and technical works and to publish the translations in multiple quantities and at affordable prices, without undue delays. The only concession available to developing countries against Article 8 was the *Berne Convention*'s general exceptions to copyright owners' rights and the reservation with regard to protection of translation rights. The general exceptions to copyright owners' rights and the reservation in respect of translation rights in the *Berne Convention*, nevertheless, were woefully inadequate to facilitate the timely and affordable translation of copyright protected scientific and technical knowledge products and the publication of these translations in large quantities in developing countries.

The latest version of the *Berne Convention* in force in the mid-twentieth century was the *Brussels Act 1948*. The *Brussels Act* contained a mixture of general exceptions to copyright protection. For instance, Article 2*bis*(1) provided that Member Countries had the discretion to exclude 'political speeches and speeches delivered in the course of legal proceedings' from the *Convention*'s protection. In terms of Article 2*bis*(2), Member Countries had the discretion to 'determine conditions under which lectures, addresses, sermons and other works of the same nature may be reproduced by the press'. Article 9(2) stated that '[a]rticles on current economic, political or religious topics may be reproduced by the press unless the reproduction thereof is expressly reserved'. According to Article 9(3), the protection of the *Berne Convention* did not apply to 'news of the day nor to miscellaneous information having the character of mere items of news'. Article 10(1) permitted Member Countries 'to make short quotations from newspaper articles and periodicals, as well as to include them in press summaries'. Article 10(2) gave the discretion for the Member Countries to grant a 'right to include excerpts from literary or artistic works in educational or scientific publications, or in chrestomathies, in so far as this inclusion is justified by its purpose'. In addition, Article 10*bis* gave Member Countries the discretion 'to determine the conditions under which recording, reproduction, and public communication of short extracts from literary and artistic works may be made for the purpose of reporting current events by means of photography or cinematography or by radio diffusion'.

Although the *Brussels Act 1948* allowed a mixture of exceptions which could have been applied against copyright owners' translation rights, these exceptions suffered from three main defects. Firstly, since the *Brussels Act* did not expressly mention translation in the general exceptions, it was not so clear whether these exceptions could be applied to translation rights.[63] As Ricketson and Ginsburg said, this omission 'impose[d] severe restrictions on persons wishing to use

62 See Carolyn Deere, *The Implementation Game: The TRIPS Agreement and the Global Politics of Intellectual Property Reform in Developing Countries* (Oxford University Press, 2009) 37.

63 The position remains the same in the *Paris Act 1971* of the *Berne Convention*.

literary and dramatic works protected under the Convention where these works [were] in other languages'.[64] Although the failure of the *Brussels Act* to mention specifically that its general exceptions to copyright owners' rights would apply to translation may have been illogical, since 'the making of reproduction of works in their original language will be of little use to populations which do not speak or understand that language',[65] there were many who supported the view that the exceptions did not cover translation.[66]

Secondly, even if it was assumed that the general exceptions under the *Brussels Act 1948* applied to translation rights, the scope of these exceptions was too narrow to facilitate the timely and affordable translation of copyright protected scientific and technical books and learning materials and the publication of these translations in large quantities. This was because all the relevant general exceptions to translation of these knowledge products was concerned with 'consumptive uses', that is, with translating parts of knowledge products for the purpose of incorporating them within another product, as opposed to 'bulk uses', that is, translating the whole knowledge product and reproducing the whole translation in large quantities which was and remains the 'most pressing need of developing countries'.[67]

The third defect with the general exceptions in the *Brussels Act 1948* concerned their clarity. In particular, the way in which the *Brussels Act* defined the exceptions was not so clear when compared with the way in which it defined copyright owners' rights. The reason for this was that the *Brussels Act* spelt out the general exceptions in a broad language with the objective of granting flexibility to Member Countries to define the precise nature and scope of these exceptions in a manner that could protect the welfare interests of their citizens. However, most of the developing countries (especially at the time of their independence) lacked expertise and institutional capacity to transform this broad language into meaningful principles in a domestic context. This problem was compounded by the absence of a uniform and well-defined set of limitations and exceptions at the international level.[68]

In addition to the general exceptions that could be applied to copyright owners' translation rights, the *Brussels Act 1948* also provided for a special exception to these rights. This special exception was the reservation that could be applied with regard to Article 8 of the *Brussels Act* which guaranteed copyright owners' right to translate their literary and scientific works. Although this reservation allowed a country to limit the duration of translation rights for a period of ten

64 Ricketson and Ginsburg, above n 24, vol 1, 835.
65 Ibid.
66 Ibid., 837–838.
67 Ruth L Okediji, 'The International Copyright System: Limitations, Exceptions and Public Interest Considerations for Developing Countries' (Issue Paper No 15, ICTSD and UNCTAD, March 2006) 6 <http://unctad.org/en/Docs/iteipc200610_en.pdf>.
68 The position remains the same with regard to the general exceptions in the *Paris Act 1971* of the *Berne Convention*. Okediji, above n 67.

years, it did little to facilitate the timely translation of copyright protected scientific and technical books and learning materials and the publication of translations. In any case, many developing countries, including Sri Lanka, were unable to make use of this reservation because of their prior commitments under the *Berne Convention*. To understand this properly, we needed to examine how the reservation in respect of translation rights in the *Berne Convention* originated and evolved up until the *Brussels Act*.

The ability of a country to make reservations in respect to copyright owners' rights, including translation rights, was first introduced to the *Berne Convention* at its Berlin revision (*Berlin Act 1908*).[69] This was with the objective of reducing the rigor created by extended standards of protection of copyright owners' rights, including translation rights, in the *Berlin Act 1908*.

The *Berlin Act 1908* allowed countries that were members of the Berne Union and who had ratified the *Berlin Act* the option of continuing with their existing obligations under the previous texts of the *Berne Convention*. This was permitted instead of undertaking the new obligations in the *Berlin Act*, as regards any specific point.[70] At the same time, countries that were not members of the Berne Union but who were acceding to the *Berne Convention* for the first time were allowed an option of undertaking obligations under provisions of either the original text of *Berne Convention* (text of 1886) or the *Paris Additional Act 1896*, as the case may be, in the place of the corresponding provisions of the *Berlin Act*.[71]

Accordingly, Member Countries of the Berne Union that were only bound by the original text of the *Berne Convention* were given an option of continuing to limit translation rights for a period of ten years as provided in Article 5 of that text. Similarly, Member Countries that were bound by the *Paris Additional Act 1896* were given the option to limit the duration of translation rights as provided in Article 1 III.[72] The new members to the *Berne Convention* (revised by the *Berlin Act 1908*) were given the option to limit the duration of translation rights either as provided under Article 5 of the original text of the *Berne Convention* or as provided under Article 1 III of the *Paris Additional Act*.

The considerable use of reservations by Member Countries in the aftermath of the *Berlin Act 1908* came to be seen as having an adverse impact on the objectives of the *Berne Convention*.[73] In particular, by 1928, 'eighteen states had availed themselves of this facility, the majority of reservations relating to translation rights'.[74] As Ricketson and Ginsburg said, '[t]his obviously gave rise to considerable complexity and confusion in determining the exact relationship between

69 Ricketson and Ginsburg, above n 24, vol 1, 105.
70 See *Berlin Act 1908* of the *Berne Convention*, art 27.
71 See Ibid., art 25.
72 See *Paris Additional Act 1896* of the *Berne Convention*, art 1III.
73 Ricketson and Ginsburg, above n 24, vol 1, 105.
74 Ibid.

different states of the [Berne] Union'.[75] Also, according to French commentators Marcel Plaisant and Oliver Pichot, these reservations 'resulted in the rupture of unity', rendering the *Berne Convention* 'no longer a tablet of the law' but 'a mosaic pavement'.[76] In short, 'the rhythm of [the *Berne Convention*] had been paralysed by these reservations'.[77]

The adverse impact of reservations on the objectives of the *Berne Convention* created a need for elimination of the system of reservations from the *Convention*. In fact, this became the prime concern of the Rome revision of the *Berne Convention* held in 1928.

Although the outcome of the Rome revision (*Rome Act 1928*) made certain changes to the system of reservations in the *Berne Convention*, the reservation with regard to translation rights survived nearly intact. In particular, while the *Rome Act 1928* allowed the existing members of the Berne Union to continue with their reservations,[78] it permitted the new members to be bound by Article 1 III of the *Paris Additional Act 1896* on the condition that the provisions in the Article applied 'only to translations into the language or languages of that country'.[79] This enabled translation rights with regard to a particular language to cease when the copyright owner had not published a translation in that language within the first ten years from the publication of the original work. The subsequent revision of the *Berne Convention* at Brussels (*Brussels Act 1948*) maintained this status quo.[80]

Even though the *Brussels Act 1948* maintained the reservation with respect to copyright owners' translation rights under which Member Countries were allowed to limit the duration of these rights, it could not be considered as an effective means that facilitated the timely translation of copyright protected scientific and technical books and learning materials. There were two main reasons for this. Firstly, the maximum effect of this reservation was to limit translation rights for a period of ten years. In other words, this meant that a country had to wait for a period of ten years if it were to allow lawful translations to be made and published out of a copyright protected knowledge product in the absence of the consent of its copyright owner. However, this waiting period was too long with regard to scientific and technical books and learning materials. Aside from these types of works becoming quickly rendered outdated because of the rapid developments in science and technology, the waiting period of ten years meant that people in developing countries (especially students) were deprived of new

75 Ibid.

76 Marcel Plaisant and Oliver Pichot, *La Conférence de Rome: Commentaire pratique de la nouvelle Convention pour la protection internationale de la propriété littéraire et artistique* (1934) 34 cited in Ricketson and Ginsburg, above n 24, vol 1, 105.

77 Ibid.

78 *Rome Act 1928* of the *Berne Convention*, art 27(2).

79 Ibid., art 25(3).

80 See *Brussels Act 1948* of the *Berne Convention*, art 25(3); *Brussels Act 1948* of the *Berne Convention*, art 27(2).

knowledge produced in developed countries. Therefore, the reservation relating to translation rights in the *Brussels Act* was virtually useless to developing countries. As Olian observed:

> Though taken advantage of by a handful of members of the Union, [the reservation in respect of translation rights in the Brussels Act] actually did very little to ensure that works of foreign authors were readily available in the national languages of all countries. The ten year duration of exclusive rights was simply too long, especially considering the need for contemporaneous learning materials and the rapid speed at which most works of a scientific or technical character become obsolete.[81]

The second reason why many developing countries, particularly former British colonies like Sri Lanka, were unable to make use of the reservation in respect of translation rights in the *Brussels Act 1948* or the *Rome Act 1928* was because of their previous commitments under the *Berne Convention*. In particular, by the time of their independence, these developing countries had already become members of the Berne Union by virtue that their former colonial masters had acceded to the *Berne Convention* without making any reservation with regard to protection of translation rights. Thus, there was no room for these countries to make new reservations, since the provisions of the *Berne Convention* did not allow it. In fact, the experience of Sri Lanka provides a good example in this connection.

Sri Lanka gained independence in 1948 and, thereafter, decided to accede to the *Rome Act 1928* of the *Berne Convention* in 1959 in its own right as an independent state. To give effect to this, the Prime Minister of Sri Lanka sent the country's 'instrument of accession' to the Swiss Federal Political Department and gave notice that Sri Lanka would be acceding to the *Rome Act 1928* of the *Berne Convention*. This was subject to the important condition that Sri Lanka 'reserve[d] for itself the right to enact local legislation for the translation of educational, scientific and technical books into the national language.'[82] Although this reservation was too vague and appeared to exceed what was allowed by the *Rome Act 1928*, even a narrow construal of it as a reservation with regard to translation rights generally allowed by the *Rome Act* was not possible because of Sri Lanka's prior commitments under the *Berne Convention*. In particular, since Sri Lanka was already a member of the Berne Union and Britain had not made any reservation on behalf of Sri Lanka in respect of translation rights at the time it acceded to the *Rome Act 1928*,[83] the provisions of the *Rome Act* did not allow

81 Irwin A Olian Jr, 'International Copyright and the Needs of Developing Countries: The Awakening At Stockholm and Paris' (1974) 7(2) *Cornell International Law Journal* 81, 95.

82 See 'Documents of the Twentieth Session including the Report of the Commission to the General Assembly' [1968] II *Yearbook of the International Law Commission* 1, 15.

83 See Chamila Talagala, 'Translation and the International Copyright Crisis: The Sri Lankan Experience During the Early Years of Independence' (2017) 39(3) *European Intellectual Property Review* 153.

Sri Lanka to make the reservation in respect of translation rights which a new member of the *Berne Convention* was generally allowed to make.[84] Thus, the reservation which Sri Lanka made in its 'instrument of accession' of 1959 was without effect. In any case, the Swiss Government interpreted this 'instrument of accession' as a 'declaration of continuity' which was eventually confirmed by the International Office of the *Berne Convention*.[85]

Like Sri Lanka, a majority of newly independent developing country Members of the *Berne Convention* gradually began to understand that the way copyright owners' translation rights were protected in the *Berne Convention* was a stumbling block for timely and affordable translations. Peter Yu observed, '[o]nce [developing] countries joined the international community following their declaration of independence, they "became more assertive of their rights and aware of their international obligations" ' under the *Berne Convention*.[86] Since developing countries were aware that the *Berne Convention* was an obstacle to solving their problem of access to scientific and technical knowledge (through timely and affordable translation of copyright protected scientific and technical books and learning materials), these countries were torn between affirming and denouncing international obligations of the *Berne Convention* into which their former colonial rulers have entered on their behalf.[87] However, Drahos and Braithwaite observed that '[e]ven after developing countries became sovereign states it proved hard to leave Berne's embrace'.[88] There were some pragmatic reasons for this.

Upon their independence, the developing country Members of the *Berne Convention* had three main options as to their obligations under the *Convention*. These were:

A) Denounce the *Berne Convention* and become a free-rider of copyright protected works, without undertaking any obligation in relation to international copyright; or
B) Denounce the *Berne Convention* and, formulate and accede to a new international copyright instrument which would be more congenial for the developing countries; or
C) Continue with the *Berne Convention* while seeking reforms that would make the *Convention* more congenial to the interests of developing countries.

4.4.1.2.1. BECOME A FREE-RIDER OF COPYRIGHT PROTECTED WORKS

The policy of granting copyright protection to authors of literary and scientific works is to promote and encourage creativity and thereby increase the

84 Ibid.
85 See 'Documents of the Twentieth Session including the Report of the Commission to the General Assembly' [1968] II *Yearbook of the International Law Commission* 1, 15.
86 Peter K Yu, 'A Tale of Two Development Agendas' (2009) 35 *Ohio Northern University Law Review* 465, 470 (emphasis added) (citations omitted).
87 Ibid.
88 Drahos and Braithwaite, above n 58, 74.

volume and quality of the production of these works.[89] Therefore, copyright protection is generally considered a *sine qua non* for countries to promote and encourage production of literary and scientific works necessary to their economic and social development. Although protection of copyright owners' rights is essential to promote and encourage production of literary and scientific works, copyright law is not exclusively concerned with protection of copyright owners' rights. It is also concerned with ensuring and encouraging wide dissemination of literary and scientific works. As was observed in chapter 1, developing countries have special problems as to the dissemination of scientific and technical works (or access to these works) owing to their level of economic development, on one hand, and the levels of scientific and technical development, on the other. As Olian pointed out, 'Of the many problems facing developing countries, none is more urgent that the need for wider dissemination of [scientific and technical] knowledge, for ultimately this will act to further the educational, cultural, and technical development of their people.'[90] Meeting the needs of developing countries for wider dissemination of scientific and technical knowledge involves two things. According to Olian, 'The first is the promotion of the rapid transfer of knowledge from advanced areas to the developing countries . . . in the fields of science and technology'.[91] The 'second is the encouragement of the growth of local publishing industries in the developing countries, through creation of incentives for authors and publishers, as well as through technical assistance.'[92]

While protection of copyright owners' rights is important for developing countries to encourage their authors and publishing industries,[93] striking a proper balance between such protection and the public access to literary and scientific works is equally important to them. This is also because access to literary and scientific works and protection of copyright owners' rights are two sides of the same coin. While protection of copyright owners' rights is a stimulus for the production of literary and scientific works, this also requires wide dissemination of literary and scientific works since it is not only the general public but also the authors who will need to use these works for the production of new works. Okediji observed that '[w]riters and creators do not exist or create in a vacuum. Indeed, certain genres of works, styles of creativity, and modes of expression specifically and deliberately incorporate, reproduce, or transform pre-existing works.'[94]

89 See Peter Drahos, 'The Regulation of Public Goods' (2004) 7(2) *Journal of International Economic Law* 321, 322.
90 Olian Jr, above n 81, 88.
91 Ibid., 88–89.
92 Ibid.
93 Ibid., 92–94.
94 See Okediji, above n 67. See also Justice Joseph Story in *Emerson v. Davies*, 8 F Cas 615, 619 (1845).

Given this predicament, becoming a free-rider of copyright protected works by abandoning copyright protection altogether does not provide optimal benefits for developing countries. Moreover, such an approach would inevitably hamper the accomplishment of their major goals, such as economic development and the advancement of science and literature.[95]

4.4.1.2.2. FORMULATE AND ACCEDE TO A NEW COPYRIGHT CONVENTION

Copyright is a European construct which remained alien to most of the developing countries prior to the nineteenth century.[96] Thus, many of these countries still lack expertise and knowledge in this field.[97] Moreover, particularly at the time of their independence, developing countries were often inexperienced new entrants to the field of international relations.[98] So formulating a new copyright convention was too heavy a burden for these countries to carry. This becomes discernible from the fact that formulation of the *Berne Convention* was not a smooth and easy process, even for the European superpowers like France, Germany and Britain.

4.4.1.2.3. CONTINUE WITH THE *BERNE CONVENTION*

In light of the problems with the previously discussed options, the only viable option for developing country Members of the *Berne Convention* was to continue their membership and attempt to revise the *Convention*'s standards of copyright protection to suit their needs and interests. In fact, a majority of developing countries, including Sri Lanka, chose this option. Factors such as the desire of these countries to be part of a 'union of civilised nations' with strong international standing, pressure from their former colonial masters, the concessions which they received and the attitude and practice of the United International Bureaux for the Protection of Intellectual Property (BIRPI) also had an impact on this choice.[99]

Agitation for reform During the 1960s, agitation among developing country Members of the *Berne Convention* to revise the *Convention*'s copyright protection standards with regard to translation rights reached a peak. There were two main reasons for this. One was the *Universal Copyright Convention* (*UCC*) which was concluded in 1952. The other was the increased bargaining power of developing countries within the Berne Union.

95 See Juan Yu, 'Can Developing Countries Benefit from Intellectual Property Protection' (2003) 10 *TFLR–IP Protection and Developing Countries* 359, 363.
96 See, e.g., Deere, above n 62, 34–36.
97 Ibid., 36.
98 Alan H Lazar, 'Developing Countries and Authors' Rights in International Copyright' (1971) 19(1) *Copyright Law Symposium* 1, 14.
99 Ibid., 14, 17–24.

4.4.1.2.4. THE *UNIVERSAL COPYRIGHT CONVENTION*

The question of whether or not developing countries needed lower standards of protection for translation rights was first raised in the *UCC*.[100] The *UCC* provided the first opportunity for the newly independent developing countries to participate and negotiate in the process of international copyright law making. Though the need for lower standards of protection for translation rights in developing countries was raised and discussed in the negotiations leading up to the *UCC*,[101] the objective of this *Convention* was a different one. Goldstein observed:

> The central object of the Universal Copyright Convention was to secure multilateral copyright relations between the countries of the Berne Union and the many countries outside the Union that found the Berne Convention's stringent minimum standards incompatible with their domestic law.[102]

These countries included the United States, 'several Latin American countries that had already entered into regional copyright treaties, the then Soviet Union, and several African and Asian nations'.[103]

The *UCC*, in particular, was an outcome of 'a *voeu*' adopted at the Rome Conference for the revision of the *Berne Convention* in 1928 'to create a bridge between the *Berne Convention* and the [*Buenos Aires Agreement 1910*], the principal Pan-American treaty to include the United States as a party'.[104] Though by 1938 the 'efforts to establish multilateral relations between Berne and non-Berne countries, particularly proposals for an entirely new convention separate from Berne had gained momentum', this was 'cut short by the outbreak of World War II'.[105]

Against this background, UNESCO initiated the *UCC* in the late 1940s[106] with the aim of establishing 'a broader-based convention that would bring together countries with widely differing levels of protection'.[107] In fact, the *UCC* was seen as a more generous framework of international copyright protection by developing countries as it provided a relatively lower level of copyright protection to that of *Berne* and for compulsory licenses in respect of translation.[108] In particular, Article V(2) of the *UCC* provided:

> [A]ny Contracting State may, by its domestic legislation, restrict the right of translation of writings, but only subject to the following provisions:

100 Ricketson and Ginsburg, above n 24, vol 2, 887.
101 Olian Jr, above n 81, 96.
102 Goldstein and Hugenholtz, above n 9, 44.
103 Ibid.
104 Ibid., (citations omitted).
105 Ibid.
106 See, e.g., Gerald R Gibbons, 'The Compulsory License System of the Universal Copyright Convention' (1956) 6 *Duke Bar Journal* 23.
107 Ricketson and Ginsburg, above n 24, vol 2, 885–886.
108 Eva Hemmungs Wirten, above n 23, 46–47; Yu, above n 86, 474–475.

> If, after the expiration of a period of seven years from the date of the first publication of a writing, a translation of such writing has not been published in the national language or languages, as the case may be, of the Contracting State, by the owner of the right of translation or with his authorization, any national of such Contracting State may obtain a non-exclusive licence from the competent authority thereof to translate the work and publish the work so translated in any of the national languages in which it has not been published . . .[109]

Even though the mechanism for compulsory translation licenses envisaged in the *UCC* provided some assistance to developing countries in addressing their needs, it can hardly be perceived as an adequate measure. There were three main drawbacks to the *UCC* compulsory licensing system which made it less congenial for the developing countries.

Firstly, a developing country that was making use of compulsory licenses provided under the *UCC* had to comply with a number of conditions. Of these, the most stringent and unfavourable for developing countries was the requirement that they had to wait until seven years from the date of publication of a copyright protected work before a translation license could be granted in respect of that work.[110] As Ricketson and Ginsburg observed:

> This provision was arguably less generous than the reservation which countries were permitted to make on acceding to the Berne Convention, the effect of which was that translation rights fell into the public domain after 10 years if no authorised translation had been published in that period.[111]

The requirement that a period of seven years had to elapse before a copyright protected work could be translated was inadequate with regard to the type of copyright protected works that were urgently needed by developing countries to promote access to scientific and technical knowledge, namely, books and learning material in the field of science and technology.[112]

The second main drawback of the compulsory licensing system in the *UCC* which made it unattractive to developing countries was the formalities and procedures that were needed to be adhered to when granting compulsory licenses.[113] In particular, these formalities and procedures were complicated and time-consuming.

109 However, this provision was subject to a number of conditions and qualifications stipulated in proviso to Article V(2) of the Universal *Copyright Convention 1952*.
110 *Universal Copyright Convention 1952*, art V(2) proviso.
111 Ricketson and Ginsburg, above n 24, vol 2, 886.
112 In particular, by the time translations of this type of copyright protected works could be published in developing countries, that is, after a minimum period of seven years, the information contained in those works would have been outdated and useless because of the rapid advancements and new findings in the field of science and technology. Also, this minimum waiting period meant that developing countries were deprived of new knowledge produced in developed countries.
113 *Universal Copyright Convention 1952*, art V(2) proviso.

Olian observed that '[s]o frustrating have such procedures turned out to be . . . that in the two decades since the UCC came into existence, not a single compulsory license has ever been issued under this provision.'[114]

Another factor which discouraged developing countries who were already Members of the *Berne Convention* from joining the *UCC* was the so called 'Berne Safeguard Clause' in the *UCC*. This clause provided that any work originating in a country that withdrew from the Berne Union after 1 January 1951 shall not be protected by the *UCC* in countries of the Berne Union.[115] In essence, this prevented countries who were Members of the *Berne Convention* from withdrawing from it after 1 January 1951, in favour of the more relaxed copyright protection standards in the *UCC*.[116]

In view of the foregoing factors, the *UCC* (in the form it was formulated) was not congenial to developing countries, particularly those who were Members of the *Berne Convention*. The reason for this can be explained with reference to the main objective of the *UCC*, which was to provide a solution to the 'problem of improving copyright protection on a worldwide basis' that existed in the mid-twentieth century,[117] without impairing international systems that were already in force.[118] Thus, addressing the needs of developing countries as a whole was a matter which fell outside the *Convention*'s scope. Nonetheless, this did not mean that developing countries gave up their attempts in persuading the *UCC* to accommodate their needs and interests. In fact, during the early 1960s certain proposals were made to revise the *UCC* in this regard. However, these proposals were rejected, since any amendments to the *UCC* were considered to be premature in view of the fact that the *Convention* had only recently come into force.[119] At the same time, developing countries also raised concerns over the possibility of deleting the Berne Safeguard Clause in the *UCC* because it was a stumbling block for countries who were also Members of the *Berne Convention* to accede to the *UCC*. Since this issue had a direct relevance to the forthcoming revision of the *Berne Convention* at Stockholm in 1967, the question of revision of the *UCC* was deferred until the Stockholm Revision had been held.[120]

4.4.1.2.5. STOCKHOLM CONFERENCE FOR THE REVISION OF THE *BERNE CONVENTION*

The Stockholm Conference for the revision of the *Berne Convention* in 1967 provided developing countries with a fitting forum to air their grievances regarding

114 Olian Jr, above n 81, 96.
115 *Universal Copyright Convention 1952*, art XVII, Appendix declaration.
116 Paul Goldstein, *International Copyright: Principles, Law, and Practice* (Oxford University Press, 2001) 29.
117 Joseph S Dubin, 'The Universal Copyright Convention' (1954) 42 *California Law Review* 89, 90.
118 *Universal Copyright Convention 1952*, Preamble.
119 Ricketson and Ginsburg, above n 24, vol 2, 898.
120 Ibid.

the stringent copyright protection standards envisaged in the *Berne Convention*. There were a number of reasons for this. Firstly, by the time of the Stockholm Conference, developing countries had formed a majority of the international community and had emerged as an identifiable bloc within the Berne Union. In particular, over a third of the Berne members were developing countries.[121] This situation forced the *Berne Convention* to take account of the needs of developing country Members who were significant in number. They also provided an important indication as to the future prospects and growth of the *Berne Convention*. In other words, while the developed country Members of the *Berne Convention* foresaw the value of persuading developing countries that were outside the Berne Union to join it, they also saw the importance of convincing developing countries who were already Members of the Union to remain within it with the broad objective of expanding 'the realm of governance for [copyright] which would potentially benefit' the export industries in developed countries.'[122] Peter Yu observed that '[t]he developed Berne members therefore were willing to offer concessions as "sweeteners" to entice these countries to join the Union'[123] without, however, unduly flexing the *Convention*'s standards. This was because the lowering of these standards in the interest of developing countries would have been an undesirable setback for those developed countries that had 'fought hard to raise the international copyright standards over the past eighty years'.[124]

Secondly, the *Berne Convention* faced significant competition from the *UCC*. The reason for this was that from the developing countries' point of view the *UCC* presented an attractive alternative to the *Berne Convention*. This was primarily because under the *UCC*, developing countries could obtain reasonable protection for their works abroad, while according lesser protection (than in the *Berne Convention*) to foreign works at home.[125] As a result, developing countries constantly referred to the less stringent provisions of the *UCC*, especially those in respect of compulsory licenses for translation, as a ground for accommodating similar provisions into the *Berne Convention*.[126] This raised concerns among BIRPI and the developed country Members of the *Berne Convention* that if the demands of the developing country Members were not met, the developing countries who were still not Members of the Berne Union might either join the *UCC* or, together with the developing country Members of the Berne Union, establish their own separate union.[127]

Thirdly, the need to revise the domestic copyright laws in developing countries along with the standards of the *Berne Convention* on which they were based

121 Ibid, vol 1, 121.
122 Yu, above n 86, 474 (citations omitted); Christopher May, *World Intellectual Property Organization (WIPO): Resurgence and the Development Agenda* (Routledge, 2007) 22.
123 Yu, above n 86, 474 (citations omitted).
124 Ibid.
125 Ibid 474–475.
126 Ibid.
127 Ibid., 475.

(to suit local needs and interests) had gained momentum by the time of the Stockholm Conference. In particular, by this time a majority of the developing country Members of the *Berne Convention* had fully realised that their national copyright laws (which were more or less based on the provisions of the *Berne Convention*) were a clear impediment for timely and affordable translation. More importantly, post-independence developments in many of these countries, particularly the expansion of provision of scientific and technical education in local languages, had triggered an urgent need to translate scientific and technical books and learning materials produced in developed countries. These concerns had paved the way for a series of events in the field of international copyright such as the African Study Meeting held in Brazzaville in 1963 (jointly organised by BIRPI and UNESCO), the Joint Session of the Permanent Committee of the Berne Union and the Intergovernmental Copyright Committee in 1963 and the East Asian Seminar on Copyright held in New Delhi in 1967 (convened by BIRPI) which had a profound impact on the Stockholm Conference.[128]

The main demands of developing countries at the Stockholm Conference were for some kind of special concession for their use of literary and scientific works, most of which originated from the developed countries. In particular, many developing countries argued that publishing houses located in developed countries charged higher prices for their copyright protected works and had little or no interest in supplying proper translations of these works to developing countries.[129] Importantly, these demands were backed by threats to the effect that if the demands were not properly met, developing countries would withdraw from the membership of the *Berne Convention*. Thus, some sort of accommodation to the demands of developing countries became unavoidable if the *Berne Convention* were to survive in the future. As a result, the Protocol regarding Developing Countries was adopted, which was intended to provide certain concessions to developing countries in respect of copyright protection. Among these concessions were the provisions which enabled developing countries to restrict the protection of translation rights in their countries.

Evaluation of the provisions in the Stockholm Protocol restricting translation rights The Protocol devised at the Stockholm Conference for the benefit of developing countries restricted translation rights in two ways: it allowed the forfeiture of translation rights in the event that they were not exercised within a period of ten years, and it also provided for the grant of compulsory licenses.[130] More specifically, the Protocol gave developing countries the option of substituting the following provisions for Article 8 of the *Berne Convention* which protected copyright owners' translation rights:

128 Ibid., 472–479.

129 Ricketson and Ginsburg, above n 24, vol 1, 129.

130 *Stockholm Act 1967* of the *Berne Convention*, Protocol Regarding Developing Countries, art 1(b); Ricketson and Ginsburg, above n 24, vol 2, 902.

> [A]uthors of literary and artistic works protected by this Convention shall enjoy in countries other than the country of origin of their works the exclusive right of making and of authorising the translation of their works throughout the term of protection of their rights in the original works. Nevertheless, the exclusive right of translation shall cease to exist if the author shall not have availed himself of it, during a term of ten years from the date of the first publication of the original work, by publishing or causing to be published, in one of the countries of the Union, a translation in the language for which protection is to be claimed.
> [I]f, after the expiration of a period of three years from the date of the first publication of a literary or artistic work, or of any longer period determined by national legislation of the developing country concerned, a translation of such work has not been published in that country into the national or official or regional language or language of that country by the owner of the right of translation or with his authorization, any national of such country may obtain a non-exclusive license from the competent authority to translate the work and publish the work so translated in any of the national or official or regional languages in which it has not been published.[131]

The Stockholm Protocol also allowed a developing country to shorten the term of protection for translation rights for a period not less than 25 years.[132] These provisions in the Protocol provided little assistance to developing countries to facilitate the translation of copyright protected scientific and technical knowledge products in order to promote access to scientific and technical knowledge. One main reason for this was the excessive waiting periods stipulated for the cease of translation rights and the granting of compulsory licenses for translation under the Protocol. In particular, limiting the duration of translation rights for 10 or 25 years suffered from the same defects that were to be seen in the *Berne Convention*'s system of reservation on translation rights. Thus, from the standpoint of developing countries, limiting the duration of translation rights was almost of no use. Olian observed:

> In view of the need of such countries for contemporaneous materials for use in education and entertainment, it became evident that the reservation permitting reduction of the post-mortem period of protection from fifty to twenty five years would affect only a small number of the highest quality works, and would result in virtually no saving in royalties paid abroad. Similar reasoning was applicable to the reservation under which an author's translation rights lapsed if he failed to publish a translation in a country's national

131 *Stockholm Act 1967* of the *Berne Convention*, Protocol Regarding Developing Countries, art 1(b).
132 Ibid., art 1(a).

> language within ten years; very few textbooks and technical works would be valuable after such a period.[133]

Although the three-year waiting period for the granting of translation licenses was an improvement compared to the *UCC*, this time period was excessive in respect to scientific and technical works.[134] The grant of these licenses was also 'still conditioned on compliance with frustrating administrative procedures, including a requirement that the applicant establish "either that he has requested, and been denied, authorisation by the proprietor of the right to make and publish the translation, or that, after due diligence on his part, he was unable to find the owner of the right" '.[135] Compliance with the formalities involved considerable expense for developing countries. Moreover, the time that was needed to comply with the formalities along with the time that was needed for a work to be properly translated, published and distributed increased the total time span for a translated work to reach the public.[136] Strba noted:

> [T]he procedural requirements of notification [in the Protocol] make the application process for a [compulsory licenses] too expensive for developing countries. Waiting periods of three or ten years are excessive for a country that is in desperate need of reading or teaching material. Even if the waiting period for application for a [compulsory license] were three years, the lengthy procedure for such an application works to make this period too long.[137]

In this sense, the system of compulsory licensing introduced in the Protocol 'suffered from the same defects which characterised the *UCC*'s system. The administrative formalities required to obtain the licenses were simply too expensive, time-consuming and frustrating.'[138] As such, from the standpoint of developing countries, almost all the provisions in the Stockholm Protocol which restricted translation rights were practically useless.[139] Thus, the Protocol developed at the Stockholm Conference was a clear setback for the developing countries. Surprisingly, it was also a setback for developed countries.

Stockholm revision and the developed countries The overall effect of the substantive revisions that occurred at the Stockholm Conference was a strengthening

133 Olian Jr, above n 81, 101.
134 Wirten noted that 'the vision of developing nations happily receiving books more or less worthless on the original market . . . smel[t] of knowledge dumping'. Eva Hemmungs Wirten, above n 23, 61.
135 Olian Jr, above n 81, 99.
136 Ibid., 101–102.
137 Susan Isiko Strba, *International Copyright Law and Access to Education in Developing Countries: Exploring Multilateral Legal and Quasi-Legal Solutions* (Martinus Nijhoff Publishers, 2012) 89 (citations omitted).
138 Olian Jr, above n 81, 101–102.
139 Ibid., 101.

of copyright protection in a number of respects. In fact, this was a bounty given to developed countries to encourage them to accept the relaxations of copyright protection standards in the Stockholm Protocol without much resistance.[140] Despite this assurance, developed countries saw the Protocol as a clear derogation from the authors' rights.[141] As such, they vehemently objected to the Protocol.[142] For instance, the United States declared that if the Protocol was adopted it would 'pose a near insurmountable barrier' to its desired accession to the *Berne Convention*.[143]

From the point of view of developed and developing countries, the Stockholm Protocol was seen as a failure: it neither addressed the needs of developing countries nor the developed countries. Olian said:

> A brief analysis of the Protocol's main provisions reveals that it was grossly defective in meeting the needs of developing nations, while at the same time highly objectionable to the more advanced countries. As such, it was nearly a complete failure.[144]

In the light of this scenario, the developed countries took maximum advantage of the mechanism provided for the ratification of the Stockholm Protocol.[145] As a result, the Protocol never came into force. Yet both the developing and developed countries understood the need for some sort of compromise, which both sides could be satisfied with, if the *Berne Convention* were to survive for the future. The Paris Conference for the revision to the *Berne Convention* came about as a result of this need.[146]

4.4.1.2.6. PARIS CONFERENCE FOR THE REVISION OF THE *BERNE CONVENTION*

The Paris Conference for the revision of the *Berne Convention* held in 1971 was a 'package deal' between developed and developing countries which involved amendments to both the *Berne Convention* and the *UCC*.[147] The need for amendment of the *UCC* arose as a result of the Berne Safeguard Clause. As noted earlier, this was because the Berne Safeguard Clause acted as a stumbling block to developing countries who preferred to accede to the *UCC*. These countries advocated for the deletion of the Berne Safeguard Clause from the *UCC*. However, developed countries were not willing to accept this proposal without raising the general level of copyright protection in the *UCC* at the same

140 Ibid., 98.
141 Ibid., 102.
142 Yu, above n 86, 480.
143 Ricketson and Ginsburg, above n 24, vol 2, 914 (citations omitted).
144 Olian Jr, above n 81, 95.
145 Ibid., 101.
146 Ricketson and Ginsburg, above n 24, vol 1, 131–132.
147 Ibid., 921.

time.[148] Thus, deliberations ensued on both the *Berne Convention* and the *UCC* which eventually led to the general agreement that 'both conventions should be revised simultaneously, with special attention being paid to the needs of developing countries.'[149]

The main outcome of the Paris revision of the *Berne Convention* is the 'Berne Appendix' (or Paris Appendix) which was introduced in the *Paris Act 1971*. In particular, the Berne Appendix in the *Paris Act 1971* contains a special copyright regime for developing countries. Among other things, it offers developing countries the option of either substituting Article 5 of the 1886 version of the *Berne Convention* as revised by the *Paris Additional Act 1896* in respect of the translations into languages of general use in these countries (the effect of which is the forfeiture of translation rights in respect of these languages in the event that the rights are not exercised within a period of ten years) or of making use of the faculty which provides for granting of compulsory licenses for translation.[150]

Evaluation of the provisions in the Paris Act on translation rights The *Paris Act 1971* of the *Berne Convention* carries the same provision that is in Article 8 of the *Berlin Act 1908*. Accordingly, copyright owners' translation rights are protected throughout the term of protection of their right of reproduction.[151]

There are certain general exceptions in the *Paris Act 1971* with regard to the copyright owners' right of reproduction. However, it is not clear whether or not these exceptions would apply to translation rights. The main general exception to copyright owners' right of reproduction in the *Paris Act 1971* is provided in Article 9(2). In particular, this Article states:

> It shall be a matter for legislation in the countries of the Union to permit the reproduction of such works in certain special cases, provided that such reproduction does not conflict with a normal exploitation of the work and does not unreasonably prejudice the legitimate interests of the author.[152]

Article 9(2) of the *Paris Act 1971* does not mention translation and only talks about reproduction. Also, there are no express provisions in other articles of the *Paris Act* stating that Article 9(2) applies to translation rights. Ricketson and Ginsburg observed:

> On its face, this omission imposes severe restrictions on persons wishing to use literary and dramatic works protected under the Convention where these

148 Ibid., 917.
149 Ibid., 921.
150 *Paris Act 1971* of the *Berne Convention*, Appendix, arts I, II, V.
151 Ibid., art 8.
152 Ibid., art 9(2).

> works are in other languages. While the Convention makes provision for the reproduction, in particular circumstances and for certain purposes, of such works in their original language, these exceptions are not expressed to be applicable where translations of those works are made in the same situation. This appears illogical, as the making of reproduction of works in their original language will be of little use to populations which do not speak or understand that language.[153]

It is pertinent to note that the (entire) provision in Article 9(2) of the *Paris Act 1971* was first introduced to the *Berne Convention* at the Stockholm Revision in 1967. The question whether this provision extended to translation rights was considered at the Stockholm Conference. In particular, the Main Committee I, which was set up with the task of considering the proposals for revising the substantive copyright provisions of the *Berne Convention*, 'considered that a general rule regarding exceptions to the right of translation was necessary and should be inserted to Article 8'.[154] However, 'It was left to the Drafting Committee to try to find a satisfactory formula and to suggest whether such a formula should be included in the text of Article 8 or merely in the part of the Report concerning that Article'.[155] Eventually, '[t]he Drafting Committee opted for the latter solution.'[156] This was mainly because [of the] 'idea that it was fairly obvious that exceptions to the other exclusive rights, such as the right of reproduction, implied corresponding exceptions in respect of the right of translation and that the Convention had generally been applied in this way.'[157] However, as Ricketson suggested, the Main Committee I had clearly made a mistake in not adopting an explicit provision in the *Berne Convention* enabling the application of the exception in Article 9(2) against translation rights.[158] In particular, he stated:

> The basis for applying the interpretation given in its Report is unclear, and is open to challenge. Thus, the relationship between reproductions and translation may be disputed; likewise, the conclusion that a contrary interpretation leads to an absurd or unreasonable result justifying reference to the unanimous view of the delegates expressed in the report may also be doubted.[159]

153 Ricketson and Ginsburg, above n 24, vol 1, 835.
154 'Report on the Work of Main Committee I' *Records of the Intellectual Property Conference of Stockholm* (11 June–14 July 1967) vol 2, [203].
155 Ibid.
156 Ibid.
157 Ibid.
158 Ricketson, above n 25, 541.
159 Ricketson and Ginsburg, above n 24, vol 1, 840 (citations omitted) (emphasis added).

As such, the question whether Article 9(2) of the *Paris Act 1971* extends to translation rights remains unclear.[160]

Be that as it may, none of the general exceptions to the copyright owners' rights in the *Paris Act 1971*, including Article 9(2), offer any material help to developing countries like Sri Lanka to facilitate the timely and affordable translation of copyright protected scientific and technical knowledge products. This is because, as Okediji noted, all these general exceptions 'pertain primarily to use-access, i.e. the freedom of others to utilise portions of the work once they are in possession of a legitimate copy.'[161] However, for developing countries like Sri Lanka 'access to legitimate copies is precisely the issue'.[162] Added to this is the need to translate the legitimate copies and reproduce the translation in large quantities at affordable prices. Okediji observed that '[n]othing in the Berne Convention addresse[s] the possibility of bulk access to protected works [except] the Berne Appendix of 1971.'[163]

The main features of the Berne Appendix (Paris Appendix) are: (1) the compulsory licensing system introduced in respect to translation and reproduction of copyright protected literary and scientific works in developing countries and (2) the alternative possibility of limiting translation rights through a special reservation.[164] These features are structurally similar to the licensing system and the special reservation in the Stockholm Protocol.[165] As a result, the Berne Appendix suffers from many of the same defects in the Protocol. Of these, the most noteworthy is the waiting period before compulsory licenses for translation can be granted. In particular, according to Article II(2), a translation license in respect of a copyright protected work can only be granted 'after the expiration of a period of three years' from the date of the first publication of that work.[166] However, there is a noteworthy exception to this in Article II(3) which makes the Appendix more favourable to developing

160 However, the question whether Article 9(2) of the *Berne Convention* applies to copyright owners' translation rights has been rendered redundant by the *TRIPS Agreement 1994* with regard to Berne members who are also members to the *TRIPS Agreement*. See *TRIPS Agreement*, art 13. See also Chamila Talagala and Leanne Wiseman, 'Copyright, Open Access and Translation' (2015) 37(8) *European Intellectual Property Review* 498, 500.

161 Okediji, above n 67.

162 Ibid.

163 Ibid., (emphasis added).

164 *Paris Act 1971* of the *Berne Convention*, Appendix, arts I, II, V. Despite the fact that the faculties in the Berne Appendix can only be made use of by developing countries, the Appendix does not provide for a clear definition of what is meant by the term 'developing country'. *Paris Act 1971* of the *Berne Convention*, Appendix, art I(1). See also Basalamah, above n 2, 511–513.

165 However, it contains several substantive changes as well as number of modifications in language. Olian Jr, above n 81, 107.

166 *Paris Act 1971* of the *Berne Convention*, Appendix, art II2*(a)*.

countries like Sri Lanka when compared with the Protocol. In particular, Article II(3)(a) provides:

> In the case of translations into a language which is not in general use in one or more developed countries which are members of the Union, a period of one year shall be substituted for the period of three years referred to in paragraph (2)(a).

Accordingly, although Article II(2)(a) of the Berne Appendix (similar to Article 1(b)(ii) of the Stockholm Protocol) generally requires an applicant for a compulsory translation license in respect of a copyright protected work to wait for a period of three years from the publication of that work, Article II(3)(a) of the Appendix enables an applicant in Sri Lanka to shorten this waiting period for one year provided that the translation is into Sinhala. This is because Sinhala is not in general use in any developed countries.

The other provisions in the Berne Appendix, nonetheless, make the compulsory licensing system restrictive and onerous for Sri Lanka (and other developing countries) in many ways.[167] In particular, these provisions (1) make it doubtful as to whether or not the compulsory licenses cover works published online, (2) restrict the purposes in respect to which licenses may be obtained, (3) impose detailed and complicated administrative procedures that should be followed when obtaining licenses, (4) prohibit granting of licenses for reproduction in respect of translations made under licenses for translation, (5) place a ban on the export of copies made under compulsory licenses and (6) strengthen the right of copyright owners' for just compensation.

4.4.1.2.7. WORKS PUBLISHED ONLINE

As the licensing system provided in the Berne Appendix is limited to 'works published in printed or analogous forms of reproduction',[168] it is questionable whether the Appendix applies to works published online. Peter Yu observed that '[p]remised on the traditional printing technologies, the [A]ppendix [does] not allow less developed countries to take advantage of new "online modes of delivery which might well be attractive to developing countries with large and widespread populations" '.[169] If this interpretation is correct (which it appears to be), the Berne Appendix completely turns a blind eye to the internet, which has become a primary means of distribution of knowledge products.[170]

167 See Eva Hemmungs Wirten, above n 23, 65.
168 *Paris Act 1971* of the *Berne Convention*, Appendix, arts II(1), (2)(a).
169 Yu, above n 86, 483 (citations omitted).
170 Talagala and Wiseman, above n 160, 503.

4.4.1.2.8. THE PURPOSES IN RESPECT OF WHICH LICENSES MAY BE OBTAINED

The purposes for which translation licenses may be obtained under the Berne Appendix are more restrictive than in the Stockholm Protocol. In particular, the Protocol allowed translation licenses for all purposes whereas according to Article II(5) of the Appendix '[a]ny license . . . shall be granted only for the purpose of teaching, scholarship or research.' Thus as Olian noted, '[l]icenses for translation, available for any purpose under the Protocol, may only be granted under the Paris Appendix "for the purpose of teaching, scholarship or research" '.[171]

4.4.1.2.9. ADMINISTRATIVE PROCEDURES

The Berne Appendix consists of many detailed and complicated administrative procedures which must be complied with before compulsory licenses can be granted. For example, in terms of Article IV(1), a compulsory license for translation may only be granted by a competent authority if the applicant, 'in accordance with the procedure of the country concerned, establishes either that he has requested, and has been denied, authorization by the owner of the right to make and publish the translation' or that, 'after due diligence on his part, he was unable to find the owner of the right'.[172] In terms of Article IV(2), if the owner of the right cannot be found, the applicant for the translation license must send copies of his application (that has been submitted to the competent authority) to the publisher of the work (in respect of which the translation license is sought) and to 'any designated national or international information centre'.[173]

More importantly, certain administrative procedures increase the waiting period before a compulsory translation license could be granted. In particular, Article II(4)(a) states:

> No license obtainable after three years shall be granted . . . until a further period of six months has elapsed, and no license obtainable after one year shall be granted . . . until a further period of nine months has elapsed
>
> (i) from the date on which the applicant complies with the requirements in Article IV (1), or
> (ii) where the identity or the address of the owner of the right of translation is unknown, from the date on which the applicant sends, as provided for in Article IV (2), copies of his application submitted to the authority competent to grant the license.

Apart from the fact that translation of scientific and technical books and learning materials after these waiting periods may become meaningless,[174] the transaction

171 Olian Jr, above n 81, 108.
172 *Paris Act 1971* of the *Berne Convention*, Appendix, art IV(1).
173 Ibid., art IV(2).
174 The additional waiting periods stipulated in Article II(4)(a) of the Berne Appendix start to run after the expiry of the general waiting periods. Basalamah, above n 2, 515.

costs involved in fulfilling the cumbersome administrative requirements in the Berne Appendix are not insignificant.[175] Both these factors reduce the incentive to translate copyright protected scientific and technical books and learning materials under the compulsory licensing system in the Berne Appendix.

4.4.1.2.10. LICENSES FOR REPRODUCTION IN RESPECT OF TRANSLATIONS MADE UNDER LICENSES FOR TRANSLATION

Under the Berne Appendix, a license to reproduce and publish a translated work cannot be granted where the translation has not been published by the owner of the right of translation or with his authorisation, or where the translation is not in a language in general use in the country in which the license is applied for.[176] The effect of this is that 'translations made under compulsory licenses cannot be the subject of a [compulsory license] for reproduction.'[177] This means that a person in Sri Lanka cannot obtain a compulsory license to reproduce or publish a translated work in India which had been translated under a compulsory license. Given that Tamil is a language of general use in both these countries, it would be beneficial for Sri Lanka if it could reproduce or publish (under a reproduction license) Tamil translations of works that had already been made under compulsory translation licenses in India, rather than translating those works into Tamil all over again. However, since the Appendix does not allow this, Sri Lanka would have to apply for each of these licenses separately, which means not only 'going through the rigorous procedural requirements twice,[178] but incurring significant expenses for translation of the work all over again.[179]

4.4.1.2.11. BAN ON EXPORTATION OF COPIES

Article IV(4)(a) of the Berne Appendix states that no compulsory license granted under it 'shall extend to the export of copies, and any such license shall be valid only for publication of the translation or of the reproduction, as the case may be, in the territory of the country in which it has been applied for.' Thus, the Appendix sets a general rule prohibiting the export of copies made under compulsory licenses. However, it provides an exception to this, subject to certain conditions, where 'a governmental or other public entity of a country which has granted a compulsory license to make a translation . . . into a language other than English, French or Spanish sends copies of a translation published under such license to another country'.[180] Nonetheless, this exception is restrictive when compared with the provisions in the Stockholm Protocol

175 Okediji, above n 67.
176 *Paris Act 1971* of the *Berne Convention*, Appendix, art III5(i), (ii).
177 Strba, above n 137, 94.
178 Ibid.
179 Talagala and Wiseman, above n 160, 502.
180 *Paris Act 1971* of the *Berne Convention*, Appendix, art IV(4)(c).

with regard to the exportation of copies made under compulsory translation licenses. This is because the Protocol allowed translated works published under a compulsory license in one country to be imported and sold in another country of the Berne Union if one of the national, official or regional languages of the other country is the same as that into which the work had been translated. This is subject to the condition that the domestic law of that other country did not prohibit such importation and sale.[181]

4.4.1.2.12. THE AUTHORS' RIGHT TO JUST COMPENSATION

The Berne Appendix strengthens the authors' right to just compensation when compared with the Stockholm Protocol. In the Protocol, this right was subject to national currency regulations. However, the Appendix provides that 'if such regulations intervene the competent authority shall nevertheless "make all efforts, by the use of international machinery, to ensure transmittal in internationally convertible currency or its equivalent" '.[182]

In view of the foregoing reasons, especially the waiting periods and the administrative burdens for obtaining compulsory translation licenses, the compulsory licensing system in the Berne Appendix too does not address the most pressing need of the developing countries, that is, timely and affordable bulk access to translations of copyright protected scientific and technical books and learning materials published in developed countries.[183] Indeed, many scholars have identified the inadequacy and the inability of the Berne Appendix to effectively meet the needs and interests of the developing countries. For instance, Ricketson and Ginsburg observed that '[i]t is hard to point to any obvious benefits that have flowed directly to developing countries from the adoption of the Appendix.'[184]

Although the Berne Appendix does not offer any direct benefits to developing countries, Ricketson and Ginsburg have asserted that the Appendix 'can be seen as an incentive to the authors and publishers in the developed countries to co-operate in the making of voluntary licensing arrangements'.[185] This is because 'the

181 *Stockholm Act 1967* of the *Berne Convention*, Protocol Regarding Developing Countries, art 1(b)(v).

182 Olian Jr, above n 81, 108.

183 Okediji, above n 67.

184 Ricketson and Ginsburg, above n 24, vol 2, 957. See also Eva Hemmungs Wirten, above n 23, 66; Alberto Cerda Silva, 'Beyond the Unrealistic Solution for Development Provided by the Appendix of the *Berne Convention* on Copyright' (Research Paper 8/2012, PIJIP, 2012) 51 <http://digitalcommons.wcl.american.edu/research/30/>; Margaret Chon, 'Intellectual Property "from Below": Copyright and Capability for Education' (2007) 40 *University of California, Davis Law Review* 803, 835; Okediji, above n 67; Laurence R Helfer and Graeme W Austin, *Human Rights and Intellectual Property: Mapping the Global Interface* (Cambridge University Press, 2011) 341.

185 Ricketson and Ginsburg, above n 24, vol 2, 958.

compulsory licenses remain in the background both as a reminder of the needs of developing countries and as a threat to be brought into operation if there is a reluctance to [cooperate]'.[186] It is to be noted that even if this assertion was accepted, it would be confined only to theory. This is because, as Strba pointed out, the 'procedural requirements in the Appendix shield copyright holders by discouraging the [potential] applicants for [compulsory licenses],' and '[t]he rights holders know this so they do not have incentive to cooperate'.[187] Thus, in practice, the authors and publishers in developed countries 'do not feel threatened' by the existence of the Appendix 'and thus they do not feel "coerced" to cooperate' with developing countries in the making of voluntary licensing arrangements for translation.[188]

Be that as it may, many developing countries, including Sri Lanka, have not made use of the faculties provided in the Berne Appendix in their domestic copyright laws. Some of these countries have not even ratified the Berne Appendix, while others have either ratified it very late or the relevant provisions are yet to be implemented into domestic law. For instance, though Sri Lanka ratified Articles 1 to 21 of the *Paris Act 1971* and the Berne Appendix in 2005, its initial ratification of the *Paris Act* in 1978 excluded these provisions.

Some scholars have argued that the reason for many developing countries not making use of the faculties provided in the Berne Appendix is a consequence of the unworkability of the mechanisms provided in it.[189] While there may be some truth in this assertion, nevertheless, it is unlikely that this situation alone has persuaded developing countries to take such an approach. This is because a number of developing countries, including Sri Lanka, have in fact ratified the Appendix even though these ratifications may have come later. Although the Appendix has certain drawbacks with regard to meeting the compelling needs of developing countries, it contains certain provisions which these countries can still use to at least make their domestic copyright laws more flexible and user friendly for translation than they are now. In these circumstances, the failure to make use of the provisions in the Appendix appears rather to be a result of a lack of knowledge or ignorance of many developing countries as far as copyright law related issues are concerned. In fact, the WIPO's involvement in the making of the WIPO model of copyright law in the *IP Code* of Sri Lanka supports this suggestion.

4.4.2. WIPO's involvement in making of the WIPO model of copyright

The involvement of the WIPO in making the WIPO model of copyright law was the main reason why Sri Lanka blindly followed the provisions of the *WIPO*

186 Ibid., (citations omitted).
187 Strba, above n 137, 97.
188 Ibid.
189 See, e.g., Silva, above n 184; Chon, above n 184.

Model Law on Copyright for Developing Countries in the copyright regime of the *IP Code*. As the *WIPO Model Law on Copyright for Developing Countries* was based on the *Berne Convention* as revised by the *Paris Act 1971*, the manner in which it seeks to protect copyright owners' translation rights is equivalent to the way in which the *Berne Convention* requires Member Countries to protect these rights.

Although Sri Lanka wanted to enact a new copyright regime in the late 1970s to suit the needs of the country, particularly by removing the old British model of copyright law, the new copyright regime had to comply with Sri Lanka's obligations under the *Berne Convention*. However, when embarking on a new copyright regime (which needed to be compatible with the *Berne Convention*) Sri Lanka had to face a major challenge. That was a lack of expertise and technical knowledge in Sri Lanka to draft a suitable copyright law which would also be compatible with the *Berne Convention*. It was against this background that Sri Lanka sought the assistance of WIPO.

WIPO is the main provider of technical assistance to developing countries in the field of intellectual property (including copyright).[190] Through its secretariat, WIPO 'provides technical assistance to developing countries in the areas of legislative advice, human resource development and training, institutional development and automation, and enforcement.'[191] However, as Strba argued, 'WIPO's role is not to promote the needs of developing countries, but the protection and enforcement of intellectual property rights.'[192] Therefore, the technical assistance offered by WIPO to developing countries like Sri Lanka can be seen as a means of incorporating stricter protection standards in the international intellectual property conventions such as the *Berne Convention* into domestic laws of these countries.[193] The adoption of the *WIPO Model Law on Copyright for Developing Countries* in the copyright regime of the *IP Code* is a good example.

The *WIPO Model Law on Copyright for Developing Countries* is a model law jointly formulated in 1976 by the WIPO and UNESCO.[194] It was adopted in 1976 by the Committee of Governmental Experts convened by the Tunisian Government in Tunis with the assistance of the WIPO and UNESCO.[195] The *WIPO Model Law on Copyright for Developing Countries* is fully compliant with the *Berne Convention* as revised by the *Paris Act 1971*.[196] When Sri Lanka sought the assistance of the WIPO to formulate a new copyright regime in the *IP Code*, the WIPO provided Sri Lanka with the *WIPO Model Law on Copyright for Developing*

190 Strba, above n 137, 182.

191 Ibid.

192 Ibid., 98.

193 Ibid.

194 See, e.g., Indunil Nirupadi Abeyesekere, *Sri Lankan Copyright Law and the TRIPS Agreement* (Mahapola Publications, 1999) 4.

195 UNESCO and WIPO, 'Tunis Model Law on Copyright for Developing Countries' (1976) 3.

196 Ibid., Indunil Nirupadi Abeyesekere, above n 194, 4.

Countries as a guide to follow. Ultimately, Sri Lanka virtually copied the provisions of the *WIPO Model Law on Copyright for Developing Countries* in the new copyright regime in the *IP Code*.

The way in which copyright owners' translation rights are protected in the *WIPO Model Law on Copyright for Developing Countries* is inimical to the timely and affordable translation of copyright protected scientific and technical works published in developed countries. According to Section 4 of this Model Law, 'the author of a protected work has the exclusive right' to 'make a translation' of that work. This right extends to a period of the 'life of the author and [50] years after his death'.[197] Section 7, which deals with fair use, provides exceptions to this exclusive right. Accordingly, this section allows translation of a work without the author's consent for limited purposes, such as the user's own personal and private use, quotations that are compatible with fair practice, or illustrations for teaching to the extent justified by the purpose. Although, Section 9 of the *WIPO Model Law on Copyright for Developing Countries* provides for a system of compulsory licenses for translation, it is severely restricted by the same cumbersome conditions that exist in the system of compulsory licenses for translation in the Berne Appendix.[198]

The *IP Code* blindly followed the *WIPO Model Law on Copyright for Developing Countries* when protecting translation rights. The only exception to this was Section 15 of the *IP Code*. Apart from this, the *IP Code* did not provide for compulsory translation licenses.

Although Sections 10 and 13 of the *IP Code* corresponded respectively to Sections 4 and 7 of the *WIPO Model Law on Copyright for Developing Countries*, Section 15 of the *IP Code* was in clear conflict with the provisions of the *WIPO Model Law on Copyright for Developing Countries*. This was because the *WIPO Model Law on Copyright for Developing Countries* does not provide for a means of limiting the duration of translation rights when translations of copyright protected works are not published in local languages within a specified period. In contrast, the only special exception to translation rights under the *WIPO Model Law on Copyright for Developing Countries* is the compulsory translation licenses provided under Section 9.[199] Be that as it may, the discrepancy between the *WIPO Model Law on Copyright for Developing Countries* and the *IP Code* caused by Section 15 of the *IP Code* (which is an innovative step on the part of the Sri Lankan Parliament) has virtually gone undetected. Even UNESCO, which was a party to the formulation of the *WIPO Model Law on Copyright for Developing Countries*, in its 'Comparative Study of the Copyright Laws in force in the States of Asia and Pacific Region in relation to Tunis Model Law on Copyright for Developing Countries', has listed Sri Lanka as one of the countries which has provisions in its copyright law for 'compulsory non-exclusive license for translation' by specifically

197 *Tunis (WIPO) Model Law on Copyright for Developing Countries 1976*, s 13.
198 Ibid., Appendix A.
199 Ibid.

referring to Section 15 of the *IP Code.*[200] As such, more often than not the copyright regime in the *IP Code* has been identified as being compliant with the *WIPO Model Law on Copyright for Developing Countries.*

Although Section 9 of the *WIPO Model Law on Copyright for Developing Countries* provided for a system of compulsory licensing for translation of copyright protected works, the *IP Code* did not provide for such a system. The reason for this was that when Sri Lanka ratified the *Paris Act 1971* of the *Berne Convention* in 1978, it excluded the Berne Appendix.[201] As a result, Sri Lanka could not make provision for the grant of compulsory licenses for translation in the *IP Code* as provided in the Berne Appendix and the *WIPO Model Law on Copyright for Developing Countries.* At the same time, Sri Lanka was also not allowed to limit the duration of copyright owners' translation rights for ten years because of this exclusion. As such, Section 15 of the *IP Code* was in breach of Sri Lanka's obligations under the *Berne Convention.* In these circumstances, it is quite pertinent to ask why Sri Lanka excluded the Berne Appendix when it ratified the *Paris Act 1971.* In the absence of any policy-based reason for such exclusion, the only plausible answer to this question is the lack of knowledge or ignorance on the part of Sri Lanka.

200 UNESCO, 'Copyright Training Course for Nationals of Asian and Pacific States, Comparative Study of Copyright Laws in Force in the States of Asia and Pacific Region in relation to Tunis Model Law on Copyright for Developing Countries' (Paris, 15 September 1982) 33.

201 When Sri Lanka deposited its instrument of ratification of the *Berne Convention* as revised by the *Paris Act 1971* on 20 June 1978 it declared that the ratification shall not apply to Article 1 to 21 and the Appendix. WIPO, *WIPO Administered Treaties—Notifications—Berne Convention*, Berne Notification No 92 <www.wipo.int/treaties/en/notifications/berne/treaty_berne_92.html>.

V TRIPS model of copyright law and translation [2003–2020]

5.1. Introduction

Sri Lanka entered the third stage of the history of copyright law in 2003 when it enacted the *Intellectual Property Act 2003*. Part II of the *Intellectual Property Act* introduced a new copyright regime which is compliant with the provisions of the *TRIPS Agreement*.[1]

The TRIPS model of copyright law contained in the *Intellectual Property Act 2003* is inimical to timely and affordable translation. The aim of this chapter is to examine the reason why Sri Lanka enacted the TRIPS model of copyright law. As demonstrated in this chapter, Sri Lanka enacted the TRIPS model of copyright law largely because of its trade and investment concerns. Apart from this, Sri Lanka's lack of awareness and transparency, as well as its ignorance with regard to copyright law, has also contributed to enacting the TRIPS model of copyright law.

5.2. The TRIPS model of copyright law

The TRIPS Model of Copyright law, which is currently in force, is the second domestic copyright regime in independent Sri Lanka. Although this regime was enacted to give effect to Sri Lanka's obligations under the *TRIPS Agreement*, the framers of the regime also sought to promote Sri Lanka's interests and needs.[2] While moving the second reading of the Intellectual Property Bill 2003 in Parliament, Minister Karunanayake said that '[i]t is only for Sri Lanka's sake that [the government is] bringing this [law]'.[3] It was also believed that the TRIPS model of copyright law would assist Sri Lanka 'to move forward in [the] knowledge based economy'.[4] Yet when we look at the stringent and unbalanced manner in

1 DM Karunaratna, *Elements of the Law of Intellectual Property in Sri Lanka* (Sarasavi Publishers, 2010) 19, n 10.
2 DM Karunaratna, *An Introduction to the Law of Copyright and Related Rights in Sri Lanka* (Sarvodaya Vishva Lekha Publication, 2006) 7.
3 Sri Lanka, *Parliamentary Debates*, 23 July 2003, col 1051.
4 Ibid., col 1047.

which copyright owners' translation rights are protected under the TRIPS model of copyright law, it is highly doubtful whether this copyright regime truly reflects the interests and needs of Sri Lanka and whether it supports Sri Lanka to move forward in the knowledge economy.

As observed in chapter 2, the way in which copyright owners' translation rights are protected in the TRIPS model of copyright law constrains the timely and affordable translation of copyright protected scientific and technical books and learning materials. Timely and affordable translation of these knowledge products is necessary for Sri Lanka to move forward in the knowledge-based economy. Since the stringent and unbalanced way in which copyright owners' translation rights are protected in the TRIPS model of copyright law was discussed in detail in chapter 2, that discussion will not be repeated here. However, it is important to note that of all the copyright regimes that have been enacted in Sri Lanka, the TRIPS model of copyright law is the one which is most hostile to translation of copyright protected works.

There are two main reasons why the TRIPS model of copyright law is the most hostile copyright regime for translation of copyright protected works. Firstly, the general exceptions to copyright owners' translation rights in the previous copyright regimes, namely, the *Copyright Ordinance 1908*, *Imperial Copyright Act 1911* and the *Code of Intellectual Property Act 1979* (*IP Code*), were more clearly and broadly articulated than in the TRIPS model of copyright law. This was particularly so in regard to the private use exception. The way in which general exceptions to translation rights had been articulated in the previous copyright regimes also appears to have given more discretion to the courts to apply those exceptions in a manner that would promote translation. Secondly, all the previous copyright regimes, except the *Imperial Copyright Act 1911* had special exceptions to copyright owners' translation rights. In contrast, the TRIPS model of copyright law does not provide for any special exception to translation rights.[5]

5.2.1. *Scope of the general exceptions*

The liberty of a person to translate copyright protected works for his or her personal use was more clearly and broadly articulated in the *Copyright Ordinance 1908*, *Imperial Copyright Act 1911* and the *IP Code*. The *Copyright Ordinance* clearly stated that '[c]opyright in a book shall not be infringed by a person making an abridgement or translation of the book for his private use (unless he uses it publicly or allows it to be used publicly by some other person)'.[6] While the *Imperial Copyright Act* did not specifically declare an exception for translation of copyright protected works for private use, it did, however, provide that '[a]ny fair dealing

5 *Intellectual Property Act No 36 of 2003* (Sri Lanka) s 13(1); *Code of Intellectual Property Act No 52 of 1979* (Sri Lanka) s 19(1); *Copyright Act 1911*, 1 & 2 Geo 5, c 46, s 3; *Copyright Ordinance No 12 of 1908* (Sri Lanka) s 12.

6 *Copyright Ordinance No 12 of 1908* (Sri Lanka) s 23.

with any work for the purposes of private study [or] research' 'shall not constitute an infringement of copyright'.[7] The *IP Code* was more specific than the *Imperial Copyright Act* with regard to the liberty of a person to translate a copyright protected work for personal use. In particular, it stated that 'the reproduction, translation, adaptation, arrangement or other transformation of [a] work exclusively for the user's own personal and private use' 'shall be permissible without the author's consent'.[8]

In contrast to the position under previous copyright regimes, the TRIPS model of copyright law restrictively articulates the liberty of a person to translate copyright protected works for private use. In particular, the fair use exception provided in Section 11 of the *Intellectual Property Act 2003* does not explicitly refer to private use or private study.[9] In addition, the specific acts of fair use stipulated in Section 12 of the *Act* do not expressly refer to translation.[10] Although it may be assumed that fair use may cover a situation where people translate copyright protected works for their private use, the conditions attached to the specific act of fair use in the *Act* which allows 'private reproduction of a published work' make this assumption highly questionable. More specifically, Section 12(1) of the *Intellectual Property Act* states:

> [T]he private reproduction of a published work in a single copy shall be permitted without the authorisation of the owner of the copyright, where the reproduction is made by a physical person from a lawful copy of such work exclusively for his own personal purposes.

However, 'private reproduction of a published work' allowed by Section 12(1) of the *Intellectual Property Act 2003* is severely curtailed by Section 12(2) which states, inter alia, that the permission under Section 12(1) 'shall not extend to the reproduction' 'in the form of reprography of the whole or a substantial part of a book' or, 'of any work, in the case of the reproduction [which] would conflict with a normal exploitation of the work or would otherwise unreasonably prejudice the legitimate interests of the owner of the copyright.'[11] Against this background, it is unlikely that the TRIPS model of copyright law would allow translation of a whole book or a substantial part of a book for personal or private use. The TRIPS model of copyright law is also unlikely to allow translation of a copyright protected work where such translation unreasonably prejudices 'the legitimate interests of the owner of the copyright.'

The way in which general exceptions to translation rights were articulated in the *Copyright Ordinance 1908, Imperial Copyright Act 1911* and the *IP Code*

7 *Copyright Act 1911*, 1 & 2 Geo 5, c 46, s 2.
8 *Code of Intellectual Property Act No 52 of 1979* (Sri Lanka) s 13.
9 *Intellectual Property Act No 36 of 2003* (Sri Lanka) s 11.
10 Ibid., s 12.
11 Ibid., s 12(2)(b), (e).

gave more discretion to the courts when applying those exceptions to promote translation. In particular, the *Copyright Ordinance* and the *Imperial Copyright Act* permitted translation of copyright protected works (without the copyright owners' consent) for certain purposes, provided that such translation constituted 'fair dealing'.[12] However, both these statutes did not define what was meant by fair dealing or stipulate guidelines, mandatory or otherwise, that the courts should/may follow when deciding the question of whether the particular dealing was fair. As a result, the courts had discretion to decide this question in a manner which promoted the interests and needs of the country, i.e. timely and affordable translation. Similarly, courts could also exercise a certain amount of discretion when applying the permitted uses that were loosely enumerated in Section 13 of the *IP Code* in relation to translation of copyright protected works.

It seems that the TRIPS model of copyright law restricts the discretion of courts when applying fair use to permit the translation of copyright protected works. This is because Section 11(1) in the *Intellectual Property Act 2003* makes it obligatory for the courts to consider the four factors stipulated in Section 11(2) when determining whether or not a translation of a copyright protected work is a fair use.[13]

The specific acts of fair use enumerated in Section 12 of the *Intellectual Property Act 2003*, moreover, seem to restrict the courts' discretion in interpreting and applying the fair use exception. For instance, according to Section 11(1) of the Act, fair reproduction of a copyright protected work (without the consent of its copyright owner) for teaching, including the making of multiples copies for classroom use, is permitted. However, the specific acts of fair use under Section 12 restrict this permission. In particular, Section 12(4) in the *Act* states that only 'the reproduction of a short part of a published work for teaching purposes by way of illustration, in writing or visual recording' is permitted.[14] Moreover, the reprographic reproduction is only permitted in respect of published articles, other short works or short extracts of works' subject to the conditions that reproduction should be only for face-to-face teaching in any educational institution, the activities of which do not serve direct or indirect commercial gain; reproduction should be 'to the extent justified by the purpose'; and, the act of such reproduction should be 'an isolated one occurring, if repeated, on separate and unrelated occasions'.[15]

Hence, it seems possible that specific acts of fair use in the *Intellectual Property Act 2003* may persuade the courts to place limits on the broad scope of the fair use exception in the *Act*. Although the specific acts of fair use in Section 12 of the

12 *Copyright Ordinance No 12 of 1908* (Sri Lanka) s 23; *Copyright Act 1911*, 1 & 2 Geo 5, c 46, s 2(1)(i); *Code of Intellectual Property Act No 52 of 1979* (Sri Lanka) s 13. *Intellectual Property Act No 36 of 2003* (Sri Lanka) s 11.

13 Karunaratna, above n 2, 80.

14 *Intellectual Property Act No 36 of 2003* (Sri Lanka) s 12(4)(a).

15 Ibid., s 12(4)(b).

Intellectual Property Act do not specifically cover translation, by analogy they may encourage the courts to place limits on the scope of the fair use exception when applied in relation to translation of copyright protected works.

5.2.2. *Special exceptions*

The TRIPS model of copyright law does not provide for special exceptions to copyright owners' translation rights. With the exception of the *Imperial Copyright Act 1911*, all of the previous copyright regimes in Sri Lanka recognised special exceptions to translation rights. For instance, the *Copyright Ordinance 1908* provided for a compulsory licensing system in respect of translation of books.[16] Section 15 of the *IP Code* provided for a special exception which enabled a person to translate freely a work into Sinhala and Tamil languages in the event such work had not been published in those languages within a period of ten years from its first publication.[17]

5.3. Trade and investment concerns: the primary reason for the TRIPS model of copyright law

The primary reason for Sri Lanka to enact the TRIPS model of copyright law, which is inimical to timely and affordable translation, was the trade and investment concerns of Sri Lanka. Because of trade and investment concerns, Sri Lanka entered into the *TRIPS Agreement* and a bilateral treaty on copyright with the United States.[18] Also, immediately preceding the enactment of the TRIPS model of copyright law, Sri Lanka was negotiating a Free Trade Agreement (FTA) with the United States to promote its exports to the United States market. All these initiatives, i.e. the *TRIPS Agreement*, bilateral treaty on copyright with the United States and the proposed FTA with the United States, required Sri Lanka to enact the TRIPS model of copyright law.

To reap the benefits of international trade, Sri Lanka had to become a member to the World Trade Organisation (WTO) in 1995, which required it to undertake the obligations of the *TRIPS Agreement*. The *TRIPS Agreement*, which advocates high standards of copyright protection (including translation rights) in the *Paris Act 1971* of the *Berne Convention*, requires all Member Countries effectively to implement these standards in their national copyright regimes.[19] Thus, Sri Lanka enacted the TRIPS model of copyright law in the *Intellectual Property Act 2003*, incorporating high standards of copyright protection (including translation rights) in the *Paris Act 1971* of the *Berne Convention*.

16 *Copyright Ordinance No 12 of 1908* (Sri Lanka) s 25.
17 *Code of Intellectual Property Act No 52 of 1979* (Sri Lanka) s 15.
18 *Agreement on the Protection and Enforcement of Intellectual Property Rights between the United States of America and the Democratic Socialist Republic of Sri Lanka 1991*.
19 Frederick M Abbott, 'The WTO TRIPS Agreement and Global Economic Development' (1996) 72 *Chicago-Kent Law Review* 385, 385.

However, at the time Sri Lanka was seeking to meet its *TRIPS* obligations, it was already under similar copyright obligations to protect the copyright owners' translation rights by virtue of a bilateral treaty entered into with the United States, that is, the *Agreement on the Protection and Enforcement of Intellectual Property Rights between the United States of America and the Democratic Socialist Republic of Sri Lanka 1991* (*US-Sri Lanka IPR Agreement*).[20] The *US-Sri Lanka IPR Agreement* is an outcome of Sri Lanka's trade and investment concerns. From the perspective of United States, it was also an interim and auxiliary measure which aided the conclusion of the *TRIPS Agreement*. Be that as it may, since the *US-Sri Lanka IPR Agreement* remained alive at the time of enactment of the *Intellectual Property Act 2003*, Sri Lanka had to give effect to the obligations under the *US-Sri Lanka IPR Agreement* in the copyright regime of the *Intellectual Property Act 2003*.[21]

On the eve of the enactment of the *Intellectual Property Act 2003*, Sri Lanka was looking to improve its trade relations with the United States to further Sri Lanka's foreign exports (particularly textile and garments) to the United States. This required Sri Lanka to explore the possibilities of concluding a FTA with the United States. It is accepted that FTAs are a means by which the United States set high standards of copyright protection, often beyond the *TRIPS* obligations (commonly referred to as TRIPS-plus standards), in foreign countries.[22] In particular, FTAs with the United States require the other parties to set TRIPS-plus standards in their copyright regimes. As such, the copyright regime in the *Intellectual Property Act* had to adopt high standards of copyright protection which included TRIPS-plus standards as a prerequisite for Sri Lanka to conclude a FTA with the United States.

5.3.1. The TRIPS Agreement

The stringent and unbalanced manner in which copyright owners' translation rights are protected in the *Intellectual Property Act 2003* is primarily an outcome of the fact that the *Act* is compliant with the *TRIPS Agreement*. The *TRIPS Agreement* is the most striking and controversial multilateral instrument that has ever been designed to protect intellectual property rights.[23] With regard to copy-

20 *Agreement on the Protection and Enforcement of Intellectual Property Rights between the United States of America and the Democratic Socialist Republic of Sri Lanka 1991*.

21 Karunaratna, above n 2, 8.

22 See especially Jakkrit Kuanpoth, 'Intellectual Property Protection after TRIPS: An Asian Experience' in Justin Malbon and Charles Lawson (eds), *Interpreting and Implementing the TRIPS Agreement: Is it Fair?* (Edward Elgar, 2008) 71.

23 Peter Drahos and John Braithwaite, *Information Feudalism: Who Owns the Knowledge Economy* (EARTHSCAN, 2002) 10; Jagdish Bhagwati, *In Defence of Globalisation* (Oxford University Press, 2004) 183; Aravind Panagariya, 'TRIPs and the WTO: An Uneasy Marriage' in Keith E Maskus (ed), *The WTO, Intellectual Property Rights and the Knowledge Economy* (Edward Elgar, 2004) 91, 91; UNDP, *Making Global Trade Work for People* (EARTHSCAN, 2003) 221; Laurence R. Helfer, 'Regime Shifting: The TRIPs Agreement

right, it extends and reinforces 'the highest level of international legal protection for copyright' (including translation rights) provided in the *Berne Convention*.[24]

Because Sri Lanka became a member to the WTO with the objective of fostering the country's trade interests, it also had to become a member to the *TRIPS Agreement*. Accordingly, the *TRIPS Agreement* imposed a further obligation on Sri Lanka (in addition to its obligations as a *Berne* member) to implement the *Berne Convention*'s standards (that advocate protection of translation rights at a higher level) into the *Intellectual Property Act 2003*.

5.3.1.1. The birth of TRIPS

The *TRIPS Agreement* is primarily a response to the inadequacies of the then existing multilateral arrangements for the protection of intellectual property rights such as the *Berne Convention* and the *Paris Convention for the Protection of Industrial Property 1883* (*Paris Convention*).[25] The *TRIPS Agreement* is an initiative of developed countries, particularly the United States, the European Union and Japan, which are net exporters of intellectual property products (including copyright protected knowledge products) to the developing world.[26]

Matthews argued that multinational companies (domiciled in developed countries) played an important role in persuading the United States, the European Union and Japan to initiate the *TRIPS Agreement*. In particular, these multinational companies that sought to secure 'trade regulation capable of protecting [their] global commercial interests to an extent not previously witnessed in relation to international protection of intellectual property rights' instigated the process which culminated in the *TRIPS Agreement* and then linked that process to government action that emerged 'most visibly in the United States . . . Europe and Japan'.[27]

Prior to the *TRIPS Agreement*, 'the protection of intellectual property rights in the international domain was perceived to be primarily a matter for the World Intellectual Property Organisation (WIPO)'.[28] In particular, from its establishment in 1967, WIPO has been responsible for the administration of the *Berne Convention* and the *Paris Convention*. However, neither these conventions nor the actions of the WIPO were effective in combating the 'growing trade in pirated

---

and New Dynamics of International Intellectual Property Lawmaking' (2004) 29(1) *The Yale Journal of International Law* 1, 3.

24 See Akhil Prasad and Aditi Agrawala, *Copyright Law Desk Book: Knowledge Access and Development* (Universal Law Publishing, 2009) 154–155.

25 See, e.g., YiJun Tian, *Re-Thinking Intellectual Property: The Political Economy of Copyright Protection in the Digital Era* (Routledge-Cavendish, 2009) 27–28.

26 See Eric H Smith, 'Worldwide Copyright Protection under the TRIPS Agreement' (1996) 29 *Vanderbilt Journal of Transnational Law* 559, 560.

27 Duncan Matthews, *Globalising Intellectual Property Rights: The TRIPs Agreement* (Routledge, 2002) 1.

28 Michael Blakeney, 'Intellectual Property in World Trade' (1995) 1(3) *International Trade Law & Regulation* 76, 76.

and counterfeited products' which became clearly apparent from the 1970s.[29] In particular, as Blakeney observed, '[f]rom the late 1970s there had been increasingly strident complaints, expressed primarily by [developed] countries, about the growth in the pirating of copyrighted works'.[30] Notably, most of the pirating happened in developing countries.[31]

From a critical point of view of the *Berne Convention*, there were three main reasons for the *Convention*'s ineffectiveness in combatting the increasing levels of piracy of copyright protected works in developing countries. They were: (1) the absence of a meaningful dispute settlement mechanism in the *Convention* that would ensure Member Countries' compliance with the *Berne* obligations, (2) the lack of effective measures in the *Convention* to enforce the *Berne* obligations at the national level and (3) the territorial coverage of the *Convention*.

5.3.1.1.1. ABSENCE OF A MEANINGFUL DISPUTE SETTLEMENT MECHANISM

The absence of a meaningful dispute settlement mechanism is one of the drawbacks of the *Berne Convention*. A meaningful dispute settlement mechanism is essential for an international convention to ensure that Member Countries comply with its obligations. When an international convention has a meaningful dispute settlement in place, each Member Country can effectively watch over the others to make sure that the convention's obligations are complied with by all members and seek definite action in the case of non-compliance. Notably, the *Berne Convention* lacks such a meaningful dispute settlement mechanism.

Although the *Berne Convention* has a dispute settlement mechanism where Member Countries can challenge each other's non-compliance with copyright protection standards in the *Convention*, this dispute settlement mechanism is so ineffective as to be 'virtually non-existent'.[32]

Under Article 33(1) of the *Berne Convention*, any dispute between Member Countries concerning the interpretation or application of the *Convention* (not settled by negotiation) can be brought before the International Court of Justice (ICJ) unless 'the countries concerned agree on some other method of settlement'.[33] However, Article 33(2) renders this provision ineffectual in the event a Member Country makes a declaration to avoid its application. In particular, Article 33(2) states:

> Each country may, at the time it signs [the Convention] or deposits its instrument of ratification or accession, declare that it does not consider

29 Ibid.

30 Ibid.

31 See Carolyn Deere, *The Implementation Game: The TRIPS Agreement and the Global Politics of Intellectual Property Reform in Developing Countries* (Oxford University Press, 2009) 46.

32 Laurence R Helfer, 'Adjudicating Copyright Claims Under the TRIPs Agreement: The Case for a European Human Rights Analogy' (1998) 38(2) *Harvard International Law Journal* 357, 375.

33 *Paris Act 1971* of the *Berne Convention*, art 33(1).

> itself bound by the provisions of [Article 33(1)]. With regard to any dispute between such country and any other country of the Union, the provisions of [Article 33(1)] shall not apply.[34]

Apart from this, as Evans observed, there is a lack of international acceptance of the dispute settlement mechanism in the *Berne Convention* particularly, because '[a]s a matter of politics, states [have] tended to avoid any form of third party adjudication that deprives them of their sovereign power of decision making' in 'matters of [copyright] where sensitive issues of national policy are likely to be involved'.[35] As a result, 'no case has ever been brought to the ICJ under this [dispute settlement] mechanism'.[36] In addition, the WIPO which administers the *Berne Convention* 'has been equally ineffective in settling disputes' with regard to non-compliance with the *Convention*'s obligations.[37]

An outcome of the absence of a meaningful dispute settlement mechanism in the *Berne Convention* was that it enabled Member Countries to deviate from the *Convention*'s rules to promote their national interests.[38] The special exception under Section 15 of the *IP Code* of Sri Lanka which enabled a person to freely translate a work into Sinhala and Tamil languages in the event such work had not been published in those languages within a period of ten years from its first publication was an example of this.[39]

As mentioned in the previous chapter, Section 15 of the *IP Code* violated Sri Lanka's obligations under the *Berne Convention*. The reason for this was that Sri Lanka had not made use of the special exceptions in the Appendix of the *Paris Act 1971 of the Berne Convention* by the time it enacted the IP Code. In particular, while the Appendix of the *Paris Act 1971* of the *Berne Convention* (which provided for special exceptions to translation rights in the case of developing countries) permitted a developing country to substitute for Article 8 of the *Paris Act 1971* 'the provisions of Article 5 of the [*Berne Convention 1886*] as completed at Paris in 1896, on the clear understanding that the said provisions are applicable only into translations into a language in general use in the said country',[40] when *IP Code* was enacted—Sri Lanka was not a country that had ratified the Appendix. Therefore, at the time the *IP Code* was enacted, Sri Lanka's obligations under the *Berne Convention* did not allow it to make provision for the special exception to translation rights that was envisaged in Section 15.

34 Ibid., art 33(2).
35 Gail E Evans, *Lawmaking under the Trade Constitution: A Study in Legislating by the World Trade Organization* (Kluwer Law International, 2000) 168.
36 Helfer, above n 32, 376.
37 Ibid.
38 See L Danielle Tully, 'Prospects for Progress: The TRIPS Agreement and Developing Countries after the Doha Conference' (2003) 26 *Boston College International & Comparative Law Review* 129, 136.
39 *Code of Intellectual Property Act No 52 of 1979* (Sri Lanka) s 15.
40 *Paris Act* of the *Berne Convention*, art 30(2)(b) read together with Appendix, arts I, V(1)(a).

5.3.1.1.2. LACK OF ADEQUATE ENFORCEMENT MEASURES

Another fundamental defect of the *Berne Convention* is the lack of adequate enforcement measures. In particular, although the *Berne Convention* requires Member Countries to adhere to high standards of copyright protection, it does not provide adequate measures to enforce these standards in the national copyright regimes of these countries.[41] During the pre-TRIPS era, this enabled a vast amount of copyright breaches to go unheeded in Member Countries to the *Berne Convention*.[42]

5.3.1.1.3. TERRITORIAL COVERAGE

The territorial coverage of the *Berne Convention* was another issue which had an impact on the growth in the pirating of copyright protected works.[43] For instance, prior to the *TRIPS Agreement*, the countries which were contracting parties to the *Berne Convention* did not exceed 100.[44] Thus, a significant number of countries opted to stay away from the *Berne Convention*. In the absence of other international copyright arrangements (such as the *UCC* or bilateral agreements) which applied to these countries and required them to protect copyright, there were ample opportunities for the pirating of copyright protected works in their territories.[45]

Large-scale copyright infringement in developing countries (including those which were members to the *Berne Convention*) became a major concern of developed countries particularly because it affected the interests of their copyright exporting businesses.[46] To remedy this, the *Berne Convention* needed to be strengthened particularly with a meaningful dispute settlement mechanism, strong enforcement measures and by increasing the territorial coverage of the *Convention*. However, the experience of the developed countries at the Stockholm and Paris Conferences for the revision of the *Berne Convention* indicated that further revisions to strengthen the *Convention* particularly through incorporating a meaningful dispute settlement mechanism and strong enforcem ent measures were improbable.[47] In fact, this indication was proved to be correct

41 Tian, above n 25, 25–26.

42 See, e.g., CBS, 'US Trade Policy: Copyright Infringement and the GATT' (Report, June 1986); Edgardo Buscaglia and Clarisa Long, *US Foreign Policy and Intellectual Property Rights in Latin America* (Hoover Institution, 1997) 11.

43 See Terence P Stewart (ed), *The GATT Uruguay Round: A Negotiating History (1986–1994)* (Kluwer Law International, 1999) vol 4, 539.

44 Christopher May, *A Global Political Economy of Intellectual Property Rights: The New Enclosures?* (Routledge, 2000) 68.

45 See Jane C Ginsburg and Edouard Treppoz, *International Copyright Law: US and EU Perspectives: Text and Cases* (Edward Elgar, 2015) 43, n 3.

46 These business entities were the primary exporters of copyright protected works to the developing world.

47 Sam Ricketson and Jane Ginsburg, *International Copyright and Neighbouring Rights: The Berne Convention and Beyond* (Oxford University Press, 2nd ed, 2006) vol 1, v.

by the breakdown of negotiations to revise the *Paris Convention* in Geneva in 1984 and the failure of 'attempts to introduce common dispute settlement provisions to cover all WIPO treaties'.[48] Matthews observed that '[f]rom the perspective of developed countries, 1984 marked a realisation that they had failed in their attempts to strengthen the enforcement mechanism of the Paris and Berne conventions'.[49]

Having realised that it was impracticable to revise the *Berne* and *Paris Conventions* to suit the interests of business entities in developed countries and also the 'impotence' of the WIPO 'to deal with burgeoning trade in infringing products',[50] developed countries began to 'turn away from consensus led WIPO initiatives to ensure international protection for intellectual property rights'.[51] The alternative course of action was to link trade with the protection of intellectual property rights through a twofold strategy involving bilateral and multilateral initiatives. Firstly, the developed countries, particularly the United States, started to use 'bilateral measures designed to ensure protection of [their] technology-based export markets' to create a 'linkage between trade and intellectual property'.[52] Secondly, developing countries led by the United States sought to link protection of intellectual property rights with a multilateral trade system particularly by bringing the protection of these rights within the framework of the *General Agreement on Tariffs and Trade 1947* (*GATT*). One main reason for this, as Helfer has noted, was that these countries 'perceived GATT's dispute settlement system as relatively effective in maintaining a stable trade regime and believed that it would be more suitable forum for adjudicating IPR disputes'.[53] Also, decision making with regard to protection of intellectual property at the *GATT* forum was more favourable for developed countries since it was 'economic power-based' in contrast to the WIPO forum with 'one-nation, one-vote decision making'.[54] Furthermore, by linking the protection of intellectual property rights to the *GATT* framework it was possible for the developed countries to establish a comprehensive set of intellectual property protection standards at the global level and get the adherence of a large part of the world (Member Countries to *GATT*) to those standards.[55]

The last phase of the Uruguay Round (the eighth round of multilateral trade negotiations conducted within the framework of *GATT* during 1986–1994) provided a suitable platform for the developed countries to effectively move forward

48 Matthews, above n 27, 12.
49 Ibid.
50 Blakeney, above n 28, 76.
51 Matthews, above n 27, 12.
52 Ibid.
53 Helfer, above n 32, 377.
54 Michael P Ryan, *Knowledge Diplomacy: Global Competition and the Politics of Intellectual Property* (Brookings Institution Press, 1988) 12.
55 Anna Lanoszka, 'The Global Politics of Intellectual Property Rights and Pharmaceutical Drug Policies in Developing Countries' (2003) 24(2) *International Political Science Review* 181, 186; May, above n 44, 68.

their agenda to link protection of intellectual property rights to world trade.[56] As will be seen later, the role played by United States here was crucial. Accordingly, the outcome of the Uruguay Round was a triumph for developed countries and their intellectual property exporting business entities that wanted to enforce intellectual property rights in the developing world through linking these rights to the world trade system.[57] In particular, this linkage was made by bringing the *TRIPS Agreement* under the purview of the WTO (that has a more effective dispute settlement mechanism than that of *GATT*) and by integrating the *TRIPS Agreement* to the WTO Agreements which Member Countries of the WTO had to accede to.[58]

5.3.1.2. Copyright protection under TRIPS

The *TRIPS Agreement* advocates and revitalises the high standards of copyright protection found in the *Berne Convention*. In addition, the *TRIPS Agreement* creates an effective dispute settlement mechanism for ensuring Member Countries' compliance with the obligations of the *Berne Convention* and adds teeth to it by providing for stronger enforcement measures. Furthermore, the *TRIPS Agreement* enhances the territorial coverage in which *Berne* obligations are applied.[59] Therefore, the *TRIPS Agreement* is inimical to promoting access to scientific and technical knowledge in developing countries. In particular, it affects the timely and affordable translation of scientific books and learning materials produced in developed countries and the reproduction of the translations in large quantities, which is essential for developing countries to promote access to scientific and technical knowledge.[60]

The *TRIPS Agreement* adapts the provisions of the *Berne Convention*, and revives and strengthens the international copyright protection standards.[61] In other words, while building upon the standards of protection in the *Berne Convention*, the *TRIPS Agreement* reinforces and extends these standards beyond the *Berne* framework.[62] In particular, Article 9(1) the *TRIPS Agreement* provides that:

> Members shall comply with Articles 1 through 21 of the Berne Convention (1971) and the Appendix thereto. However, Members shall not have rights

56 Ryan, above n 54, 92.
57 Matthews, above n 27, 7.
58 Lanoszka, above n 55, 183.
59 Lionel Bently and Brad Sherman, 'Great Britain and the Signing of the *Berne Convention* in 1886' (2000–2001) 48 *Journal of the Copyright Society of the USA* 311, 311.
60 See Ruth L Gana, 'Prospects for Developing Countries Under the TRIPs Agreement' (1996) 29 *Vanderbilt Journal of Transnational Law* 735, 740.
61 Peter-Tobias Stoll, Jan Busche and Katrin Arend (eds), *WTO—Trade-Related Aspects of Intellectual Property Rights* (Martinus Nijhoff Publishers, 2009) 213.
62 Helfer, above n 32, 360.

or obligations under this Agreement in respect of the rights conferred under Article 6*bis* of that Convention or of the rights derived therefrom.[63]

As Helfer observed, instead of attempting to restructure the international copyright protection standards from the ground up, the *TRIPS Agreement* acknowledges the existing standards contained in the latest version of the *Berne Convention* as a starting point.[64] The Agreement then adds to, subtracts from, and reinforces these standards in several ways.[65] The exclusion of moral rights conferred under Article 6*bis* of the *Berne Convention* (*Paris Act 1971*) is a notable subtraction from the *Berne* standards. However, the additions made by the *TRIPS Agreement* to the *Berne* standards outweigh the subtractions from it.[66] In particular, the *TRIPS Agreement* contains a substantial number of additional obligations on matters where the *Berne Convention* is silent or was seen as being inadequate. For instance, the Agreement requires Member Countries to protect computer programs and compilations of data or other material as literary works. It also 'establishes new minimum standards, including the right of authors of computer programs and cinematographic works "to authorize or to prohibit the commercial rental to the public of originals or copies of their copyright works"'.[67] In view of this, the *TRIPS Agreement* is said to promote *Berne*-plus standards.[68]

The *TRIPS Agreement* reinforces the copyright protection standards in the *Berne Convention* in two ways: through the enforcement measures and through the dispute settlement procedure. As mentioned earlier, the *Berne Convention* lacks measures to enforce copyright protection standards at the national level. It also lacks a meaningful dispute settlement procedure at the international level which enables Member Countries to effectively challenge each other's compliance with the copyright protection standards in the *Convention*. The *TRIPS Agreement* addresses these defects. In particular, Part III of the Agreement specifies a strong and a detailed set of enforcement measures which Member Countries should give effect to in their national copyright regimes. These enforcement measures include civil and administrative procedures and remedies,[69] provisional measures,[70] special requirements related to border measures[71] and criminal procedures.[72] Article 41 of the *TRIPS Agreement* obliges all Member Countries to ensure that these enforcement measures are available under their respective

63 Stoll, Busche and Arend, above n 61, 211.
64 Helfer, above n 32, 378.
65 Ibid., 379.
66 Ibid.
67 Ibid.
68 L Bently, B Sherman, D Gangjee and P Johnson, *Intellectual Property Law* (Oxford University Press, 5th ed, 2018) 47.
69 *TRIPS Agreement 1994*, arts 42–49.
70 Ibid., art 50.
71 Ibid., art 51–60.
72 Ibid., art 61.

laws to 'permit effective action against an act of infringement of intellectual property rights covered by [the] Agreement, including expeditious remedies to prevent infringements and remedies which constitute a deterrent to further infringements'.[73]

The *TRIPS Agreement* links protection of copyright to the WTO dispute settlement system.[74] In particular, Article 64(1) states:

> The provisions of Article XXII and XXIII of GATT 1994 as elaborated and applied by the Dispute Settlement Understanding shall apply to consultations and the settlement of disputes under this Agreement except as otherwise specifically provided herein.

The WTO dispute settlement system introduced at the Uruguay Round negotiations is a much more effective dispute settlement mechanism than that provided for in the *Berne Convention*.[75] It is also more effective than the dispute settlement mechanism under *GATT*.[76] As the WTO website claims:

> The WTO's [dispute settlement] procedure underscores the rule of law, and it makes the trading system more secure and predictable. The system is based on clearly defined rules, with timetables for completing a case. First rulings are made by a panel and endorsed (or rejected) by the WTO's full membership. Appeals based on points of law are possible.[77]

Moreover, as Ginsburg and Treppoz noted, when a country which is in breach of WTO obligations (including those under the *TRIPS Agreement*) 'does not comply with the panel's decision, the complaining state may ask the Dispute Settlement Body for permission to impose limited trade sanctions ("suspend concessions or obligations") against the other side.'[78] Thus, the WTO system enables 'centrally authorized sanctions against recalcitrant violators of WTO trade agreements', including the *TRIPS Agreement*.[79]

Since all WTO members should adhere to their obligations under the *TRIPS Agreement*, it enhances the territorial coverage in which *Berne* obligations are

73 Stoll, Busche and Arend, above n 61, 208.
74 Helfer, above n 32, 365.
75 Indunil Nirupadi Abeyesekere, *Sri Lankan Copyright Law and the TRIPS Agreement* (Mahapola Publications, 1999) 9.
76 See Lynne Puckett and William L Reynolds, 'Rules, Sanctions and Enforcement under Section 301: At Odds with WTO?' (1990) 90(4) *The American Journal of International Law* 675, 687.
77 WTO, 'A Unique Contribution' (2015) *Understanding the WTO: Settling Disputes* <www.wto.org/english/thewto_e/whatis_e/tif_e/disp1_e.htm>.
78 Ginsburg and Treppoz, above n 45, 23.
79 Warren F Schwartz and Alan O Sykes, 'The Economic Structure of Renegotiation and Dispute Resolution in the World Trade Organisation' (2002) 31(S1) *The Journal of Legal Studies* S179, S179.

applied.[80] Tian observed that '[a]s part of the [WTO] access requirements, all countries wishing to join the WTO must abide by the TRIPS Agreement' and accordingly, 'the number of member states to the *Berne Convention* nearly doubled between 1986 and 1995 (during the period of WTO negotiations).'[81]

5.3.1.3. Why developing countries like Sri Lanka accepted TRIPS

Although many developing countries initially objected to linking the protection of intellectual property rights to world trade and thus into the WTO Agreements, eventually they accepted the *TRIPS Agreement*.[82] Several factors contributed to this acceptance. Of these, the main factors were the lack of awareness and negotiation strength of developing countries, the role played by the United States (particularly through the Generalized System of Preferences, the coercion exercised under Section 301 of the United States *Trade Act 1974* (as amended), and bilateral initiatives), the glossy picture portrayed by developed countries with regard to the significance of affording protection for intellectual property rights in developing countries for their rapid economic development and the trade benefits (sweeteners) that were shown to be available to developing countries in the event they became members to the WTO.

5.3.1.3.1. LACK OF AWARENESS AND NEGOTIATION STRENGTH

During the eight years of the Uruguay Round negotiations, '[f]or almost 3 years, from 1986 until May 1989, developing countries refused to negotiate an agreement on intellectual property.'[83] However, this position changed from the second half of 1989 as it no longer became possible 'politically, to avoid the discussion'.[84] In particular, the Mid-Term Review of the Uruguay Round in April 1989 produced a text that gave 'the go-ahead to a full-blown agreement on TRIPS'.[85] This was followed by two draft agreements on TRIPS tabled by the European Community and the United States in 1990.[86] In addition, Switzerland and Japan also submitted draft negotiating proposals. Around this time, '[a] core group of fourteen developing countries conceded [that] they would have no choice but to participate more fully in the TRIPS discussions'.[87]

80 See Stoll, Busche and Arend, above n 61, 208.
81 Tian, above n 25, 29.
82 Abbott, above n 19, 387.
83 Karin Timmermans and Togi Hutadjulu (eds), 'The TRIPS Agreement and Pharmaceuticals' (Report of an ASEAN Workshop on the TRIPS Agreement and its Impact on Pharmaceuticals, Jakarta, 2–4 May 2000) 11.
84 Ibid.
85 Drahos and Braithwaite, above n 23, xiv.
86 Ibid., xv.
87 Carolyn Deere-Birkbeck, 'Developing Countries in the Global IP System before TRIPS: The Political Context for the TRIPS Negotiations' in Carlos M Correa (ed), *Research Handbook*

Although developing countries participated in the TRIPS negotiations, they 'faced increasing difficulty in countering the pro-TRIPS agenda' advocated by the developed countries.[88] One of the reasons for this was the lack of knowledge and negotiating strength on the part of developing country delegates vis-à-vis the delegates from the developed countries to deal with extremely complex matters that were involved in the negotiation process. In particular, as Matthews observed, there was 'a lack of real understanding among developing country delegations about how far-reaching the economic and social implications of the TRIPS Agreement were likely to be.'[89] Moreover, as Balasubramaniam noted:

> Developing countries sent a senior official of the Trade Ministry [as a delegate]. There was no technical support. Several small developing countries were represented by the Trade Counsellors in Geneva being driven from one committee to another.[90]

In contrast, delegations sent from developed countries to the TRIPS negotiation process had with them 'teams comprised of hundreds of experts and specialists who were very knowledgeable in the issue under discussion'.[91] Matthews noted that these delegations 'had access to the highest level of business advice, this proving to be the most effective method for delegates to acquire the negotiating expertise they required.'[92] In view of this asymmetrical way in which the delegates of developed and developing countries carried out the TRIPS negotiation process, Balasubramaniam observed that '[t]here was hardly any "negotiations" in the real sense of the word' and, 'the so-called "negotiating process" did not involve any give and take'.[93]

5.3.1.3.2. ROLE PLAYED BY THE UNITED STATES

The United States played a crucial role at the Uruguay Round to bring the developing countries to the negotiation table in relation to the linking of intellectual property with trade and ultimately persuade them to accept the *TRIPS Agreement*. As Matthews stated, the approach adopted by the United States in this connection was one of 'carrot and stick'.[94] In pursuing this approach, the United States strategically used the Generalized System of Preferences, Section 301 of the United

---

on the Protection of Intellectual Property under WTO Rules: Intellectual Property in the WTO (Edward Elgar Publishing, 2010) vol 1, 43.

88 Ibid., 43–44.

89 Matthews, above n 27, 44 (citations omitted).

90 K Balasubramaniam, 'Globalisation and Liberalisation of Healthcare Services: WTO and the General Agreement on Trade in Services' (Issue Paper, People's Health Assembly, 2000) 8.

91 Ibid.

92 Matthews, above n 27, 44.

93 Balasubramaniam, above n 90, 8.

94 Matthews, above n 27, 33.

States *Trade Act 1974* (as amended) and bilateral treaties relating to trade and investment interchangeably or in combination to ease the developing countries' opposition to integrating protection of intellectual property rights with the world trading system and persuade these countries to accept the *TRIPS Agreement.*

Generalized System of Preferences The Generalized System of Preferences (GSP) was one of the important reasons why developing countries like Sri Lanka accepted the *TRIPS Agreement.* As Drahos and Braithwaite noted, '[T]he Generalized System of Preferences (GSP) allowed [the] US to develop a carrot and stick approach [towards developing countries] to the globalization of the standards of intellectual property it wanted'.[95] In particular, when the GSP program was originally designed in the United States, 'protection of intellectual property was not a criterion of eligibility for receiving benefits under it'.[96] However, on the eve of the Uruguay Round, the United States specifically revised its GSP program with the aim of using GSP as a carrot and stick to support its agenda for negotiating a multilateral intellectual property protection framework in the nature of the *TRIPS Agreement.* Thereby, on the one hand, the United States could provide incentives to those developing countries which accepted its agenda, and on the other hand, penalise those who were opposed.

The GSP in the United States is a 'program designed to promote economic growth in the developing world' by providing a preferential duty-free treatment for a wide number of products exported from selected developing countries to the United States.[97] As Palmeter observed, by 1984, 'most imports from most developing countries' received the duty-free treatment under the GSP program.[98] In particular, '[b]y 1984 roughly 3000 products from 140 developing countries and territories were part of the [United States GSP] scheme'.[99]

In view of the large size of the United States market, the duty-free treatment provided by the GSP program is very important for developing countries like Sri Lanka to enhance export earnings crucial for its economic development.[100] Perhaps, the magnitude of the importance of the duty-free treatment under the United States GSP program for developing countries during the period of TRIPS negotiations can be best illuminated in the huge losses suffered by India in 1992 when the United States suspended the duty-free privileges provided under the GSP for about US$80 million worth of exports from India.[101]

95 Drahos and Braithwaite, above n 23, 86.
96 Ibid.
97 Office of the USTR, *US Generalised System of Preferences: Guidebook* (2013) 3.
98 N David Palmeter, 'The Trade and Tariff Act of 1984: From the Customs Treatment of Manhole Covers to the Return of Goods from Outer Space' (1984) 11(3) *Syracuse Journal of International Law and Commerce* 487, 523.
99 Drahos and Braithwaite, above n 23, 86.
100 Ibid., (citations omitted).
101 Gail E Evans, 'Intellectual Property as a Trade Issue: The Making of the Agreement on Trade-Related Aspects of Intellectual Property Rights' (1994) 18(2) *World Competition*

The GSP program was originally introduced as part of the United States *Trade Act 1974*.[102] In particular, Section 501 of the *Act* stated '[t]he President may provide duty-free treatment for any eligible article from any beneficiary developing country in accordance with the provisions of [title V of *the Trade Act*]'. In taking such action, the President was required to 'have due regard for': (1) the effect of such action on furthering the economic development of developing countries, (2) the extent to which other major developed countries are undertaking a comparable effort to assist developing countries by granting GSP with respect to imports of products of such countries and (3) the anticipated impact of such action on the United States producers of like or directly competitive products.[103]

Except for the 'countries that were excluded statutorily from the designation as beneficiary developing countries', the *Trade Act 1974* gave the President 'virtual *carte blanche* in designating countries as eligible for GSP treatment'.[104] However, in exercising this discretion the President was required to take four factors into account, namely: (1) the expression by such country of its desire to be so designated, (2) the level of economic development of such country, (3) whether or not other major developed countries are extending generalised preferential tariff treatment to such countries and (4) the extent to which such country has assured the United States that it will provide equitable and reasonable access to the markets and basic commodity resources of such country.[105]

The GSP program introduced in the *Trade Act 1974* 'had to be reviewed by the Congress on a periodical basis' and '[i]n 1984 the GSP was due to expire in one year'.[106] Accordingly, in 1984, the United States enacted the *Generalised System of Preferences Renewal Act 1984 (GSP Renewal Act 1984)*[107] by bringing significant revisions to the GSP program introduced by the *Trade Act 1974*. One such revision was the linkage of protection of intellectual property rights with the GSP program. In particular, the *GSP Renewal Act 1984* declared that one of its purposes was to '[e]ncourage developing countries to provide effective means under which foreign nationals may secure, exercise, and enforce exclusive intellectual property rights'.[108] More importantly, it amended the beneficiary developing country criteria for GSP in the *Trade Act 1974* by incorporating appropriate protection of intellectual property rights in developing countries as an additional criterion for GSP eligibility. More specifically, to be eligible for designation as a beneficiary developing country for GSP under the *GSP Renewal Act*, the

---

137, 155; Gail E Evans, *India Business Law Handbook: Strategic Information and Basic Laws* (International Business Publications, 2013) vol 1, 117.

102 Palmeter, above n 98, 523; *Trade Act 1974*, Title V.

103 *Trade Act 1974*, s 501.

104 Palmeter, above n 98, 524 (citations omitted).

105 *Trade Act 1974*, s 502C.

106 Drahos and Braithwaite, above n 23, 86.

107 *Trade and Tariff Act 1984* (United States) Title V.

108 Ibid., s 501(b)9(B).

President was required to consider 'the extent to which a particular country "is providing adequate and effective means under its law for foreign nationals to secure, to exercise, and to enforce exclusive rights in intellectual property, including patents, trademarks and copyrights".'[109]

As Palmeter observed, the reference to intellectual property rights in the *GSP Renewal Act 1984* reflected one of the 'areas of particular importance to the United States for the world trade agenda' at the Uruguay Round of *GATT* negotiations.[110] In particular, the revised GSP program in the *GSP Renewal Act* could be used by the United States 'in the manner of a carrot and stick' against developing countries, in that, [the] United States was able to reward the developing countries who were complying with its agenda with GSP benefits while penalising the others by depriving them of these benefits.[111] Thus, as Drahos and Braithwaite pointed out:

> Singapore was given a favourable GSP Package in 1987 because of its good efforts in copyright essentially, while Mexico (1987), Thailand (1989) and India (1992) came for the GSP losses (US$50 million, US$165 million and US$80 million respectively) because they failed to meet certain standards of intellectual property protection.[112]

Section 301 of the United States Trade Act 1974 Another strong reason which persuaded developing countries to accept the *TRIPS Agreement* was Section 301 of the United States *Trade Act 1974* (as amended). This section provides a mechanism through which the United States can unilaterally take action and impose trade sanctions against countries that do not afford adequate protection for intellectual property rights.

The United States strategically used Section 301 to persuade developing countries to accept the *TRIPS Agreement* in two ways. On the one hand, it used the threat of action under Section 301 to push developing countries to the TRIPS negotiating table and to counter their resistance to the *TRIPS Agreement*.[113] On the other hand, it gave hope to developing countries that the 'dispute settlement procedures within the package of measures for TRIPS implementation' would offer 'some respite from the [much more severe] threat of US trade sanctions' under Section 301.[114]

As Bhagwati noted, 'Section 301 of the [Trade Act 1974] is the original piece of legislation that provides, in popular parlance, the shorthand for the current

109 Palmeter, above n 98, 524 (citations omitted); *Trade and Tariff Act 1984* (United States) s 503(c)(3).
110 Palmeter, above n 98, 524–525.
111 Drahos and Braithwaite, above n 23, 88.
112 Ibid.
113 Ryan, above n 54, 13.
114 Matthews, above n 27, 44.

US policy of aggressive unilateralism.'[115] The unilateral mechanism which the United States can adopt under Section 301 to settle its trade disputes with foreign countries is very severe and rigorous when compared with the dispute settlement mechanisms in the old *GATT* system and the present WTO system. As Puckett and Reynolds observed, Section 301 'reaches beyond the [*GATT*] to give the United States unilateral power to penalize countries that threaten American interests'.[116] According to these critics, it was the 'dearth of enforcement power' in the *GATT* system which 'left the vacuum that section 301 was designed to fill'.[117]

When the *Trade Act 1974* was first enacted, although Section 301 of the *Act* empowered the President of the United States to take unilateral retaliatory action and impose trade sanctions against foreign countries that carried out certain unreasonable, unjustifiable or discriminatory trade practices against the United States, it did not allow action to be taken against foreign countries for failure to protect intellectual property rights in their countries.[118] However, closer to and during the Uruguay Round negotiations, two significant amendments were brought to the *Trade Act 1974* to incorporate protection of intellectual property rights under the purview of Section 301.

The amendment brought to Section 301 of the *Trade Act 1974* in 1984 through the *Trade and Tariff Act 1984* was the first significant move which grafted intellectual property onto the Section 301 process.[119] Matthews observed that '[t]he effect of the amended Section 301 was threefold'.[120] Firstly, it empowered the Office of the United States Trade Representative (USTR) to 'investigate the appropriateness of another country's intellectual property without waiting for a complaint from a US company'.[121] Secondly, it incorporated failure to protect intellectual property rights as a criterion that would allow action under Section 301.[122] Thirdly, 'it included intellectual property protection as a new criterion for elimination of tariff privileges for imports into the US from designated developing countries under the Generalised System of Preferences (GSP)'.[123]

The second set of significant amendments to Section 301 was introduced in 1988 by the *Omnibus Foreign Trade and Competitiveness Act 1988*, which further

115 Jagdish Bhagwati, 'Aggressive Unilateralism: An Overview' in Jagdish Bhagwati and Hugh T Patrick (eds), *Aggressive Unilateralism: America's 301 Trade Policy and the World Trading System* (University of Michigan Press, 1990) 1, 2.
116 Lynne Puckett and William Reynolds, 'Rules, Sanctions and Enforcement under Section 301: At Odds with the WTO?' (1996) 90(4) *The American Journal of International Law* 675, 675.
117 Ibid., 687.
118 *Trade Act 1974* (United States) s 301(a).
119 Ryan, above n 54, 73; Drahos and Braithwaite, above n 23, xi.
120 Matthews, above n 27, 15.
121 Ibid.
122 Ibid.
123 Ibid.

linked intellectual property protection to the Section 301 process by introducing 'Special 301'. Under 'Special 301' the USTR is required to identify countries that deny adequate and effective protection of intellectual property rights or deny fair and equitable market access to United States persons who rely upon intellectual property protection within 30 days after the annual report is submitted to the Congress and select (out of the identified countries) the 'priority foreign countries'.[124] The 'priority foreign countries' that USTR should select are those countries that have the most onerous or egregious acts, policies or practices that have the greatest adverse impact on the relevant United States products and that do not enter into good faith negotiations or make significant progress in bilateral and multilateral negotiations to provide adequate and effective protection of intellectual property rights.[125] The effect of selection as 'priority foreign countries' is that it 'triggers a 30 day countdown during which targeted countries must "(enter) into good faith negotiations" or "(make) significant progress in bilateral or multilateral negotiations" or face sanctions determinations under the Section 301 process'.[126]

As Blakeney pointed out, 'Special 301' 'was explicitly introduced as a supplement to the US TRIPs negotiating strategy'.[127] As such, at the Uruguay Round of negotiations, the United States used the new 'Special 301' together with Section 301 sanctions as a powerful weapon to sway the hard-line developing countries (who were strongly opposed to linking intellectual property with world trade) to participate at the TRIPS negotiating table as well as weaken their opposition to the provisions of the *TRIPS Agreement*. Ultimately, Section 301 became one of the main reasons for the lukewarm approach of the developing countries towards the *TRIPS Agreement* during the latter stage of the Uruguay Round negations.[128]

By the time the Uruguay Round of negotiations started, the United States had already 'initiated [Section 301] actions over intellectual property against Korea and Brazil in 1985 to get them to the [Uruguay Round negotiating] table'.[129] With the creation of 'Special 301' in 1988, the United States was able to effectively use this new tool to weaken the opposition of many developing countries that strongly stood against pro-*TRIPS* proposals by initiating 'Special 301' actions and threatening them with sanctions.[130] In particular, when the USTR released

124 *Omnibus Foreign Trade and Competitiveness Act 1988* (United States) s 1303.

125 Ibid.

126 Sean M Flynn, 'Special 301 of the Trade Act of 1974 and Global Access to Medicine' (2010) 7 *Journal of Generic Medicines* 309, 310–311.

127 Michael Blakeney, 'The Impact of the TRIPs Agreement in the Asia Pacific Region' (1996) 18(10) *European Intellectual Property Review* 544, 545; Michael Blakeney, *Intellectual Property Enforcement: A Commentary on the Anti-Counterfeiting Trade Agreement (ACTA)* (Edward Elgar, 2012) 35.

128 Matthews, above n 27, 33.

129 Ryan, above n 54, 13.

130 Matthews, above n 27, 15–17, 25–28.

its Fact Sheet—*'Special 301' on Intellectual Property* in May 1989, it placed on a 'Priority Watch List' India and Brazil—the two countries which led the 'group of ten developing nations' who 'at first opposed the US proposal to make a code on intellectual property a negotiating item' in the Uruguay Round,[131] and thereafter 'continued to argue for a narrow interpretation of the Ministerial mandate on the negotiation of intellectual property'.[132] In addition, the USTR also placed Argentina, Egypt and Yugoslavia, which belonged to the same group ('group of ten developing nations') in the 'Watch List'.[133]

The impact of the USTR 'Special 301' listing had a profound impact on developing countries that were opposed to the pro-*TRIPS* proposals. This can be explained with regard to the context of India, which was a chief opponent of the *TRIPS Agreement.* While both India and Brazil continued to be in USTR's 'Priority Watch List' in 1990, in 1991 India was identified by the USTR as a 'Priority Foreign Country' due to its inadequate level of patent protection and the level of piracy of copyright protected works.[134] The identification as a 'Priority Foreign Country' under 'Special 301' led to a nine-month investigation on India that was initiated in May 1991. At the conclusion of this investigation in February 1992, the 'USTR determined that India's denial of adequate and effective patent protection [was] unreasonable and burden[ed] or restrict[ed] US commerce'.[135] In light of this finding, in April 1992, the United States 'suspended duty free privileges under the Generalized System of Preferences (GSP) for $60 million in trade from India' which was 'applied principally to pharmaceuticals, chemicals, and related products'.[136] Also, 'benefits on certain chemicals added to GSP in June 1992 were withheld from India, increasing the trade for which GSP [was] suspended to approximately $80 million'.[137] Matthews noted that '[i]n the face of potential losses of this magnitude India, a chief opponent of the TRIPS Agreement, saw its resolve weakened'.[138]

At the same time, the Indian example and the other instances of the widespread use of 'Special 301' persuaded the recalcitrant developing countries to change

131 Peter Drahos, 'BITS and BIPS: Bilateralism in Intellectual Property' (2001) 4(6) *The Journal of World Intellectual Property* 791, 793.

132 Peter Drahos, 'Negotiating Intellectual Property Rights: Between Coercion and Dialogue' in Peter Drahos and Ruth Mayne (eds), *Global Intellectual Property Rights: Knowledge, Access and Development* (Palgrave Macmillan, 2002) 161, 170; Office of the USTR, '"Special 301" on Intellectual Property' (Fact Sheet, 25 May 1989) 3.

133 Ibid.

134 Office of the USTR, '"Special 301" on Intellectual Property' (Fact Sheet, 27 April 1990); Office of the USTR, '"Special 301" on Intellectual Property' (Fact Sheet, 26 April 1991) 2.

135 Office of the USTR, *1992 National Trade Estimate Report on Foreign Trade Barriers* (1992) 116.

136 Evans, above n 101, 155.

137 Ibid.

138 Matthews, above n 27, 31.

their stance and 'to seek agreement in the Uruguay Round on the content of a TRIPS Agreement'.[139] In view of this, Matthews said:

> In the face of developing country opposition, the most important stimulus for progress in negotiations came not through multilateral discussions in the Uruguay Round, but through the threat of bilateral trade sanctions being brought by the United States under Special 301 of the Omnibus Trade and Traffic Act of 1988.[140]

The austerity of the unilateral dispute settlement process under Section 301 persuaded developing countries to seek out a less onerous mechanism of dispute settlement for trade-related issues. Against this backdrop, these countries saw the dispute settlement procedures negotiated at the Uruguay Round and offered as a package with the *TRIPS Agreement* as a more suitable method for dispute settlement of trade issues. Ryan observed that '[w]ithin the context of the TRIPS agreement, the Dispute Settlement Understanding offered countries some respite from the threat of US trade sanctions under authority of the section 301 policy'.[141] In other words, developing countries believed that once the dispute settlement mechanism negotiated at the Uruguay Round was put in place, the United States would refrain from initiating its unilateral dispute settlement process under Section 301.[142] Drahos and Mayne observed that '[a]t least if developing countries negotiated multilaterally there was the possibility that they would be able to obtain some limits on the use of 301 actions'.[143] In fact, this 'was what they were being told by developed country negotiators and the GATT Secretariat'.[144]

As observed earlier, the *TRIPS Agreement* came in a single package that incorporated all the WTO Agreements, including the Dispute Settlement Understanding.[145] As such, to implement the dispute settlement mechanism negotiated at the Uruguay Round which developing countries believed would restrict the use of action under Section 301, they had to accept the entire package of WTO Agreements, including the *TRIPS Agreement.*[146]

Bilateral treaties Entering into bilateral treaties with developing countries that required the protection of intellectual property rights was another mechanism which the United States used to persuade countries to accept the *TRIPS*

139 Ibid., 32–33 (citations omitted).
140 Ibid., 31 (citations omitted).
141 Ryan, above n 54, 13.
142 Indunil Nirupadi Abeyesekere, above n 75, 9.
143 Drahos, above n 132, 172.
144 Ibid.
145 Ryan, above n 54, 13.
146 Abbott, above n 19, 388–389.

Agreement. In particular, once developing countries with whom these treaties were entered into accepted the treaty obligations to protect intellectual property rights, often set at a higher level to those under the *TRIPS Agreement* (TRIPS-plus), these countries were more inclined to accept the *TRIPS Agreement* than to oppose it.

Bilateral treaties on intellectual property entered into by the United States with other countries during the 1980s and early 1990s were mainly a response to the United States 'failure to obtain an agreement on trade and counterfeit goods at the end of the Tokyo Round (1979) and the resistance of developing countries in the first half of the 1980s to including intellectual property as a negotiating item in the new GATT Round'.[147]

By entering into bilateral treaties on intellectual property with developing countries, the United States believed that not only could the resistance of these countries for bringing intellectual property as an item of the Uruguay Round negotiating table be effectively circumvented, but it also could persuade these countries to concede to the pro-TRIPS proposals put forward by the developed countries. In setting up the ground for this new strategy, the United States effectively interlinked its new model BIT program, economic power, scientific and technological know-how, and Section 301 of the *Trade Act 1974* (as amended) to the bilateral treaty scheme.

The model BIT program which the United States developed in the 1980s linked it 'to the goal of adequate and effective protection for intellectual property'.[148] This meant that the United States could use BITs 'as a carrot to get developing countries to sign bilateral intellectual property agreements'.[149] To apprehend how this became possible, it is important to first understand the developing countries' perception on BITs with the United States.

The core purpose of BITs is 'to protect and promote foreign investments'.[150] For developing countries, foreign investment (particularly foreign direct investment [FDI]) is a crucial matter for economic development. In particular, FDI brings a wide range of economic benefits, including 'increased levels of investment and economic activity, work training, well-paid jobs and technology transfers that enhance the productivity of local firms' in developing countries.[151] Given that the United States is an economic superpower in the world, attracting FDI from the United States is beneficial for developing countries not only because these countries can enhance their investment inflow but also because they can tap

147 Drahos, above n 131, 793.

148 Ibid.

149 Ibid., 795.

150 Lauge Skovgaard Poulsen, 'The Importance of BITs for Foreign Direct Investment and Political Risk Insurance' (2009–2010) *Yearbook on International Investment Law & Policy* 539, 539.

151 Deborah L Swenson, 'Why do Developing Countries Sign BITs?' (2005) 12 *University of California, Davis Journal of International Law and Policy* 131, 131–132.

into the scientific and technological know-how of the United States that comes with FDI. Thus, even today, many developing countries are keen to enter into BITs with the United States. So it is in this context that many developing countries like Sri Lanka entered into BITs with the United States closer to and during the Uruguay Round negotiations.

Pursuant to its new model BIT program introduced in 1980s, which linked BITs with adequate and effective protection for intellectual property, the United States has often made BITs conditional upon the other country signing a bilateral intellectual property agreement with it. This can be seen, for example, in the context of Nicaragua and Sri Lanka. For instance, as Drahos noted, when Nicaragua signed a BIT with the United States in July 1995, the BIT was 'made conditional upon Nicaragua signing a [bilateral intellectual property agreement] providing adequate and effective protection for US intellectual property rights'.[152] Similarly, (as will be more fully described later) when Sri Lanka signed a BIT with the United States on 20 September 1991, it signed a bilateral intellectual property agreement with that country on the same day.

Section 301 of the *Trade Act 1974* (as amended) also played an important role in facilitating the United States to enter into bilateral treaties on intellectual property with developing countries. As Drahos observed, an investigation under Section 301 can be used to bring about a bilateral agreement for protection of intellectual property rights between the United States and the target state.[153] Section 301 can also be used as means to accelerate the conclusion of intellectual property agreements between the United States and developing countries that are under way, especially when the negotiations in that connection are getting or are likely to get stalled. The case of Nicaragua provides a good example in this connection. In particular, although the BIT signed in July 1995 between the United States and Nicaragua was conditional upon Nicaragua signing a bilateral intellectual property agreement, the negotiations for concluding such an agreement were ongoing even in 1996. However, when the USTR placed Nicaragua in the 'Special 301 Observation list' in April 1997, it signed the agreement in January 1998.[154] Drahos noted, in the Nicaraguan example, that '[t]he 301 process was wheeled in presumably to speed up the negotiating cycle on the [bilateral intellectual property agreement] which had been proceeding too slowly for the United States'.[155]

The United States strategy of entering into bilateral treaties with developing countries which required these countries to protect intellectual property rights (in the way that United States wanted) proved to be a highly successful strategy in persuading these countries to accept the *TRIPS Agreement*. Evans noted that

152 Drahos, above n 131, 796.
153 Ibid., 792.
154 Ibid., 796.
155 Ibid., 797.

'[b]etween 1989 and 1994, the United States concluded bilateral agreements for the protection of intellectual property with at least twelve countries'.[156] Many of these bilateral agreements contained TRIPS-plus features which went beyond the standards of intellectual property protection prescribed by the *TRIPS Agreement*. The bilateral agreement on intellectual property entered into between the United States and Sri Lanka is a classic example of this.[157] As such, when developing countries had already undertaken more onerous obligations to protect intellectual property rights under the bilateral agreements with the United States (than required by the *TRIPS Agreement*) they were less inclined to be opposed to the *TRIPS Agreement* and also 'were no longer likely to support other developing nations that were continuing to resist the proposals for a TRIPs Agreement'.[158] Matthews observed that '[o]nce the United States had bilaterally persuaded a sufficient number of countries to act on intellectual property rights, it could expect little resistance in the multilateral GATT forum that led to the adoption of the TRIPS Agreement'.[159]

5.3.1.3.3. INTELLECTUAL PROPERTY AND ECONOMIC DEVELOPMENT

The hypothesis offered by developed countries about the significance of intellectual property for rapid economic development was another reason which inclined developing countries to accept the *TRIPS Agreement*. Abbott noted that during the *TRIPS Agreement* negotiation process, developed countries 'promoted the idea that higher levels of IPRs would be in the best interests of the developing countries'.[160] To this end, the developed countries cleverly linked their economic prosperity with their high standards of intellectual property protection. In particular, they attributed their economic prosperity to high levels of innovation and pointed out that high levels of innovation require high standards of intellectual property protection. Developed countries thus claimed that it was in the best interests of developing countries to accept the *TRIPS Agreement* because by adopting higher standards of intellectual property protection prescribed in the *Agreement*, the developing countries could promote innovation through which they could achieve rapid economic development. Developed countries also maintained that if developing countries did not adopt high standards of intellectual property protection, 'their scientists and other innovators will leave because they will not be adequately rewarded for their innovation' and the 'industrialised country IPRs-holders will not transfer technology to them'.[161]

156 Evans, above n 101, 152.
157 Kanchana Kariyawasam, 'Developing a Regulatory Framework for the Protection of Intellectual Property Rights in Plant Genetic Resources in Sri Lanka' (PhD Thesis, School of Law, Griffith University, 2005) 84–85.
158 Matthews, above n 27, 33.
159 Ibid.
160 Abbott, above n 19, 390.
161 Ibid.

5.3.1.3.4. TRADE BENEFITS IN THE WTO PACKAGE-DEAL

Perhaps the most important and persuasive reason why developing countries like Sri Lanka accepted the *TRIPS Agreement* was the trade benefits which came as sweeteners in the package deal of WTO Agreements. Because these trade benefits were incorporated in a single package in which the *TRIPS Agreement* was a part, to receive the benefits, it was necessary for Sri Lanka (and other developing countries) to accept the entire package, which included the *TRIPS Agreement*. Thus, Ryan observed that '[w]hen the [*TRIPS Agreement*] was finally achieved as part of the Uruguay Round, it appeared that linkage-bargain diplomacy explained the outcome'.[162]

The Uruguay Round provided a fitting forum for developed countries to offer many trade benefits to developing countries as part of a bargain to get them to accept the *TRIPS Agreement*. This was because the proposed agenda for the Uruguay Round included a range of areas relating to trade that were very important to many developing countries (particularly Sri Lanka), such as textiles and apparel, agriculture, services, foreign direct investment and government procurement.[163] As Abbott noted, the trade benefits offered by developed countries to developing countries as part of the bargain at the Uruguay Round included agreements to 'reduce levels of agricultural export subsidies' and to 'gradually phase out quotas on textile products'.[164] In addition to these concessions, developing countries also made 'substantial concessions with respect to imports of tropical products'.[165] Ryan said that '[m]any developing countries had much to gain from liberalized trade in textiles and apparel and agricultural products'.[166] Thus, 'they eventually accepted TRIPs in exchange for "a global package deal" that included greater access to industrialised markets and new treaties on trade in agriculture and textiles'.[167]

5.3.1.4. Sri Lanka's accession to the TRIPS Agreement

From Sri Lanka's perspective, the overall outcome of the Uruguay Round of negotiations was seen to be favourable to the country. This was particularly because of the potential trade benefits which Sri Lanka could gain from the new framework created at the Uruguay Round. In particular, the Central Bank of Sri Lanka—the advisor to the Sri Lankan government on economic affairs—said:

> The Uruguay Round . . . concluded after seven years on December 15, 1993 . . . covered a range of issues including Agriculture, Textile & Clothing,

162 Ryan, above n 54, 92.
163 Ibid.
164 Abbott, above n 19, 387.
165 Ibid.
166 Ryan, above n 54, 92.
167 Helfer, above n 32, 377.

> Trade in Services, Trade Related Investment Measures and Trade Related Aspects of Intellectual Property Rights. The overall impact of the agreement is expected to be beneficial to all developing countries including Sri Lanka as reduced tariff and non tariff measures together with strengthened trade rules and disciplines would result in an expansion in global trade.[168]

As an initial measure, Sri Lanka signed the *Final Act Embodying the Results of the Uruguay Round of Multilateral Trade Negations 1994* (*Final Act*), the first of the WTO Agreements, on 15 April 1994. This was '[w]ith a view of achieving the benefits of expansion in global trade by way of lowering tariff and non-tariff barriers and strengthening rules and disciplines in international trade'.[169]

The *Final Act* specifically stated in Article 3 that '[t]he representatives agree on the desirability of acceptance of the WTO Agreement by all participants in the Uruguay Round Multilateral Trade Negotiations with a view to its entry into force by 1 January 1995'. As the Central Bank observed in its 1994 Annual Report:

> The implementation of the rules of the [*Final Act*] is crucially important for the Sri Lankan economy since it covers not only measures to lower tariff and non-tariff barriers, but also a wide spectrum of issues including the integration of textiles and clothing into the [WTO], trade in agriculture and services, trade related investment measures and intellectual property rights. According to the changes in tariffs, Sri Lanka's major export items would considerably benefit from implementation of the [*Final Act*].[170]

In view of this situation, on 1 June 1994 Sri Lanka ratified the *WTO Agreement*.[171] With the ratification of the *WTO Agreement*, Sri Lanka also became a member to the *TRIPS Agreement*. Thus, it became mandatory for Sri Lanka to implement a TRIPS-compliant copyright regime.

5.3.1.5. Implementing the TRIPS obligations in Sri Lankan Law

The *TRIPS Agreement* is very clear about the need to implement its provisions into national copyright regimes of its members. The *TRIPS Agreement* requires WTO members to implement TRIPS-compliant copyright regimes within stipulated time frames. At the same time, the Council for Trade-Related Aspects of Intellectual Property Rights (Council for TRIPS) monitors the compliance of WTO members to their TRIPS-obligations. Because failure of a WTO member to carry out its obligations under the *TRIPS Agreement* can be a subject matter of

168 Central Bank of Sri Lanka, *Annual Report 1993* (1994) 101.
169 Central Bank of Sri Lanka, *Annual Report 1994* (1995) 105.
170 Ibid.
171 *Agreement Establishing the World Trade Organisation 1994.*

dispute settlement,[172] one WTO member can invoke the WTO dispute settlement mechanism when another member has failed to implement a TRIPS-compliant copyright regime within the stipulated period in the *Agreement*.[173] Since the outcome of the WTO dispute settlement mechanism can result in trade sanctions, the *TRIPS Agreement* creates an effective deterrent to ensure that Member Countries comply with the TRIPS copyright obligations in their national copyright regimes. In addition, the constant surveillance of the Council for TRIPS also creates pressure for WTO members to implement TRIPS-compliant copyright regimes within the stipulated period in the *TRIPS Agreement*. Against this background, it became necessary for Sri Lanka to give effect to a TRIPS-compliant copyright regime in the *Intellectual Property Act 2003*.

The *TRIPS Agreement* obliges all Member Countries to give effect to its provisions in their national laws. However, the Member Countries are not obliged to 'implement in their law more extensive protection than is required by the *TRIPS Agreement*' although they have the discretion to do so.[174] Moreover, the Member Countries must implement TRIPS-compliant intellectual property regimes before expiry of a general period of one year following the date of entry into force of the *WTO Agreement*.[175] However, developing countries are given a grace period of a further four years and the least developing countries are given a grace period of ten years (except in the case of Articles 3, 4 and 5 of the Agreement) with regard to implementation of the TRIPS obligations into their national intellectual property regimes.[176] The upshot of this was that Sri Lanka was required to give effect to TRIPS obligations in its intellectual property law (including copyright law) before 1 January 2000.

As Matthews observed, the Council for TRIPS performs the 'formal role of carrying out scrutiny and surveillance of national measures implementing the TRIPS Agreement.'[177] More specifically, the *TRIPS Agreement* grants the Council for TRIPS the authority to 'monitor the operation of [the] Agreement and, in particular, Members' compliance with their obligations [thereunder]'.[178] In addition, the Council for TRIPS is vested with the authority to carry out reviews on the implementation of the obligations of the *TRIPS Agreement* in the national laws of Member Countries after the deadline stipulated in the *Agreement* for such implementation, two years after the deadline for such implementation and at identical intervals thereafter.[179] The Council also has the authority to 'undertake reviews in the light of any relevant new developments which might warrant

172 Justin Malbon, Charles Lawson and Mark Davison, *The WTO Agreement on Trade-Related Aspects of Intellectual Property Rights: A Commentary* (Edward Elgar, 2014) 734.
173 *TRIPS Agreement 1994*, art 64.
174 Ibid., art 1.
175 Ibid., art 65(1).
176 Ibid., arts 65(2), 66(1).
177 Matthews, above n 27, 79.
178 *TRIPS Agreement 1994*, art 68.
179 Ibid., art 71(1).

modification or amendment of the [TRIPS] Agreement'.[180] Moreover, the Member Countries are obliged to notify the laws and regulations made effective by them pertaining to the subject matter of the *TRIPS Agreement* to the Council for TRIPS to assist the Council in its review of the operation of the Agreement.[181] The *TRIPS Agreement* further requires each Member Country to be prepared to supply, in response to a written request from another Member Country, information regarding its laws, regulations, final judicial decisions and administrative rulings of general application.[182]

With the accession to the WTO and the *TRIPS Agreement*, Sri Lanka's intellectual property law came under the scrutiny and surveillance of the Council for TRIPS. As a result, Sri Lanka was closely monitored by the Council for TRIPS as to whether the country was enacting a copyright regime which complied with the TRIPS obligations within the given deadline. In light of this, there was pressure on Sri Lanka to introduce a TRIPS-compliant copyright regime.

Although from 1996 Sri Lanka had been 'doing its best' to 'update' its intellectual property regime (including copyright) in compliance with the *TRIPS Agreement*, the process of finalising the updates was delayed due to '[c]ertain unavoidable technical reasons such as translation of the English version of the draft bill into official languages'.[183] As a result of these delays, the deadline prescribed by the *TRIPS Agreement* for Sri Lanka to enact a TRIPS-compliant copyright regime lapsed. However, in observing the requirement under Article 63(2) of the *TRIPS Agreement* to notify all the laws and regulations relating to the Agreement to the Council for TRIPS, on 26 November 2001, Sri Lanka placed a copy of a 'Proposed Act to Amend the Code of Intellectual Property Act' (Proposed Act to amend the *IP Code*) before the Council for TRIPS.[184] This proposed amending Act was intended to be in compliance with the *TRIPS Agreement*. Its provisions relating to copyright owners' translation rights were the same as those in the *Intellectual Property Act 2003* except for the duration of these rights which was limited to the 'life of the author and for fifty years after his death'.[185]

Although the Proposed Act to amend the *IP Code* was a fair indication that Sri Lanka was on the move to enact a TRIPS-compliant copyright regime in the near future, many developed Member Countries to the *TRIPS Agreement* constantly raised questions about Sri Lanka in the Council for TRIPS. Specific issues raised regarded the provisions in the *IP Code* that were against TRIPS obligations and

180 Ibid.
181 Ibid., art 63(2).
182 Ibid., art 63(3).
183 *Sri Lanka—Review of Legislation*, WTO Doc IP/Q/LKA1, IP/Q2/LKA1, IP/Q3/LKA1, IP/Q4/LKA1 (13 October 2003) 2.
184 *Sri Lanka—Main Dedicated Intellectual Property Laws and Regulations Notified under Article 63.2 of the Agreement*, WTO Doc IP/N/1/LKA/C/1/Add.1, IP/N/1/LKA/I/1/Add.1 (26 November 2001).
185 Proposed Act to Amend the Code of Intellectual Property Act No 52 of 1979 (Sri Lanka) s 14.

the new provisions that were needed to be introduced to make the *IP Code* compliant with these obligations. Notably, one such question related to the protection of translation rights. In particular, on 30 November 2001 the European Communities and their Member States specifically posed a question to Sri Lanka on the consistency of Section 15 of the *IP Code* (which enabled a person to freely translate a work into Sinhala and Tamil languages in the event such work had not been published in those languages within a period of ten years from its first publication) with the TRIPS obligations.[186] Sri Lanka's reply to this question was simply that '[t]his Section has been removed under the proposed law'.[187] In the midst of questions of this nature by developed countries at the Council for TRIPS and their constant reminders on Sri Lanka to comply with the *TRIPS Agreement*, Sri Lanka ultimately enacted the *Intellectual Property Act 2003* on 12 November 2003, thereby giving effect to a TRIPS-compliant copyright regime in the country.

5.3.2. The US-Sri Lanka IPR Agreement

The *US-Sri Lanka IPR Agreement*,[188] which was a result of Sri Lanka's trade and investment concerns, is another reason for the stringent and unbalanced manner in which copyright owners' translation rights are protected in the *Intellectual Property Act 2003*. At the time Sri Lanka undertook the copyright obligations under the *TRIPS Agreement*, it had already undertaken similar obligations under the *US-Sri Lanka IPR Agreement*.[189] Although Sri Lanka did not give effect to these obligations by the deadline stipulated in the *US-Sri Lanka IPR Agreement*, this *Agreement* played a fairly important role in rendering the *Intellectual Property Act 2003* inimical for the translation of copyright protected works required for promoting access to scientific and technical knowledge in Sri Lanka.

The main aim of the *US-Sri Lanka IPR Agreement* is to 'provide adequate and effective protection and enforcement of intellectual property rights in patents, trademarks, copyrights, trade secrets, and layout designs for integrated circuits'.[190] As Kariyawasam noted, the *US-Sri Lanka IPR Agreement* 'set[s] higher intellectual property standards than the TRIPS Agreement.'[191] However, as far

186 *European Communities—Review of Legislation: Questions Posed by the European Communities and Their Member States*, WTO Doc IP/C/W/320/Add.2 (30 November 2001) 3.
187 *Sri Lanka—Responses from Sri Lanka to Questions Posed by the European Communities and Their Member States*, WTO Doc IP/C/W/324/Add.4 (23 January 2002) 2.
188 *Agreement on the Protection and Enforcement of Intellectual Property Rights between the United States of America and the Democratic Socialist Republic of Sri Lanka 1991*.
189 The *US-Sri Lanka IPR Agreement* was signed on 20 September 1991 and it entered into force 30 days after signing. *Agreement on the Protection and Enforcement of Intellectual Property Rights between the United States of America and the Democratic Socialist Republic of Sri Lanka 1991*, art 8.
190 *Agreement on the Protection and Enforcement of Intellectual Property Rights between the United States of America and the Democratic Socialist Republic of Sri Lanka 1991*, Preamble.
191 Kariyawasam, above n 101, 81.

as standards in regard to protection of copyright owners' translation rights are concerned, the *US-Sri Lanka IPR Agreement* appears to contain similar standards to those advocated by the *TRIPS Agreement*.

In terms of the *US-Sri Lanka IPR Agreement*, Sri Lanka is required to adhere to the *Paris Act 1971* of the *Berne Convention* and to observe certain other 'commitments' stipulated in the Agreement.[192] This means that under the *US-Sri Lanka IPR Agreement*, there is an additional obligation on Sri Lanka (apart from its obligations as a *Berne* member) to give effect to the *Berne Convention*'s standards of protection of translation rights in Sri Lanka's national copyright regime. More importantly, certain other 'commitments' stipulated in the *US-Sri Lanka IPR Agreement* require Sri Lanka to protect translation rights beyond the standards required by the *Berne Convention*. In particular, the *US-Sri Lanka IPR Agreement* requires each party to the Agreement to protect 'works listed in Article 2 of the Berne Convention and any other works now known or later developed, that embody original expression within the meaning of the Berne Convention.'[193] In this connection, the Agreement specifically states that both parties should protect 'all types of computer programs' (expressed in any language), 'works created within the use or assistance of computers',[194] and 'collections or compilations of protected or unprotected material or data whether in print, machine readable or any other medium including data bases'.[195] Certainly, this is a Berne-plus obligation which requires copyright owners' translation rights to be extended to these types of works as well.

Apart from this, the *US-Sri Lanka IPR Agreement* deals with certain exceptions that are applicable to copyright owners' translation rights. In particular, Article 2(a)(vii) states that the parties to the *US-Sri Lanka IPR Agreement* should confine 'any limitations upon and exceptions to the exclusive rights' provided under the *Berne Convention* and the Agreement (including any limitations or exceptions that restrict such rights to 'public activity') to 'certain special cases which do not conflict with a normal exploitation of the work and do not unreasonably prejudice the legitimate interests of the right holder'. In addition, Article 2(a)(vii) of the *US-Sri Lanka IPR Agreement* states:

> Each party shall limit resort to compulsory licensing to those works, rights and utilizations permitted under the Berne Convention; and further permitted shall ensure that any legitimate compulsory or non-voluntary license or restriction of exclusive rights to a right of remuneration shall provide means to ensure payment and remittance of royalties at a level consistent with what would be negotiated on a voluntary basis.

192 *Agreement on the Protection and Enforcement of Intellectual Property Rights between the United States of America and the Democratic Socialist Republic of Sri Lanka 1991*, art 2.
193 Ibid., art 2 (a)(i).
194 Ibid., art 2(a)(i)(2).
195 Ibid., art 2(a)(i)(3).

As far as standards of protection of translation rights are concerned, the purpose of these provisions appears to be to reinstate the obligations under the *Berne Convention*. Moreover, these provisions also seem to be in line with the obligations of the *TRIPS Agreement*.

The *US-Sri Lanka IPR Agreement* came into force 'thirty days after it [was] signed by the Parties', that is, in October 1991, and it still remains in force.[196] Although the *US-Sri Lanka IPR Agreement* required Sri Lanka to 'submit for enactment no later than 1 September 1993 the legislation necessary to carry out the obligations of [the] Agreement and to exert best efforts to enact and implement this legislation by that date',[197] as far as its obligations relating to protection of translation rights under the Agreement were concerned, Sri Lanka did not enact and implement a legislation that complied with the Agreement by 1 September 1993.[198] One possible reason for this is that the United States meant the *US-Sri Lanka IPR Agreement* to only be a conduit to persuade Sri Lanka to accept the *TRIPS Agreement*. Be that as it may, Sri Lanka was obliged to give effect to the provisions in the *US-Sri Lanka IPR Agreement* in its national intellectual property regime at the time of the enactment of the *Intellectual Property Act 2003*. Thus, as well as complying with the provisions of the *TRIPS Agreement*, the copyright regime in the *Intellectual Property Act* also gave effect to the obligations under the *US-Sri Lanka IPR Agreement*.[199]

Apart from its broad impact on the stringent and unbalanced manner in which copyright owners' translation rights are protected in the *Intellectual Property Act 2003*, the *US-Sri Lanka IPR Agreement* also has a specific impact on the scope and extent of the general exceptions to these rights recognised in the *Intellectual Property Act*. In particular, the fair use exception in Section 11(1) of the *Intellectual Property Act*, which is 'almost a verbatim reproduction of Section 107 of the US Copyright Act',[200] is presumably a result of the *US-Sri Lanka IPR Agreement*. This is because the *US-Sri Lanka IPR Agreement* has opened room for the United States to get involved in the process of making the national intellectual property regime of Sri Lanka compatible with the obligations of the *US-Sri Lanka IPR Agreement*. As Article 6 of the *Agreement* states:

> Prior to submission of legislation necessary to carry out the obligations of the Agreement, the Parties agree to consult and jointly identify by the exchange of letters or otherwise all matters in the Agreement which are at variance with current law or need supplementing or amendment to such law

196 Ibid., art 8.
197 Ibid., art 7.
198 For instance, Section 15, which was contrary to the provisions of the *Paris Act 1971* of the *Berne Convention* and the *US-Sri Lanka IP Agreement*, remained in force even after this date.
199 Karunaratna, above n 2, 8.
200 Ibid., 77.

and to take all necessary steps to bring these matters into conformity with the Agreement.

Thus, the adoption of a fair use exception in the *Intellectual Property Act 2003*, which is very similar to that in the United States *Copyright Act 1976*, is presumably a result of the *US-Sri Lanka IPR Agreement*.[201]

This *US-Sri Lanka IPR Agreement* is an outcome of Sri Lanka's trade and investment interests. In particular, it was an attached commitment to the *Treaty between the United States of America and the Democratic Socialist Republic of Sri Lanka concerning the Encouragement and Reciprocal Protection of Investment 1991* (*US-Sri Lanka BIT*) which was signed on the same date on which the *US-Sri Lanka IPR Agreement* was signed. The main objective of the *US-Sri Lanka BIT* is to promote investment between the United States and Sri Lanka through providing protection for investment in both countries.

From the point of view of Sri Lanka, the most important purpose of entering into the *US-Sri Lanka BIT* was to attract from the United States foreign investment crucial for the country's economic development.[202] The importance of foreign investment, particularly FDI, for economic development of Sri Lanka is well recognized. In particular, FDI is important for Sri Lanka to bridge the gap between low level of domestic savings and investment that is required to promote economic growth.[203] As Mustafa and Santhirasegaram observed, 'FDI plays a major role in contributing to [Sri Lanka's] local resource base available for investment to obtain sufficient rates of economic growth which will improve standard of living of the people.'[204] Also, FDIs strengthen external reserves of Sri Lanka to help the country to 'withstand any potential external vulnerability'.[205] Moreover, as the World Bank notes, 'Sri Lanka's economy depends on FDI to bring innovation.'[206] In addition, FDIs contribute to creating better employment opportunities and increasing domestic competition and other positive externalities in Sri Lanka.[207] As such, attracting FDIs has been a major goal of Sri Lanka ever since its economy was

201 The Proposed Act to amend the *IP Code* that was placed before the Council for TRIPS by Sri Lanka on 26 November 2001 also contained a fair use exception which is very similar to that in the United States *Copyright Act 1976*. Proposed Act to Amend the Code of Intellectual Property Act No 52 of 1979 (Sri Lanka) s 12.

202 See Yusuf Caliskan, 'The Development of International Investment Law: Lessons from the OECD MAI Negotiations and Their Application to a Possible Multilateral Agreement on Investment' (Juris Scientiae Doctris Thesis, Washington University School of Law, 2002) 37.

203 Central Bank of Sri Lanka, *Annual Report 2012* (2013) 7.

204 AMM Mustafa and S Santhirasegaram, 'The Impact of Foreign Direct Investment on Economic Growth in Sri Lanka' (2013) 8(1) *Journal of Management* 27, 27.

205 Central Bank of Sri Lanka, *Annual Report 2012* (2013) 122.

206 World Bank, 'Context' (23 June 2015) *Sri Lanka: Overview* <www.worldbank.org/en/country/srilanka/overview>.

207 PPA Wasantha Athukorala, 'The Impact of Foreign Direct Investment for Economic Growth: A Case Study in Sri Lanka' (Paper submitted for the 9th International Conference on Sri Lankan Studies, Matara, 28–30 November 2003) 2.

liberalised in 1977. In fact, even in 2015 the World Bank has pointed out that 'Sri Lanka needs to attract FDI—in order to maintain its high growth rate'.[208]

Given the status of economic development that the United States has achieved and its intellectual strength in the field of science and technology, Sri Lanka's desire to attract FDI from the United States hardly needs any explanation. Also, the employment conditions and other externalities which Sri Lanka could gain from FDI from the United States are very attractive. As Robert O Blake, United States Ambassador to Sri Lanka from 2006–2009, observed:

> US investment and trade plays a very important role in enhancing Sri Lanka's economic development. US investment also increases wages and creates opportunities for local labourers to advance.
> US companies frequently offer amongst the highest salaries to both managers and line workers . . . US investment has brought to Sri Lanka, cutting edge technology that makes the economy globally competitive.
> US investors also tend to be good citizens in their host communities. For US companies, corporate social responsibility is not just a marketing exercise, it is at the core of corporate values.[209]

For the United States, there were three main reasons for entering into the *US-Sri Lanka BIT*. Firstly, to protect American investment in Sri Lanka.[210] Secondly, to set in Sri Lanka the standards of intellectual property rights protection which the United States wanted as part of its strategy to achieve enhanced protection of these rights around the world. Thirdly, to persuade Sri Lanka to accept the *TRIPS Agreement*.

5.3.2.1. Protection of investment

Protection of the investments of the United States investors in Sri Lanka was one of the key reasons why the United States entered into the *US-Sri Lanka BIT*. Protection of investments does not only mean safeguarding the physical property of the investors. It also means protection of intangible property such as intellectual property rights.[211] Because of this, during the 1980s, the United States designed the model BIT program to cover protection of intellectual property rights.[212] The *US-Sri Lanka BIT*, which was entered in the aftermath of this

208 World Bank, 'South Asia Economic Focus: Making the Most of Cheap Oil' (Report, 2015) 62.
209 Robert O Blake, 'Importance of Investment and Trade in Sri Lanka' (Speech delivered at the Sri Lanka Economic Summit 2007, Cinnamon Grand, 6–8 June 2007) <http://businesstoday.lk/cover_page.php?article=4602&issue=272>.
210 See Caliskan, above n 202, 37.
211 See, e.g., Abbott, above n 19, 386.
212 Drahos, above n 131, 793; Frederick M Abbott, 'Protecting First World Assets in the Third World: Intellectual Property Negotiations in the GATT Multilateral Framework' (1989) 22(4) *Vanderbilt Journal of Transnational Law* 689, 710, n 71.

model BIT program, defines 'investment' and investment 'associated activities' to include intellectual property rights. In particular, Article I1(a) of the *US-Sri Lanka BIT* states:

> 'investment' means every kind of investment in territory of one Party . . . and includes: . . . intellectual property which includes, inter alia, rights relating to: literary and artistic works, including sound recordings, patentable inventions in all fields of human endeavour, industrial designs, semiconductor mask works, trade secrets, know-how, and confidential business information, and trademarks, service marks, and trade names.

5.3.2.2. Globalising intellectual property rights

Another reason why the United States entered into *US-Sri Lanka BIT* was to enhance the protection of intellectual property rights in Sri Lanka which was part of a bigger program of enhancing global protection of these rights.[213] As Buthe and Milner noted, prior to commencing serious negotiations for a BIT, the United States assesses 'whether the potential treaty partner is "politically willing and administratively ready or capable" to sign up to the major obligations that a BIT entails, including a "real commitment to [protect] intellectual property rights" '.[214] Moreover, the United States often makes BITs conditional upon signing bilateral intellectual property agreements. This was particularly the case with regard to the *US-Sri Lanka BIT*.

5.3.2.3. Persuasion to accept TRIPS

As noted earlier, the United States increasingly used bilateral treaties to persuade developing countries to accept the *TRIPS Agreement*. The *US-Sri Lanka BIT* served a similar purpose to persuade Sri Lanka to accept the *TRIPS Agreement*. In particular, once Sri Lanka accepted the TRIPS-plus obligations in the *US-Sri Lanka IPR Agreement*, which was an attached commitment to the *US-Sri Lanka BIT*, there was less reason for Sri Lanka to decline the *TRIPS Agreement*.

5.3.3. Proposed US-Sri Lanka Free Trade Agreement

The proposed Free Trade Agreement between the United States and Sri Lanka (the proposed US-Sri Lanka FTA), the negotiations of which started on the eve of the enactment of the *Intellectual Property Act 2003*, is another reason for the

213 Drahos, above n 131, 798.

214 Tim Buthe and Helen V Milner, 'Bilateral Investment Treaties and Foreign Direct Investment: A Political Analysis' in Karl P Sauvant and Lisa E Sachs (eds), *The Effect of Treaties on Foreign Direct Investment: Bilateral Investment Treaties, Double Taxation Treaties, And Investment Flows* (Oxford University Press, 2009) 171, 211.

stringent and unbalanced manner in which copyright owners' translation rights are protected in the TRIPS model of copyright law.

5.3.3.1. *Background to the proposed US-SRI Lanka Free Trade Agreement*

Kelegama observed that '[s]ince the beginning of 2002, a possible US-Sri Lanka FTA has been discussed'.[215] The reason for this was Sri Lanka's trade concerns. On the one hand, Sri Lanka needed to gain more benefits from international trade to recover from the economic crisis which it faced during the early 2000s. On the other hand, Sri Lanka needed a preferential trade arrangement with the United States to offer support to its garment industry, which was predicted to be affected by the expiry of the *Multi Fibre Agreement 1974* (*MFA*) on 1 January 2005. To achieve these ends, it was important for Sri Lanka to enter into a FTA with the United States.

An important reason for the negotiation of the proposed US-Sri Lanka FTA was Sri Lanka's economic crisis in the early 2000s. At the dawn of the twenty-first century, Sri Lanka was 'in the thick of an economic crisis' resulting from 'deep indebtedness'.[216] For the first time in its history, Sri Lanka also reported negative economic growth in 2001.[217] To overcome this economic crisis, Sri Lanka implemented a new economic policy which sought to further integrate its economy to the global economy, particularly through trade relations at the 'regional and bilateral level'.[218] In fact, as one of the priority actions of this policy, Sri Lanka needed to 'pursue an aggressive program to explore bilateral trade opportunities . . . and develop and implement bilateral and regional free trade agreements that offer improved market access for Sri Lankan exports'.[219] To this end, Sri Lanka took several actions in 2002. As the 2002 Annual Report of the Central Bank of Sri Lanka stated:

> One of the main strategies during 2002 was to identify countries of significance to Sri Lanka's bilateral trade relations. Ministerial level trade promotion missions were undertaken by the Ministry of Trade and Consumer Affairs to consolidate existing trade relations and to explore trade potential and new opportunities for mutual cooperation with countries such as India,

215 Saman Kelegama, 'A Possible US-Sri Lanka Free Trade Agreement to Support the Garment Industry?' in Saman Kelegama (ed), *Ready-Made Garment Industry in Sri Lanka: Facing the Global Challenge* (Institute of Policy Studies, 2004) 215, 215; JB Kelegama, 'Proposed FTA between Lanka and US' *The Island* (online), 18 August 2004 <www.island.lk/2004/08/18/featur01.html>.

216 Government of Sri Lanka, *Regaining Sri Lanka: Vision and Strategy for Accelerated Development* (Government of Sri Lanka, 2002) 1.

217 Central Bank of Sri Lanka, *Annual Report 2001* (2002) 1.

218 Government of Sri Lanka, above n 216, 1, 12, 15.

219 Ibid., 15.

Pakistan, USA, Thailand, China, Vietnam, Japan, Egypt, and Saudi Arabia, Iraq, UAE, Belgium, and UK.[220]

Accordingly, Sri Lanka was able to conclude two bilateral trade agreements, with Pakistan and the United States in 2002, namely, the *Pakistan-Sri Lanka Free Trade Agreement* (*PSLFTA*) signed on 1 August 2002 and the *United States-Sri Lanka Trade and Investment Framework Agreement* (*USSLTIFA*) signed on 25 July 2002.[221]

The *USSLTIFA* is the first Trade and Investment Framework Agreement (TIFA) that the United States signed with a country in the South Asian region.[222] More importantly, the signing of the *USSLTIFA* was a precursor towards the creation of a FTA between the United States and Sri Lanka.[223] Given that the United States has been the largest single buyer of Sri Lanka's exports since 1979, a possible FTA between the United States and Sri Lanka was believed to offer improved market access for Sri Lankan exports.[224]

Another important reason for Sri Lanka to negotiate the proposed US-Sri Lanka FTA was the potential impact of the expiry of the *MFA* on its garment industry. In the early 2000s, the garment industry was the largest net foreign exchange earner to Sri Lanka and recruited 'close to 330 000 people directly'.[225] Given that the *MFA* was to expire on 1 January 2005, the future of the garment industry was of 'particular concern to both the government and the industry'.[226] In particular, the Central Bank of Sri Lanka warned that 'Sri Lanka may face reduced demand for textile and garments with the proposed phasing out of the MFA in 2005 unless strong corrective measures are taken in advance'.[227] In addition, it was predicted that 'post-2004 restructuring of [the] garment industry would lead to a number of job losses'.[228] Moreover, it was also projected that 'the phase-out of *MFA* will result in approximately 50,000 Sri Lankan workers in garment industries in Middle East, Mauritius, Madagascar, and other countries coming back to Sri Lanka'.[229]

Given that the United States was Sri Lanka's largest export market for garments, the signing of a FTA with the United States was very important for Sri Lanka to shape the future of its garment industry. In particular, in 2001, 64 percent of Sri Lankan garment exports were destined for the United States market.[230]

220 Central Bank of Sri Lanka, *Annual Report 2002* (2003) 229.
221 Ibid.
222 Ibid.
223 Kelegama, above n 215, 217.
224 Central Bank of Sri Lanka, *Annual Report 2003* (2004) 195; Central Bank of Sri Lanka, *Annual Report 2002* (2003) 213.
225 Kelegama, above n 215, 216.
226 Ibid.
227 Central Bank of Sri Lanka, *Annual Report 2002* (2003) 207.
228 Kelegama, above n 215, 216.
229 Ibid.
230 Ibid.

Of the total Sri Lankan exports to the United States market, garments amounted to 78 percent ($ 1.5 billion).[231]

However, despite the importance of the United States to Sri Lanka as a prime export market for its garments, the United States did not make certain benefits which other countries, such as the European Union, made available to Sri Lankan garment exports. For instance, 47 percent of Sri Lankan garments for the United States market were 'quota-based and subject to a tariff rate of 15–20 percent for cotton garments'.[232] In contrast, in the European Union market, 'not only . . . Sri Lanka enjoy[ed] a quota free regime since early 2001 but also benefit[ted] from [the] Generalized System of Preferences'.[233] Sri Lanka needed similar benefits from the United States to protect the future of its garment industry. This was particularly important in light of projected adverse impacts of the expiry of *MFA* on the industry. As Kelegama observed:

> It [was] believed that an FTA with USA will give some support to the garment industry to maintain a significant level of employment and also to absorb the trained garment workers returning to the country. In other words, it [was] believed that an FTA will facilitate the garment industry to absorb the post-2004 shock with some ease.[234]

5.3.3.2. Impact of the proposed US-SRI Lanka Free Trade Agreement

The proposed US-Sri Lanka FTA had an important impact on the TRIPS model of copyright law, adopting high standards of copyright protection. This can be explained with reference to the TRIPS-plus copyright protection standards in the *Intellectual Property Act 2003*.

Ruse-Khan has stated that '[s]ince the mid-nineties, countries interested in higher IP standards have successfully shifted IP negotiations away from WIPO and WTO towards Free Trade Agreements (FTAs)'.[235] FTAs are used as primary means by the United States to promote protection of intellectual property in other countries. More specifically, provisions in FTAs which the United States has entered into with other countries oblige them to adhere to standards of intellectual property rights protection beyond those in the *TRIPS Agreement* (TRIPS-plus standards). The *Chile-United States Free Trade Agreement 2003*, the *United States-Singapore Free Trade Agreement 2003*, the *Dominican Republic-Central America Free Trade Agreement 2004* and the *United States-Australia Free Trade Agreement 2004* are some examples. All these FTAs require copyright owners'

231 Ibid., 215.
232 Ibid., 216.
233 Ibid.
234 Ibid., 217.
235 Henning Grosse Ruse-Khan, 'The International Law Relation Between TRIPS and Subsequent TRIPS-Plus Free Trade Agreements: Towards Safeguarding TRIPS Flexibilities?' (2011) 18(2) *Journal of Intellectual Property Law* 1, 3.

exclusive rights, including translation rights, to be protected stringently and for an extended period.[236]

As Kelegama said, at the time the proposed US-Sri Lanka FTA was negotiated the anticipation was that 'it will be modelled on the Singapore and Chile [FTAs]—these being the most recently concluded and the most comprehensive.'[237] As mentioned earlier, both these FTAs require TRIPS-plus standards of copyright protection, in particular, copyright owners' exclusive rights, including translation rights, to be protected stringently and for a period of the life of the author and 70 years. As such, strengthening of the national copyright regime by introducing higher standards was important for Sri Lanka if it were to enter into a FTA with the United States. This was also important because copyright piracy of American works was a major concern of the United States.[238]

5.4. Lack of awareness, transparency and ignorance

Lack of awareness, transparency and general ignorance on the part of Sri Lanka with regard to copyright law has contributed to rendering the TRIPS model of copyright law inimical to timely and affordable translation. Lack of awareness about intellectual property in general and copyright in particular is a relatively long-standing issue in Sri Lanka. In fact, when moving the second reading of the Code of Intellectual Property Bill in 1979, Minister Athulathmudali observed that:

> The Bill is not something that is widely understood, naturally, because it is really a specialist's field: but it really is revolutionary in terms of this particular class of property so necessary for the commercial development of Sri Lanka.[239]

Moreover, in a paper published by the WIPO in 2006 the then Director General of Intellectual Property in Sri Lanka stated that 'the poor awareness' on intellectual property 'is still a major issue in Sri Lanka, which needs constructive and pro-active attention'.[240] As he observed, lack of awareness about intellectual property 'is not an issue limited only to enforcement of IP rights. It is an issue

236 *Chile-United States Free Trade Agreement 2003*, art 17.5; *United States-Singapore Free Trade Agreement 2003*, art 16.4; *Dominican Republic-Central America Free Trade Agreement 2004*, art 15.5; *United States-Australia Free Trade Agreement 2004*, art 17.4.

237 Kelegama, above n 215, 223.

238 See Office of the USTR, *2012 National Trade Estimate Report on Foreign Trade Barriers* (2012) 353–354. Also see Siva Vaidhyanathan, *Copyrights and Copywrongs: The Rise of Intellectual Property and How It Threatens Creativity* (New York University Press, 2001) 2.

239 Sri Lanka, *Parliamentary Debates*, 25 May 1979, col 507.

240 DM Karunaratna, 'Issues Related to the Enforcement of IP Rights: National Efforts to Improve Awareness of Decision Makers and Education of Consumers' (Document presented to the WIPO Advisory Committee on Enforcement WIPO/ACE/3/5, Third Session, Geneva, 15–17 May 2006) 4.

that spreads through the entire IP regime—nature of IP rights, creation, acquisition and management of IP rights, their relevance'.[241] Hemaratne observed that '[l]ack of awareness of intellectual property is not confined to the public in general but to government officials [in Sri Lanka] who are involved directly or indirectly in protection of intellectual property rights of the country'.[242]

One of the reasons for the lack of awareness about intellectual property in Sri Lanka seems to be that intellectual property regimes in Sri Lanka, particularly copyright, have always been directly adopted and transplanted from either Britain, WIPO or from other countries. As a result, there is less discussion on intellectual property law at the local level in Sri Lanka. Another reason for the lack of awareness about intellectual property in Sri Lanka is the acute shortage of literature on Sri Lankan intellectual property jurisprudence. As Hemaratne observed:

> The first and most important impediment to the development of intellectual property jurisprudence in Sri Lanka is the lacuna of literature . . . [T]here is little academic writings on the intellectual property rights in Sri Lanka. A few studies have been undertaken often aimed at gaining academic qualifications. Nevertheless, hardly any attempts have been made to study, as a piece, to understand the intellectual property in Sri Lanka by seeking the possibilities to introduce a system where social values have impacted the law.[243]

A related issue that has arisen as a result of direct adoption and transplantation of intellectual property norms from other countries or international instruments to the Sri Lankan law is the lack of inclination and opportunity for the Sri Lankan courts to develop local judicial norms to determine issues relating to intellectual property. Instead of developing local judicial norms to suit the needs and interests of the country, the common approach of the Sri Lankan courts has been to follow the norms that have been set by the courts in other countries that have similar intellectual property laws to that of Sri Lanka.

The upshot of the lack of awareness, the lacuna of literature and the absence of local judicial norms on intellectual property in Sri Lanka is that there is less pressure from the courts, academia and other stakeholders to reform or revise the intellectual property law of Sri Lanka to suit the needs and interests of the country. The fact that up until this book, there has not been any attention on how the present Sri Lankan copyright regime impacts on one of the most crucial aspects of access to scientific and technical knowledge in Sri Lanka, namely, timely and affordable translation of copyright protected scientific and technical books and learning materials, is a good example of this.

241 Ibid.
242 TSK Hemaratne, 'Intellectual Property Law and E-Commerce in Sri Lanka: Towards a Jurisprudence based on Constitution, Roman-Dutch Law and Buddhist Principle' (PhD Thesis, Queen Mary, University of London, London, 2005) 38.
243 Ibid., 23–24.

The lack of transparency in the process of copyright law making in Sri Lanka is another contributing factor for high standards of protection of copyright owners' translation rights in the *Intellectual Property Act 2003.* In developed countries such as Britain, Australia and the United States, the process of copyright law making is transparent and open. In particular, these countries have allowed the participation of almost all the relevant stakeholders in the process of copyright law making, and their views and responses have largely been taken into consideration. In contrast, the copyright law making process in Sri Lanka has never been transparent. As Rodrigo observed, 'in Sri Lanka, there was hardly any fruitful discussion or debate before the *Code of Intellectual Property Act* 1979 and the *Intellectual Property Act* 2003 were passed by Parliament.'[244] Because of this, 'the stakeholders of intellectual property, including copyright, were shut out of the law making process and were given little opportunity to contribute by expressing their views and commenting upon those others.'[245] The upshot of this was the mere transplanting in Sri Lanka of 'the [copyright] laws of what either the WIPO has generally prescribed for developing countries or what other countries have enacted'.[246]

The general ignorance on the part of Sri Lanka on how best to mould its copyright regime to meet the needs and interest of the country whilst adhering to the international obligations is another explanation for why Sri Lanka adopted stringent protection over translation rights in the *Intellectual Property Act 2003.* The fact that Sri Lanka did not ratify the Appendix to the *Paris Act 1971* of the *Berne Convention* until 2005, and that even after this ratification it did not introduce the special exceptions to translation rights allowed in the Berne Appendix into the *Intellectual Property Act*, clearly explains this position.

As was observed in the previous chapter, the Berne Appendix, which was the main outcome of the Paris Conference for the revision of the *Berne Convention* held in 1971, introduced certain special exceptions to translation rights in developing countries. Accordingly, developing countries could either introduce a compulsory licensing system for translation or a limitation on the duration of translation rights. Yet Sri Lanka specifically excluded the Appendix when it ratified the *Paris Act 1971* in 1978. The reason for this exclusion remains unknown. One possible reason is that Sri Lanka may have thought that the special exceptions allowed under the Berne Appendix were unworkable. However, Sri Lanka's subsequent ratification of the Berne Appendix in 2005 and the declaration to the effect that 'it avails itself of the faculties provided for in Articles II and III of the Appendix' suggest otherwise.[247] More importantly, this subsequent

244 WD Rodrigo, 'Access to Information for Educational Purposes: The Role of Educational Exceptions to Copyright in a Developing Country like Sri Lanka' (2008) 14(1) *The Bar Association Law Journal* 57, 61.

245 Ibid.

246 Ibid.

247 WIPO, *WIPO Administered Treaties—Notifications—Berne Convention*, Berne Notification No 92 <www.wipo.int/treaties/en/notifications/berne/treaty_berne_92.html>.

ratification and the declaration suggest that the reason for Sri Lanka's exclusion of the Berne Appendix from its initial ratification of the *Paris Act 1971* in 1978 was its ignorance. This is particularly so because Sri Lanka ought to have been aware of the faculties in the Berne Appendix since a delegation from Sri Lanka not only participated at the Paris Conference 1971 but also the head of that delegation acted as one of the Vice-Presidents of that Conference.[248] Aside from this, the fact that even after the 2005 ratification and declaration, Sri Lanka has not done anything to implement the provisions of the Berne Appendix into its copyright regime is further suggestive of Sri Lanka's ignorance on how best it should mould its copyright regime to meet the needs and interests of the country.

248 General Report, *Records of the Diplomatic Conference for the Revision of the Berne Convention* (Paris, 5–24 July 1971) [3], [12].

VI Conclusion and the way forward

6.1. Conclusion

The aim of this book was to explore the reason why developing countries have failed to strike a proper balance in their copyright laws between the protection of translation rights and the ability of people to access translations of copyright protected scientific and technical books and learning materials. In that connection, the relationship between copyright law and translation, and its impact on access to scientific and technical knowledge were examined by placing emphasis on the context of Sri Lanka. However, as explained in the introductory chapter of this book and as will be seen later in this chapter, the focal points of the discussion relating to Sri Lanka are equally applicable to other developing countries, such as India and Bangladesh in general.

In the previous chapters, it was stated that the translation of scientific and technical books and learning materials (that are usually copyright protected) produced in developed countries and the reproduction of the translations in large quantities in a timely and affordable manner is crucial to promoting access to scientific and technical knowledge in Sri Lanka. However, the copyright law of Sri Lanka restricts the timely and affordable translation of these knowledge products and the reproduction of the translations in large quantities because it protects copyright owners' translation rights stringently without providing adequate exceptions. In particular, the way in which translation rights are protected in Sri Lankan copyright law makes it illegal for people to translate copyright protected scientific books and learning materials and to reproduce the translations in large quantities without the authorisation of the copyright owners. Obtaining copyright owners' authorisation for translation can be expensive, which can make the translations as well as their reproduction unaffordable to people. Also, since obtaining authorisation from copyright owners may be a slow process, it can affect timely translation and reproduction of the translations. The upshot of this is that the way in which translation rights are protected in the copyright law of Sri Lanka restricts the ability of its people to get access to scientific and technical knowledge. This is the bitter reality in most of the WTO-member developing countries where there is a multiplicity of languages or where a single local language dominates all spheres of life. India and Bangladesh are good examples in this connection.

The core objective of copyright law is to promote knowledge. To achieve this objective, copyright law should strike a proper balance between copyright owners' rights and the exceptions to these rights in a manner that would enhance people's ability to access copyright protected works. Like many other developing countries in the world, the way in which translation rights are protected in Sri Lankan copyright law clearly shows that Sri Lanka has failed to strike this balance.

The primary reason for the failure of the Sri Lankan copyright law to have struck a proper balance between the copyright owners' translation rights and the people's ability to access translations of copyright protected works in a manner that promotes public access to scientific and technical knowledge is that Sri Lanka has never taken into consideration the needs and interests of the country and its people when devising its copyright laws. From its inception, copyright law in Sri Lanka has been devised to suit foreign interests rather than the interests of the country. In particular, when copyright law was first introduced to Sri Lanka, it was a colonial instrument which reflected the needs and interests of Britain. Furthermore, from the introduction of the first copyright statute in 1908 up to now, all the copyright statutes in Sri Lanka have complied with the international copyright obligations in the *Berne Convention*, which predominantly reflects the needs and interests of copyright-exporting countries in the West. In addition, from 2003, the copyright law of Sri Lanka has complied with the obligations of the *TRIPS Agreement* and the *US-Sri Lanka IPR Agreement*, which predominantly reflect the needs and interests of the United States and other copyright-exporting countries.

Similar to Sri Lanka, India and Bangladesh (as a part of larger British India) were also under the shackles of British colonialism from the eighteenth century up until the mid-twentieth century. While copyright law was first introduced to British India during this period, as Bently's account of the history of translation rights in British India amply demonstrates, it was a colonial instrument which furthered the British interests to the detriment of the needs and interests of the Indians.[1] Like in the case of almost all the countries which were under British colonial occupation at that time, India also was made a party to the *Berne Convention* by Britain in 1887. Even after their declaration of independence, most of these countries, including India and Bangladesh, continued with their *Berne*-membership despite the fact that certain principles and standards advocated by the *Berne Convention* (such as translation rights) were pernicious to their own interests. While these countries became obliged to devise their domestic copyright laws in compliance with the *Berne* obligations as a result, acceding to the *TRIPS Agreement* meant that such compliance is more intense than ever.

The fact that copyright law is a balancing act between the copyright owners' rights and the public's ability to access copyright protected works is recognised by the *Berne Convention*, the *TRIPS Agreement* and the *US-Sri Lanka IPR*

1 See Lionel Bently, 'Copyright, Translations, and Relations between Britain and India in the Nineteenth and Early Twentieth Centuries' (2007) 82(3) *Chicago-Kent Law Review* 1181.

Agreement. In particular, all these instruments strive to strike a proper balance between copyright owners' rights and the people's ability to access copyright protected works by entrenching rights of copyright owners and providing for exceptions to those rights. However, the problem is that the balance struck by these instruments only suits the developed world. This is because, in striving to strike a proper balance, what these instruments only have taken into consideration is the factual matrix which is applicable to their architects—that is, developed countries which produce and export copyright protected works such as the United States and those in the European Union. In contrast, the factual matrix that is applicable to developing countries like Sri Lanka, India and Bangladesh, which are the main users and importers of copyright protected works, has been by and large, if not totally, ignored by these instruments when striving to strike a proper copyright balance.

Uniform standards of copyright protection which ensue from the copyright balance that is struck by the *Berne Convention*, the *TRIPS Agreement* and the *US-Sri Lanka IPR Agreement* have different significance in different contexts. In particular, the copyright balance that is struck by the *Berne Convention*, the *TRIPS Agreement* and the *US-Sri Lanka IPR Agreement* is tilted in favour of the protection of copyright owners' rights. The reason for this (as noted earlier) is that this copyright balance has been struck by taking into consideration the needs and interests of developed countries that produce and export copyright protected works. As such, the uniform standards of copyright protection in the *Berne Convention*, the *TRIPS Agreement* and the *US-Sri Lanka IPR Agreement* would be suitable and work well for developed countries which produce and export copyright protected works. The issue, however, is that the socio-economic and political context of developing countries like Sri Lanka is different to the context of these developed countries. Developing countries like Sri Lanka, India and Bangladesh are users and importers of copyright protected works and therefore the standards of copyright protection which ensue from a copyright balance which is tilted in favour of copyright owners are grossly unsuitable for these countries, particularly for their access to scientific and technical knowledge.

The fact that copyright protection does not have the same meaning in different contexts is clearly discernible from the way in which protection of translation rights has evolved in the copyright law of Britain (as was examined in chapter 3). In particular, one of the main reasons for Britain's refusal to protect copyright owners' translation rights until the mid-nineteenth century and the reluctance to accord these rights the same status of the right of reproduction until the early twentieth century was the socio-economic and political context of Britain at that time.

As observed in chapter 3, until the mid-nineteenth century British copyright law did not protect translation rights of copyright owners. This was despite the fact that in Britain by the latter half of the eighteenth century it was acknowledged that unauthorised translation of books and other printed materials was injurious to the interests of the authors of these works. One of the main reasons for Britain's refusal to protect copyright owners' translation rights until 1852 (despite the fact that unauthorised translation was injurious to the interests of authors) was the importance of translation of books and other printed materials for promoting access to knowledge of the people in that country. In particular, especially during its early period of printing, Britain considered that translation was important to further the interests of printers, translators and the reading public which would ultimately promote public access to knowledge. Notably, Britain appears to have carried this idea (to a more or lesser extent) into the nineteenth century. Indeed, this becomes discernible from the fact that the 1838 and 1844 International Copyright Acts, specifically excluded copyright owners' translation rights from copyright protection[2] partly for the reason that protection of a right of translation 'would fetter the transmission of literature and of discoveries in science from one country to another'.[3] In addition, the Copyright Bill 1837 introduced by Sergeant Talfourd and other subsequent Bills that culminated in the *Copyright Act 1842* specifically stated that translation of a copyright protected work would not amount to infringement of copyright.[4]

Although Britain started to protect copyright owners' translation rights in 1852, that protection was confined to certain foreign authors. Also, the protection of translation rights was subject to certain cumbersome conditions and the duration of these rights was limited to five years.[5] This shows that even in 1852 Britain was reluctant to accord translation rights the same status of the right of reproduction despite that the modern copyright law which emerged in Britain during the 1850s or thereabouts recognised on principle that unauthorised translation was clearly an infringement of copyright in the original work. Notably, one of the main reasons for this reluctance was the British Parliament's view of the importance of translations to facilitate access to knowledge of the people in Britain. In fact, this becomes evident from the proceedings of the British Parliament on the enactment of the *International Copyright Act 1852*, particularly where Lord Beaumont observed that the translation rights sought to be protected through

2 *International Copyright Act 1838*, 1 & 2 Vict, c 59, s 13; *International Copyright Act 1844*, 7 & 8 Vict, c 12, s 18.
3 United Kingdom, *Hansard*, House of Commons, 20 March 1838, vol 41, col 1107.
4 A Bill to Consolidate and Amend the Laws relating to Copyright in Printed Books, Musical Compositions, Acted Dramas, and Engravings, to provide Remedies for the Violation thereof, and to extend the Term of its Duration 1837 (380), s 13 proviso; A Bill to Amend the Law relating to Copyright 1837–38 (164), s 19 proviso; A Bill to Amend the Law relating to Copyright 1837–38 (461), s 17 proviso; A Bill to Amend the Law relating to Copyright 1839 (19) s, 17 proviso; A Bill to Amend the Law of Copyright 1840 (61), s 15 proviso; A Bill to Amend the Law of Copyright 1841 (29 January 1841), s 15 proviso; A Bill to Amend the Law of Copyright 1842 (79), s 15 proviso; A Bill to Amend the Law of Copyright 1842 (139), s 15 proviso; A Bill to Amend the Law of Copyright 1842 (194), s 15 proviso. See also Catherine Seville, *Literary Copyright Reform in Early Victorian England: The Framing of the 1842 Copyright Act* (Cambridge University Press, first published 1999, 2003) 240, 245–247.
5 *International Copyright Act 1852*, 15 & 16 Vict, c 12 ss 2–11.

the *International Copyright Act* were 'very injurious to literature and to the progress of science'.[6]

In 1911, British copyright law fully accommodated the principle that translation rights were an exclusive right of copyright owners, as was the exclusive right of reproduction. This accommodation was mainly an outcome of the changed socio-economic and political conditions in Britain by the twentieth century. By this time, in particular, Britain had become a major producer and exporter of books. Thus, British copyright law and the balance which it had earlier struck between the copyright owners' rights and the public's ability to access copyright protected works had to be changed in line with the country's new economic, social and political conditions.

As its book industry blossomed, from the nineteenth century Britain was concerned with protecting the interests of its copyright owners (authors and publishers) against unauthorised copying of their books in foreign countries. To this end, Britain entered into bilateral copyright arrangements with several countries, including France, in which unauthorised reprinting of British books frequently occurred. The bilateral treaty entered into between Britain and France, popularly known as the *Anglo-French Copyright Treaty 1851*, with the aim of, inter alia, preventing unauthorised reprinting of British books in France, demanded Britain protect the translation rights of certain French copyright owners for a period of five years, subject to certain conditions.[7] As such, Britain had to enact the *International Copyright Act 1852* which recognised copyright owners' translation rights for the first time in British copyright law.

The bilateral copyright arrangements were not an effective mechanism to protect the interests of the British copyright owners against unauthorised copying of their books in foreign countries. Moreover, Britain was unable to conclude a bilateral copyright arrangement with the United States, which constituted a large market for British books and in which there was an unprecedented level of piracy against the copyright owners in Britain. In this context, Britain foresaw the benefit of acceding to the *Berne Convention* to protect the interests of British copyright owners in the United States and in other countries. In particular, Britain thought that ratifying the *Berne Convention* would be favourable to creating copyright relations with the United States or at least 'would not prejudice potential Anglo-American relations'.[8] At the same time, ratifying the *Berne Convention* 'seemed necessary to maintain existing levels of protection in European markets' because it was felt probable that once a multilateral copyright arrangement was established through the *Berne Convention*, the existing bilateral copyright arrangements 'could all be terminated'.[9]

6 United Kingdom, *Hansard*, House of Lords, 30 April 1852, vol 121, col 4.

7 *Convention between Her Majesty and the French Republic for the Establishment of International Copyright* signed at Paris on 3 November 1851, art III.

8 Lionel Bently and Brad Sherman, 'Great Britain and the Signing of the *Berne Convention* in 1886' (2000–2001) 48 *Journal of the Copyright Society of the USA* 311, 335.

9 Ibid., 334.

The outcome of Britain's decision to accede to the *Berne Convention* was the *International Copyright Act 1886*, which recognised translation rights of foreign copyright owners for a period of ten years. In particular, the original version of the *Berne Convention* required Member Countries to protect translation rights of the authors in other Member Countries for a period of ten years.

Towards the latter part of the nineteenth century, another issue which copyright owners in Britain, particularly the 'respectable, educational publishers',[10] encountered was the unauthorised translation of their books in India. To rectify this problem, these copyright owners, among other things, lobbied the British Parliament to enact a copyright law protecting the translation rights of British authors in Britain and its colonial possessions. However, British authors had to wait till the enactment of the *Imperial Copyright Act 1911* for their translation rights to be protected under the copyright law of Britain.

The impetus for enactment of the *Imperial Copyright Act 1911* came from the Berlin revision of the *Berne Convention* in 1908 (*Berlin Act 1908*). The *Berlin Act 1908* of the *Berne Convention* extended the protection afforded to copyright owners' translation rights to accommodate the principle that translation rights were an exclusive right of copyright owners as was the right of reproduction. Britain gave effect to its obligations under the *Berlin Act 1908* in the *Imperial Copyright Act 1911*. Thus, the *Imperial Copyright Act* protected translation rights of both foreign and domestic copyright owners for the full term of their copyright protection.

The fact that copyright protection does not have the same meaning in different contexts is also clearly discernible from the way in which protection of translation rights has evolved in the *Berne Convention*. As examined in chapter 4, when the *Berne Convention* was concluded in 1886, it limited the protection of copyright owners' translation rights for a period of ten years because of the differences in socio-economic and political conditions of the countries who participated at the Berne negations. In particular, countries like Norway and Sweden (who were mainly users and importers of literary and scientific works) did not agree with the views of developed countries like France (who were producers and exporters of copyright protected works) that copyright owners' translation rights should be protected in the same way as reproduction rights.[11] Norway and Sweden were only prepared to accept a shorter term of protection in respect of translation rights for the reason that 'readily available translations were of great importance to the Scandinavian countries in view of their small, dispersed populations and educational needs'.[12] In addition, Japan, which played a very active role at the Uruguay Round of *GATT* negotiations and which supported the higher standards of copyright protection (including translation rights) advocated by the

10 Bently, above n 1, 1204–1205.

11 Sam Ricketson and Jane Ginsburg, *International Copyright and Neighbouring Rights: The Berne Convention and Beyond* (Oxford University Press, 2nd ed, 2006) vol 1, 67 (citations omitted).

12 Ibid.

TRIPS Agreement, claimed in 1908 (when it was a developing country) that '[t]he translation into Japanese of a work written in a European language and vice versa [should] be completely free'.[13] As Ricketson and Ginsburg observed, 'Japanese desire, as a developing country to gain ready access to European technical and other literature was obvious, and many European countries had only recently been in that position themselves.'[14]

The desire of developing countries, particularly India, during the 1960s and early 1970s to lower the standards of copyright protection (including translation rights) in the *Berne Convention* is another example of the fact that copyright protection does not have the same meaning in different contexts. As observed in chapter 4, developing countries at the 1967 Stockholm Conference for the revision of the *Berne Convention* demanded some kind of special concession for their use of copyright protected works, most of which originated from the developed countries. In particular, many developing countries argued that publishing houses located in developed countries charged high prices for their copyright protected works and had little or no interest in supplying proper translations to developing countries.[15] The revision of the *Berne Convention* (*Stockholm Act 1967*) recognised that as the economic, social and political conditions of developing countries differ to those of developed countries, the developing countries needed a special scheme of copyright protection. The result was the Stockholm Protocol which provided special concessions with regard to copyright protection in developing countries. While the Stockholm Protocol was a total failure from the point of view of the developing countries because it never came in to effect, the subsequent Paris revision of the *Berne Convention* in 1971 also gave developing countries certain special concessions with regard to copyright protection. These concessions were provided in the Appendix to the *Paris Act 1971* of the *Berne Convention*.

Although at the Stockholm and Paris conferences the *Berne Convention* recognised that developing countries needed lower standards of copyright protection than those in developed countries, the lower standards of copyright protection (the special concessions) ultimately introduced in the Appendix to the *Paris Act 1971* are not adequate for developing countries. In particular, the compulsory licensing system for translation introduced by the Appendix hardly provides any assistance to developing countries for the timely and affordable translation of scientific and technical books and learning materials. It also does not facilitate the reproduction of the translations in large quantities in a timely and affordable manner. There are three main reasons for this. Firstly, translations under compulsory licenses can only be made from works 'published in printed and analogous forms of reproduction'[16] and except for broadcasting, translations made under compulsory licenses can only be published in 'printed or analogous forms of

13 Ibid., 98.
14 Ibid.
15 Ibid., 129.
16 *Paris Act 1971* of the *Berne Convention*, Appendix, art II (1).

reproduction'.[17] This seems to exclude translation of online copyright protected works and online publication of translations made under compulsory licenses. Secondly, the time period that an applicant has to wait before applying for compulsory licenses for translation—which is one year and nine months or three years and six months (as the case may be)—is excessive. Thirdly, the administrative procedures that have to be followed to obtain compulsory licenses for translation are burdensome, expensive and time-consuming.

Given that different countries have different needs vis-à-vis copyright protection, setting global uniform standards of copyright protection (including protection of translation rights) is unrealistic. It is illogical to assume that standards of copyright protection can be articulated in a 'one size fits all' manner. And this is exactly what the *Berne Convention*, the *TRIPS Agreement* and the bilateral arrangements such as the *US-Sri Lanka IPR Agreement* have done. Although it might be argued in view of the special faculties provided in its Appendix in favour of developing countries that the *Berne Convention* sets different standards of copyright protection between developed and developing countries, since these special faculties are inadequate and unworkable, there does not appear to be an actual distinction in the way in which *Berne Convention* requires developed and developing countries to protect copyright. In short, the actual manner in which standards of copyright protection in the *Berne Convention* work is effectively a 'one size fits all' model.

Moreover, needs differ even among developing countries themselves because of diverse economic, social and political conditions. These differences require different standards of copyright protection in countries. However, the *Berne Convention*, the *TRIPS Agreement* and bilateral arrangements such as the *US-Sri Lanka IPR Agreement* do not recognise this. Thus, if copyright laws of countries are to reflect their needs and interests, there needs to be an overall change in the ongoing process of globalising uniform copyright norms that does not look at the economic, social and political conditions (context) of each country when setting the uniform copyright standards which all countries in the world are required to adhere to.

A related aspect of the globalising uniform copyright norms through the *Berne Convention*, the *TRIPS Agreement* and bilateral arrangements such as the *US-Sri Lanka IPR Agreement* is that developing countries like Sri Lanka, India and Bangladesh accommodate these norms into their national copyright laws without the will of the people. In the same way in which colonisation compelled these countries to accommodate alien copyright norms to their laws, today the trade and commercial interests of these countries have also compelled them to accommodate alien copyright norms to their laws. As shown in chapter 3, uniform copyright norms were first introduced to Sri Lanka under the political coercion of colonisation. The situation was the same in the case of British India. As demonstrated in chapter 5, developing countries such as Sri Lanka, India and

17 Ibid., arts II(2)(a), 9(a).

Bangladesh have accommodated the *TRIPS Agreement* and bilateral arrangements such as the *US-Sri Lanka IPR Agreement* because of economic coercion, namely, the trade incentives and sanctions applied by developed countries, particularly the United States. The copyright norms introduced by the *TRIPS Agreement* and bilateral arrangements such as the *US-Sri Lanka IPR Agreement* revive and reinforce the copyright norms in the *Berne Convention*. Indeed, according to von Lewinski, '[t]he Berne Convention has experienced the strongest boost in its "career" through the incorporation of its substantive law into the TRIPS Agreement and into bilateral and regional trade agreements.'[18]

It is an accepted norm that laws of a country should reflect the will of its people. When laws are made and implemented without the will of the people, they remain alien to the people. As a result, people typically remain ignorant and unaware of these laws. This is what appears to have happened to the copyright law of Sri Lanka. As shown in chapters 3, 4 and 5, all the copyright laws of Sri Lanka have constantly reflected the will of copyright owners in developed countries that export copyright protected works rather than the will of the people in Sri Lanka, the users and importers of copyright protected works. In fact, this is exactly what the *Berne Convention*, the *TRIPS Agreement* and the *US-Sri Lanka IPR Agreement* have mandated Sri Lanka to do.

To date, there has not been any public participation in the process of copyright law making in Sri Lanka. In contrast, it appears that authorities in Sri Lanka, due to a mixture of ignorance and a lack of awareness, have merely transplanted provisions into the copyright law of Sri Lanka from model laws or copyright laws from foreign countries like Britain, Australia and the United States. However, the authorities in Sri Lanka cannot be totally blamed for this because they must meet their international obligations under the *Berne Convention*, the *TRIPS Agreement* and the *US-Sri Lanka IPR Agreement* and enact them into the national copyright law. Yet when copyright law is made in this manner there is a possibility that authorities miss the chance to define copyright law as best as they can meet the needs and interests of the country, while staying within the country's international obligations. The failure of Sri Lanka to make use of the facilities provided under the *Berne Convention* for compulsory licensing exemplifies this point well.

In the final analysis, it can be concluded that the primary reason why Sri Lankan copyright law operates to restrict access to scientific and technical knowledge is the international copyright obligations that have been imposed on Sri Lanka by the *Berne Convention*, the *TRIPS Agreement* and the *US-Sri Lanka IPR Agreement*. The situation is the same in the case of India, Bangladesh and other developing countries which are Member Countries to the *Berne Convention*, the *TRIPS Agreement* and other international/bilateral agreements similar to the *US-Sri Lanka IPR Agreement*.

18 Silke von Lewinski, *International Copyright Law and Policy* (Oxford University Press, 2008) 585.

6.2. The way forward

To change the existing situation, either the obligations imposed by the *Berne Convention*, the *TRIPS Agreement* and other similar international/bilateral agreements have to be altered or developing countries should denounce these obligations. However, in a globalised world, where the economic development of these countries is highly dependent on integration with other countries, especially developed countries, denouncing the obligations of the *Berne Convention*, the *TRIPS Agreement* and other initiatives such as the *US-Sri Lanka IPR Agreement* would not be in their best interest. Thus, the only available alternative for developing countries is to seek reform of these instruments through a concerted effort towards amicable negotiation. However, two major obstacles that developing countries, particularly smaller countries like Sri Lanka and Bangladesh, would inevitably have to encounter in this connection are the 'inequalities of power' between developed and developing countries and the 'lack of an effective democratic legislative bargaining mechanism' at the international level.[19]

Tian said that '[a]t the international level, the power of developed nations is much stronger than that of developing nations.'[20] This was quite evident at the proceedings for the last two revisions of the *Berne Convention* in 1967 and 1971 as well as the Uruguay Round negotiations for the *TRIPS Agreement*. As observed in chapters 4 and 5, despite the strong involvement of a giant country like India, the developed countries were still able to effectively subdue and supress the demands of developing countries through various means, including economic coercion. This was particularly so at the Uruguay Round, the outcome of which was a triumph for developed countries and their intellectual property exporting business entities that wanted to enforce intellectual property rights in the developing world.

Also, as the United Kingdom Commission on Intellectual Property Rights observed, '[t]oo often the interests of the "producer" dominate in the evolution of IP policy, and that of the ultimate consumer is neither heard nor heeded.'[21] The result is that IP policy 'tends to be determined more by the interests of the commercial users of the system, than by an impartial conception of the greater public good', thus creating an imbalance in 'IPR discussions between developed and developing countries'.[22] Apart from the economic factors which give the developed countries an edge over the developing nations in the process of setting global intellectual property standards, another main reason for the dominance of the developed countries in this sphere is the fact that 'developing countries, are less able to identify and represent their own interests against those of the

19 YiJun Tian, *Re-Thinking Intellectual Property: The Political Economy of Copyright Protection in the Digital Era* (Routledge-Cavendish, 2009) 82–92.
20 Ibid., 83.
21 Commission on Intellectual Property Rights, *Integrating Intellectual Property Rights and Development Policy*, Report of the Commission on Intellectual Property Rights (2002) 7.
22 Ibid.

developed nations'.[23] As Tian stated, '[a]t the international IP standard-setting process, pressures from developed nations, added to the relatively disorganised structure of developing country bargaining groups, often means developing countries cannot conduct effective international bargaining.'[24] While there might be multiple causes which contribute towards the less effective and disorganised manner in which developing countries conduct their international bargaining, one contributory factor seems to be the lesser importance attached to piecemeal bargaining, that is, negotiating over each individual matter or issue (for instance, translation of scientific and technical knowledge products) one at a time, rather than submitting a comprehensive package of proposals.

Piecemeal bargaining would be particularly important in the context of international copyright reform towards facilitating access to scientific and technical knowledge through translation. The present international copyright standards formulated in instruments such as the *Berne Convention* recognise and provide copyright protection for subject matter in broad terms. For the most part, copyright protection yardsticks in these instruments do not distinguish between factual works and fiction, scientific works and non-scientific works, etc. Instead, copyright protection is afforded to 'every [original] production in the literary, scientific and artistic domain' in very broad terms.[25]

The general exceptions recognised for copyright protection in these instruments take a similar form, whereas these exceptions are not specific to the subject matter that is sought to be protected through copyright. For instance, Article 9(2) of the *Berne Convention* (*Paris Act 1971*), which provides for the main general exception to authors' rights, allows the exception for all works but does not distinguish between subject matter of copyright according to their nature (i.e. factual, fictional, scientific or non-scientific). This makes it difficult and more challenging for the developing countries to seek concessions from the developed nations with regard to translation of scientific and technical books and learning materials either by reduction of the term of copyright protection in general or by enlargement of the scope of the general exceptions to copyright because that would inevitably affect and weaken the copyright protection afforded to other subject matter (for instance, computer programs, films, music) which would have a major economic significance to those developed countries.

The better and more viable alternative for the developing countries seems to be to bargain piecemeal for copyright concessions which are limited to specified uses (i.e. translation and reproduction of translations), subject matter (i.e. scientific and technical books and learning materials) and users (for example students). This is because authors and copyright industries in developed countries would be less opposed to specific copyright concessions or exceptions that would, for instance, allow free translation of scientific and technical books and learning material into

23 Ibid.

24 Tian, above n 19, 83.

25 *Berne Convention (Paris Act 1971)* art 2(1).

certain local languages used in developing countries—such as Sinhala, the usage of which is geographically very limited. Since the market size for works in such languages is small, there would hardly be any substantial deprivation of economic benefit caused to the copyright owners by allowing free translation of their works into such languages. Moreover, because scientific and technical books and learning material get outdated soon, it is less likely that copyright owners of these types of works would be much keen in translating their works to cater to small markets. Further, copyright owners would be less opposed to allow free translation and the reproduction of translations for the use of selected categories of persons (for example students) in developing countries than to a general exception that would allow free translation and the reproduction of translations for the use of all. The *Marrakesh Treaty to Facilitate Access to Published Works for Persons Who Are Blind, Visually Impaired, or Otherwise Print Disabled 2013* (*Marrakesh VIP Treaty*) provides a good example in this connection.

As authors of *Copinger and Skone James on Copyright* observed, *Marrakesh VIP Treaty* 'is unique in the copyright field, in that it is the first international copyright instrument which obliges countries to introduce an exception or limitation to rights established under other international copyright treaties and domestic laws'.[26] Also, it is the 'first treaty that established obligations with respect to exceptions and limitations for a particular group of beneficiaries, namely persons who are blind or suffer from other print disability, and for specific acts in relation to copyright-protected works'.[27]

The *Marrakesh VIP Treaty* addresses not only the '[s]ignificant concern that has been expressed about the potential impact of copyright law on the ability of people with disabilities to access cultural materials' but also the potential of copyright law to deprive users of copyright protected works when their market size is small (i.e. market failures).[28] The problem of small markets is particularly relevant in the context of access to translations of copyright protected scientific and technical works in certain local languages used in developing countries. For instance, the use of a language like Sinhala is geographically limited to Sri Lanka and because of that the size of the market for Sinhala readership is small. Consequently, authors and copyright industries in developed nations would be less inclined to cater to such a small market through making available translations of their scientific and technical works in Sinhala because of economic interests. An international instrument similar to the *Marrakesh VIP Treaty* would be highly desirable for developing countries like Sri Lanka to promote access to translations of scientific and technical knowledge produced in the West because it would not only create a specific exception to translation of these knowledge products but would also address market failures created by copyright law.

26 Gillian Davies, Nicholas Caddick and Gwilym Harbottle, *Copinger and Skone James on Copyright* (Sweet & Maxwell-South Asian, 17th ed, 2019) vol 1, 1764.

27 Ibid.

28 L Bently, B Sherman, D Gangjee and P Johnson, *Intellectual Property Law* (Oxford University Press, 5th ed, 2018) 49.

While the exceptions and flexibilities in the *Berne Convention*, the *TRIPS Agreement* and other initiatives such as the *US-Sri Lanka IPR Agreement* do not provide assistance to developing countries to promote access to translations of copyright protected scientific and technical books and learning materials, they might provide assistance to developing countries in other respects such as broadening access to translations of non-scientific material and fiction. Besides, India and Bangladesh have incorporated the flexibilities provided in the Appendix of the *Berne Convention* into their domestic copyright laws. As such, for the time being, it would be prudent for Sri Lanka to at least try to gain the maximum benefits out of the flexibilities provided in the *Berne Convention*, the *TRIPS Agreement* and the *US-Sri Lanka IPR Agreement*. Although there are number of problems with the special exceptions contained in the Berne Appendix, a useful starting point in the meantime might be for Sri Lanka to make use of these exceptions for whatever purpose they may serve, as Sri Lanka will not lose anything by doing so.

Bibliography

Abbott, Frederick M, 'Protecting First World Assets in the Third World: Intellectual Property Negotiation in the GATT Multilateral Framework' (1989) 22(4) *Vanderbilt Journal of Transnational Law* 689

Abbott, Frederick M, 'The WTO TRIPS Agreement and Global Economic Development' (1996) 72 *Chicago-Kent Law Review* 385

Abeyesekere, Indunil Nirupadi, *Sri Lankan Copyright Law and the TRIPS Agreement* (Mahapola Publications, 1999)

Alexander, Isabella, 'All Change for the Digital Economy: Copyright and Business Models in the Early Eighteenth Century' (2010) 25 *Berkeley Technology Law Journal* 1351

Altbach, Philip G and Edith S Hoshino (eds), *International Book Publishing: An Encyclopaedia* (Garland Publishing, 1995)

Amarasuriya, Harini and Dileepa Witharana, 'Conflicting Agendas: Implications of Intellectual Property Rights on Access to Knowledge in Education and Research' (Paper presented at the 7th National Conference on Library and Information Science, Colombo, 25 June 2009) <http://eprints.rclis.org/13385/>

Amarasuriya, Nirmala R, *Publishing Scientific & Technical Journals in Sri Lanka: Report of a National Survey* (Natural Resources, Energy and Science Authority, 1987)

Arber, Edward, *A Transcript of the Registers of the Company of Stationers of London: 1554–1640 AD* (1894) vol 5

Ariyadasa, KD, *The Curriculum Development Centre of Sri Lanka* (UNESCO, 1977)

Asian Development Bank, *Innovative Strategies for Accelerated Human Resource Development in South Asia: Teacher Professional Development* (Report, ADB, 2017)

Askerud, Pernille, *A Guide to Sustainable Book Provision* (UNESCO, 1997)

Athukorala, PPA Wasantha, 'The Impact of Foreign Direct Investment for Economic Growth: A Case Study in Sri Lanka' (Paper submitted for the 9th International Conference on Sri Lankan Studies, Matara, 28–30 November 2003)

Aturupane, Harsha et al., *Transforming School Education in Sri Lanka: From Cut Stones to Polished Jewels* (World Bank, 2011)

Aturupane, Harsha et al., 'Sri Lanka: Investment in Human Capital' (Report No 69, World Bank, 2014)

Auchter, Dorothy, *Dictionary of Literary and Dramatic Censorship in Tudor and Stuart England* (Greenwood Press, 2001)

Balasubramaniam, K, 'Globalisation and Liberalisation of Healthcare Services: WTO and the General Agreement on Trade in Services' (Issue Paper, People's Health Assembly, 2000)

Baldsing, LindZay, 'Making English the Lynchpin for Globalisation of Education in Sri Lanka: Quality versus Equality' (PhD Thesis, Edith Cowan University, 2013)
Banks, JA, 'Population Change and the Victorian City' (1968) 11(3) *Victorian Studies* 277
Barker, Ronald and Robert Escarpit (eds), *The Book Hunger* (UNESCO, 1973)
Basalamah, Salah, 'Compulsory Licensing for Translation: An Instrument of Development?' (2000) 40(4) *IDEA: The Journal of Law and Technology* 503
Baugh, Albert C and Thomas Cable, *A History of the English Language* (Routledge, 5th ed, 2002)
Bennett, HS, *English Books & Readers 1558 to 1603: Being a Study in the History of the Book Trade in the Reign of Elizabeth I* (Cambridge University Press, 1965)
Bennett, HS, *English Books & Readers 1475 to 1557: Being a Study in the History of the Book Trade from Caxton to the Incorporation of the Stationers' Company* (Cambridge University Press, 2nd ed, 1969)
Bennett, HS, *English Books & Readers 1603 to 1640: Being a Study in the History of the Book Trade in the Reigns of James I and Charles I* (Cambridge University Press, 1970)
Bently, Lionel, 'Copyright and Translations in the English Speaking World' (1993) 12(4) *Translatio—FIT Newsletter* 491
Bently, Lionel, 'Copyright, Translations, and Relations Between Britain and India in the Nineteenth and Early Twentieth Centuries' (2007) 82(3) *Chicago-Kent Law Review* 1181
Bently, Lionel and M Kretschmer (eds), *Primary Sources on Copyright (1450–1900)* <www.copyrighthistory.org>
Bently, Lionel and Brad Sherman, 'Great Britain and the Signing of the Berne Convention in 1886' (2000–2001) 48 *Journal of the Copyright Society of the USA* 311
Bently, Lionel and Brad Sherman, *Intellectual Property Law* (Oxford University Press, 3rd ed, 2009)
Bently, Lionel, Brad Sherman, D Gangjee and P Johnson, *Intellectual Property Law* (Oxford University Press, 5th ed, 2018)
Bently, Lionel, Uma Suthersanen and Paul Torremans (eds), *Global Copyright: Three Hundred Years Since the Statute of Anne, from 1709 to Cyberspace* (Edward Elgar, 2010)
Bhagwati, Jagdish, *In Defence of Globalisation* (Oxford University Press, 2004)
Bhagwati, Jagdish and Hugh T Patrick (eds), *Aggressive Unilateralism: America's 301 Trade Policy and the World Trading System* (University of Michigan Press, 1990)
Bhattacharya, Lokenath, *Books and Reading in India* (UNESCO, 1985)
Bhattacharya, Usree, 'Mediating Inequalities: Exploring English-Medium Instruction in a Suburban Indian Village School' (2013) 14(1) *Current Issues in Language Planning* 164
Birrell, Augustine, *Seven Lectures on the Law and History of Copyright in Books* (Cassell, 1899)
Blagden, Cyprian, *The Stationers' Company: A History, 1403–1959* (Stanford University Press, 1977)
Blake, Robert O, 'Importance of Investment and Trade in Sri Lanka' (Speech delivered at the Sri Lanka Economic Summit 2007, Cinnamon Grand, 6–8 June 2007) <http://businesstoday.lk/cover_page.php?article=4602&issue=272>
Blakeney, Michael, 'Intellectual Property in World Trade' (1995) 1(3) *International Trade Law & Regulation* 76

Blakeney, Michael, 'The Impact of the TRIPs Agreement in the Asia Pacific Region' (1996) 18(10) *European Intellectual Property Review* 544

Blakeney, Michael, *Intellectual Property Enforcement: A Commentary on the Anti-Counterfeiting Trade Agreement (ACTA)* (Edward Elgar, 2012)

Bowers, Jennifer and Peggy Keeran, *Literary Research and the British Renaissance and Early Modern Period: Strategies and Sources* (Scarecrow Press, 2010)

Bracha, Oren, 'Owning Ideas: A History of Anglo-American Intellectual Property' (JSD Thesis, Harvard Law School, 2005)

Bracha, Oren, 'The Adventures of the Statute of Anne in the Land of Unlimited Possibilities: The Life of a Legal Transplant' (2010) 25 *Berkeley Technology Law Journal* 1427

Bragg, Melvyn, *The Adventure of English 500AD to 2000: The Biography of a Language* (Sceptre, first published 2003, 2004 ed)

Briggs, William, *The Law of International Copyright* (Stevens & Haynes, 1906)

Brohier, RL, *Ancient Irrigation Works in Ceylon* (Government Publications Bureau, 1934) vol 1

Brown, Michael E and Sumit Ganguly (eds), *Fighting Words: Language Policy and Ethnic Relations in Asia* (MIT Press, 2003)

Buscaglia, Edgardo and Clarisa Long, *US Foreign Policy and Intellectual Property Rights in Latin America* (Hoover Institution, 1997)

Cabral, Harsha, *Intellectual Property Law in Sri Lanka: The Act No 36 of 2003, the TRIPS Agreement and a Case Digest* (2004)

Caliskan, Yusuf, 'The Development of International Investment Law: Lessons from the OECD MAI Negotiations and Their Application to a Possible Multilateral Agreement on Investment' (JSD Thesis, Washington University School of Law, 2002)

Canagarajah, AS, 'Dilemmas in Planning English/Vernacular Relations in Post-Colonial Communities' (2005) 9(3) *Journal of Sociolinguistics* 418

Cary, E, 'Translation in the Modern World' *The UNESCO Courier*, April 1958, 9

Castro, Rocio et al., 'Sri Lanka Development Forum: The Economy, Regional Disparities, and Global Opportunities' (Report No 38388-LK, World Bank, 12 January 2007)

CBS, 'US Trade Policy: Copyright Infringement and the GATT' (Report, June 1986)

Central Bank of Sri Lanka, *Annual Report 1993* (1994)

Central Bank of Sri Lanka, *Annual Report 1994* (1995)

Central Bank of Sri Lanka, *Annual Report 2001* (2002)

Central Bank of Sri Lanka, *Annual Report 2002* (2003)

Central Bank of Sri Lanka, *Annual Report 2003* (2004)

Central Bank of Sri Lanka, *Annual Report 2012* (2013)

Central Bank of Sri Lanka, *Sri Lanka Socio-Economic Data 2019* (2019)

Central Intelligence Agency, *The World Fact Book: Sri Lanka* (18 May 2015) <www.cia.gov/library/publications/the-world-factbook/geos/ce.html>

Ceylon, Royal Commission to Examine and Report upon the Present State of the Laws, Regulations and Usages in the Settlements of the Cape of Good Hope and the Island of Mauritius and Ceylon, *Report of Lieutenant-Colonel Colebrooke, one of His Majesty's Commissioners of Inquiry, upon the Administration and Government of Ceylon* (1831)

Chamberlen, Paul, *An Impartial History of the Life and Reign of Our Late Most Gracious Sovereign Queen Anne* (1738)

Chon, Margaret, 'Intellectual Property "from Below": Copyright and Capability for Education' (2007) 40 *University of California, Davis Law Review* 803

Clair, William St, *The Reading Nation in the Romantic Period* (Cambridge University Press, 2004)

Commission on Intellectual Property Rights, *Integrating Intellectual Property Rights and Development Policy*, Report of the Commission on Intellectual Property Rights (2002)

Coperahewa, Sandagomi, 'The Language Planning Situation in Sri Lanka' (2009) 10(1) *Current Issues in Language Planning* 69

Coperahewa, Sandagomi, 'Colonialism and Problems of Language Policy: Formulation of a Colonial Language Policy in Sri Lanka' (2011) 1(1) *Sri Lanka Journal of Advanced Social Studies* 27

Copinger, Walter Arthur and JM Easton, *The Law of Copyright* (Stevens and Haynes, 5th ed, 1915)

Copyright Law Review Committee, *Report of the Committee Appointed by the Attorney General of the Commonwealth to Consider What Alterations Are Desirable in the Copyright Law of the Commonwealth* (1959)

Correa, Carlos M (ed), *Research Handbook on the Protection of Intellectual Property under WTO Rules: Intellectual Property in the WTO* (Edward Elgar Publishing, 2010) vol 1

Curtis, George Ticknor, *A Treatise on the Law of Copyright* (A Maxwell & Son, 1847)

Daskon, Chandima D, 'Are Cultural Traditions Real "Assets" for Rural People? An Analysis from A Livelihood Perspective' (2010) 10(3) *Global Journal of Human Social Science* 13

Davies, Gillian, Nicholas Caddick and Gwilym Harbottle, *Copinger and Skone James on Copyright* (Sweet & Gillian Maxwell, 17th ed South Asian, 2019) vol 1

Davis, Caroline, *Creating Postcolonial Literature: African Writers and British Publishers* (Palgrave Macmillan, 2013)

Day, Gary, *Literary Criticism: A New History* (Edinburgh University Press, 2008)

de Silva KM, 'The Transfer of Power in Sri Lanka—A Review of British Perspectives' (1974) 4(1&2) *The Ceylon Journal of Historical and Social Studies* 8

de Silva, KM (ed), *Sri Lanka: A Survey* (University Press of Hawaii, 1977)

de Silva, KM, *A History of Sri Lanka* (C Hurst, 1981)

De Silva, MU, 'Land Tenure, Caste System and the Rajakariya under Foreign Rule: A Review of Change in Sri Lanka Under Western Powers, 1597–1832' (1992–1993) 37 *Journal of the Royal Asiatic Society of Sri Lanka* 1

Deazley, Ronan, *On the Origin of the Right to Copy: Charting the Movement of Copyright Law in Eighteenth-Century Britain (1695–1775)* (Hart Publishing, 2004)

Deckelbaum, Richard J, James M Ntambi and Debra J Wolgemuth, 'Basic Science Research and Education: A Priority for Training and Capacity Building in Developing Countries' (2011) 25(3) *Infectious Disease Clinics of North America* 669 <www.id.theclinics.com/article/S0891-5520%2811%2900044-4/abstract>

Deere, Carolyn, *The Implementation Game: The TRIPS Agreement and the Global Politics of Intellectual Property Reform in Developing Countries* (Oxford University Press, 2009)

Department of Census & Statistics, *Census of Population and Housing 2012* (Final Report, 2015)

Department of Cultural Affairs, 'Sinhala Parivarthana Sahithya' [Sinhala Translation Literature] (Report and Proceedings of the Conference on Sinhala Translation, Colombo, 16–25 February 1965)

Desai, Sonalde B et al., *Human Development in India: Challenge for a Society* (Oxford University Press, 2010)
DeVotta, Neil, *Blowback: Linguistic Nationalism, Institutional Decay and Ethnic Conflict in Sri Lanka* (Stanford University Press, 2004)
'Documents of the Twentieth Session including the Report of the Commission to the General Assembly' [1968] II Yearbook of the International Law Commission 1
Drahos, Peter, 'BITS and BIPS: Bilateralism in Intellectual Property' (2001) 4(6) *The Journal of World Intellectual Property* 791
Drahos, Peter, 'The Regulation of Public Goods' (2004) 7(2) *Journal of International Economic Law* 321
Drahos, Peter and John Braithwaite, *Information Feudalism* (EARTHSCAN, 2002)
Drahos, Peter and Ruth Mayne (eds), *Global Intellectual Property Rights: Knowledge, Access and Development* (Palgrave Macmillan, 2002)
Dubin, Joseph S, 'The Universal Copyright Convention' (1954) 42 *California Law Review* 89
Edirisinghe, Dasun, 'SL Undergrads' English Proficiency Woefully Low, A Study Reveals' *The Island* (online), 30 May 2013 <www.island.lk/index.php?page_cat=article-details&page=article-details&code_title=80148>
Erling, Elizabeth J, 'Language Planning, English Language Education and Development Aid in Bangladesh' (2017) 18(4) *Current Issues in Language Planning* 388
European Commission Directorate-General for Translation, *Contribution of Translation to the Multilingual Society in the EU* (2010)
European Commission Directorate-General for Translation, *Lingua France: Chimera or Reality?* (2011)
European Communities—Review of Legislation: Questions Posed by the European Communities and Their Member States, WTO Doc IP/C/W/320/Add.2 (30 November 2001)
Evans, Gail E, 'Intellectual Property as a Trade Issue: The Making of the Agreement on Trade-Related Aspects of Intellectual Property Rights' (1994) 18(2) *World Competition* 137
Evans, Gail E, *Lawmaking Under the Trade Constitution: A Study in Legislating by the World Trade Organization* (Kluwer Law International, 2000)
Ezeife, Anthony N and T Arivalagan, 'Technology Education and Economic Competitiveness in Developing Countries: The Sri Lankan Experience' (2006) 35(1) *Canadian and International Education Journal* 12
Feather, John, *A History of British Publishing* (Routledge, 1988)
Feather, John, *Publishing, Piracy and Politics: A Historical Study of Copyright in Britain* (Mansell, 1994)
Fernando, JN Oleap, 'Sri Lankan Experience in School Science Education' (Proceedings of the Asian Regional IAP Seminar on the Generation of Experimental Materials and Learning Modules for Science Education, New Delhi, 24–25 October 2002) <http://insaindia.org/pdf/proceeding.pdf>
Floud, Roderick and Paul Johnson (eds), *The Cambridge Economic History of Modern Britain: Economic Maturity, 1860–1939* (Cambridge University Press, 2004) vol 2
Flynn, Sean M, 'Special 301 of the Trade Act of 1974 and Global Access to Medicine' (2010) 7 *Journal of Generic Medicines* 309
Gana, Ruth L, 'Prospects for Developing Countries under the TRIPs Agreement' (1996) 29 *Vanderbilt Journal of Transnational Law* 735

Garnett, Kevin, Gillian Davies and Gwilym Harbottle, *Copinger and Skone James on Copyright* (Sweet & Maxwell, 16th ed, 2011)

Gervais, Daniel, *The TRIPS Agreement: Drafting History and Analysis* (Sweet & Maxwell, 3rd ed, 2008)

Gibbons, Gerald R, 'The Compulsory License System of the Universal Copyright Convention' (1956) 6 *Duke Bar Journal* 23

Ginsburg, Jane C and Edouard Treppoz, *International Copyright Law: US and EU Perspectives: Text and Cases* (Edward Elgar, 2015)

Goldstein, Paul, *International Copyright: Principles, Law, and Practice* (Oxford University Press, 2001)

Goldstein, Paul and Bernt Hugenholtz, *International Copyright: Principles, Law, and Practice* (Oxford University Press, 2013)

Gomez, Mario, 'Keeping Rights Alive: Reform and Reconciliation in Post-War Sri Lanka' (2011) 17 *Asian Yearbook of International Law* 117

Goold, Patrick R, 'The Statute of Anne and Translations' (Unpublished Paper, Selected Works of Patrick R Goold, March 2013) <http://works.bepress.com/patrick_goold/1>

Government of India, 'Report of the Working Group on Higher Education for the XII Year Plan' (Department of Higher Education, September 2011)

Government of Sri Lanka, *Regaining Sri Lanka: Vision and Strategy for Accelerated Development* (Government of Sri Lanka, 2002)

Graham, M, SA Hale and M Stephens, *Geographies of the World Knowledge*, Corinne M Flick (ed), (Corinne M Flick, Convoco Foundation and Oxford Internet Institute, Convoco! ed, 2011)

Greg, WW and E Boswell (eds), *Records of the Court of the Stationers' Company (1576 to 1602—From Register B)* (Bibliographical Society, 1930)

Grosheide, Willem (ed), *Intellectual Property and Human Rights: A Paradox* (Edward Elgar, 2010)

Gunasena, HPM, 'Universities Should Focus More on Researches Meant for Public Good' *The Island* (online), 25 May 2014 <www.island.lk/index.php?page_cat=article-details&page=article-details&code_title=103920>

Gupta, BM, 'Sri Lanka S & T Output during 2001–2010: A Scientometric Assessment' (2012) 17(3) *Malaysian Journal of Library & Information Science* 49

Harris, Roy and Talbot J Taylor, *Landmarks in Linguistic Thought I: The Western Tradition from Socrates to Saussure* (Routledge, 2nd ed, 1997)

Harvey, David, 'Law and the Regulation of Communications Technologies: The Printing Press and the Law 1475–1641' (2005) *Australian and New Zealand Law & History Society E Journal* 160 <www.anzlhsejournal.auckland.ac.nz/other papers/otherpapers_2005/Harvey.pdf>

Helfer, Laurence R, 'Adjudicating Copyright Claims Under the TRIPs Agreement: The Case for a European Human Rights Analogy' (1998) 38(2) *Harvard International Law Journal* 357

Helfer, Laurence R, 'Regime Shifting: The TRIPs Agreement and New Dynamics of International Intellectual Property Lawmaking' (2004) 29(1) *The Yale Journal of International Law* 1

Helfer, Laurence R and Graeme W Austin, *Human Rights and Intellectual Property: Mapping the Global Interface* (Cambridge University Press, 2011)

Hemaratne, TSK, 'Intellectual Property Law and E-Commerce in Sri Lanka: Towards a Jurisprudence based on Constitution, Roman-Dutch Law and Buddhist Principle' (PhD Thesis, Queen Mary, University of London, 2005)

Henderson, Felicity, 'Faithful Interpreters? Translation Theory and Practice at the Early Royal Society' (2013) 67 *Notes and Records of the Royal Society* 101

Huntington, Ray L and W Jeffrey Marsh, 'Revisiting William Tyndale, Father of the English Bible' (2011) 12(2) *Religious Educator* 12

India Business Law Handbook: Strategic Information and Basic Laws (International Business Publications, 2013) vol 1

Intellectual Property Office, *Copyright Act 1956* <www.ipo.gov.uk/types/copy/c-about/c-history/c-history-1956.htm>

Irangani, MKL and Yoshiharu Shiratake, 'Indigenous Techniques Used in Rice Cultivation in Sri Lanka: An Analysis from an Agricultural History Perspective' (2013) 12(4) *Indian Journal of Traditional Knowledge* 638

Islam, MN, 'Historical Evolution of English in Bangladesh' (2019) 10(2) *Journal of Language Teaching and Research* 247

Jayasuriya, JE, *Educational Policies and Progress during British Rule in Ceylon (Sri Lanka) 1796–1948* (Associated Educational Publishers, 1977)

Jayathilaka, K, 'Pitapath Aithiwasikam Panatha' [Copyright Act], *Dina Dina Sangarawa* (Ceylon), 25 October 1956

Jayaweera, Swarna, 'Language and Colonial Educational Policy in Ceylon in the 19th Century' (1971) 2(2) *Modern Ceylon Studies* 151

Jayaweera, Swarna and Chandra Gunawardena, *Social Inclusion: Gender and Equity in Education SWAPS in South Asia: Sri Lanka Case Study* (UNICEF, 2007)

Jeffries, Sir Charles, *Ceylon: The Path to Independence* (Pall Mall Press, 1962)

Karim, M Saiful, 'Implementation of the MARPOL Convention in Developing Countries' (2010) 79 *Nordic Journal of International Law* 303

Kariyawasam, Kanchana, 'Developing a Regulatory Framework for the Protection of Intellectual Property Rights in Plant Genetic Resources in Sri Lanka' (PhD Thesis, School of Law, Griffith University, 2005)

Karunaratna, DM, *An Introduction to the Law of Copyright and Related Rights in Sri Lanka* (Sarvodaya Vishva Lekha, 2006)

Karunaratna, DM, 'Issues Related to the Enforcement of IP Rights: National Efforts to Improve Awareness of Decision Makers and Education of Consumers' (Document presented to the WIPO Advisory Committee on Enforcement WIPO/ACE/3/5, Third Session, Geneva, 15–17 May 2006)

Karunaratna, DM, *Elements of the Law of Intellectual Property in Sri Lanka* (Sarasavi Publishers, 2010)

Kearney, Robert N, 'Language and the Rise of Tamil Separatism in Sri Lanka' (1978) 15(5) *Asian Survey* 521

Kelegama, JB, 'Proposed FTA between Lanka and US' *The Island* (online), 18 August 2004 <www.island.lk/2004/08/18/featur01.html>

Kelegama, Saman (ed), *Economic Policy in Sri Lanka: Issues and Debates* (Sage Publications 2004)

Kelegama, Saman (ed), *Ready-Made Garment Industry in Sri Lanka: Facing the Global Challenge* (Institute of Policy Studies, 2004)

Khan, Abdul Waheed, 'Universal Access to Knowledge as a Global Public Good' on Global Policy Forum (June 2009) <www.globalpolicy.org/social-and-economic-policy/global-public-goods-1-101/50437-universal-access-to-knowledge-as-a-global-public-good.html>

Khan, Hameed Ahmed, *Education, Science and Technology in Developing Countries: Some Thoughts and Recollections* (COMSATS, 2004)

Kharbe, Ambreen Safder, *English Language and Literary Criticism* (Discovery Publishing House, 2009)
Khong, Dennis WK, 'The Historical Law and Economics of the First Copyright Act' (2006) 2(1) *Erasmus Law and Economics Review* 35
Krikorian, Gaelle and Amy Kapczynski (eds), *Access to Knowledge in the Age of Intellectual Property* (Zone Books, 2010)
Langley, Mark A, 'The Power of Knowledge' in 'Pulse of Profession: Capturing the Value of Project Management through Knowledge Transfer' (Report, Project Management Institute, March 2015)
Lanoszka, Anna, 'The Global Politics of Intellectual Property Rights and Pharmaceutical Drug Policies in Developing Countries' (2003) 24(2) *International Political Science Review* 181
Law of Copyright Committee, *Report of the Committee on the Law of Copyright 1909* (Cd 4976, 1910)
Lazar, Alan H, 'Developing Countries and Authors' Rights in International Copyright' (1971) 19(1) *Copyright Law Symposium* 1
Lewinski, Silke von, *International Copyright Law and Policy* (Oxford University Press, 2008)
Lievrouw, Leah A and Sharon E Farb, 'Information and Equity' (2003) 37 *Annual Review of Information Science and Technology* 499
Little, Angela W and Siri T Hettige, *Globalisation, Employment and Education in Sri Lanka: Opportunity and Division* (Routledge, 2013)
MacGillivray, EJ, *A Treatise upon the Law of Copyright* (John Murray, 1902)
Madanipour, Ali, *Knowledge Economy and the City: Spaces of Knowledge* (Routledge, 2011)
Malbon, Justin and Charles Lawson (eds), *Interpreting and Implementing the TRIPS Agreement: Is it Fair?* (Edward Elgar, 2008)
Malbon, Justin, Charles Lawson and Mark Davison, *The WTO Agreement on Trade-Related Aspects of Intellectual Property Rights: A Commentary* (Edward Elgar, 2014)
Maskus, Keith E (ed), *The WTO, Intellectual Property Rights and the Knowledge Economy* (Edward Elgar, 2004)
Matthews, Duncan, *Globalising Intellectual Property Rights: The TRIPs Agreement* (Routledge, 2002)
May, Christopher, *A Global Political Economy of Intellectual Property Rights: The New Enclosures?* (Routledge, 2000)
May, Christopher, *World Intellectual Property Organization (WIPO): Resurgence and the Development Agenda* (Routledge, 2007)
May, Christopher and Susan K Sell, *Intellectual Property Rights: A Critical History* (Lynne Rienner Publishers, 2006)
McKitterick, David (ed), *The Cambridge History of the Book in Britain 1830–1914* (Cambridge University Press, 2009) vol 6
Mendis, GC, *Ceylon under the British* (Asian Educational Services, first published 1952, 2005 ed)
Meneghini, Rogerio and Abel L Packer, 'Is there Science Beyond English' (2007) 8(2) *EMBO Reports* 112
Mitch, David, 'The Spread of Literacy in Nineteenth-Century England' (1983) 43(1) *Journal of Economic History* 287
Mustafa, AMM and S Santhirasegaram, 'The Impact of Foreign Direct Investment on Economic Growth in Sri Lanka' (2013) 8(1) *Journal of Management* 27

National Intellectual Property Office of Sri Lanka, *Statistics* <www.nipo.gov.lk/satistic.htm>

National Science Foundation, *National Survey of Research and Development in Sri Lanka 2004* (National Science Foundation, 2007)

National Science Foundation, *Sri Lanka Science, Technology & Innovation: Statistical Handbook 2015* (National Science Foundation, 2018)

The National Translation Mission, 'About NTM' <www.ntm.org.in/languages/english/aboutus.aspx>

The National Translation Mission, *A Detailed Project Report* (Central Institute of Indian Languages, February 2008)

The National Translation Mission, 'Origin' <www.ntm.org.in/languages/english/origin.aspx>

Nimmer, David, '"Fairest of them All" and Other Fairy Tales of Fair Use' (2003) 66 *Law and Contemporary Problems* 263

Nimmer, Melville B, 'Does Copyright Abridge the First Amendment Guarantees of Free Speech and Press?' (1970) 17 *UCLA Law Review* 1180

Nimmer, Melville B, Matthew Bender, *Nimmer on Copyright* (at Release 4)

Noronha, Frederick and Jeremy Malcolm (eds), *Access to Knowledge: A Guide for Everyone* (Consumers International, 2010)

Office of the USTR, '"Special 301" on Intellectual Property' (Fact Sheet, 25 May 1989)

Office of the USTR, '"Special 301" on Intellectual Property' (Fact Sheet, 27 April 1990)

Office of the USTR, '"Special 301" on Intellectual Property' (Fact Sheet, 26 April 1991)

Office of the USTR, *1992 National Trade Estimate Report on Foreign Trade Barriers* (1992)

Office of the USTR, *2012 National Trade Estimate Report on Foreign Trade Barriers* (2012)

Office of the USTR, *US Generalised System of Preferences: Guidebook* (2013)

Okediji, Ruth L, 'Africa and the Global Intellectual Property System: Beyond the Agency Model' (2004) 12 *African Year Book of International Law* 207

Okediji, Ruth L, 'The International Copyright System: Limitations, Exceptions and Public Interest Considerations for Developing Countries' (Issue Paper No 15, ICTSD and UNCTAD, March 2006) <http://unctad.org/en/Docs/iteipc200610_en.pdf>

Olian Jr, Irwin A, 'International Copyright and the Needs of Developing Countries: The Awakening at Stockholm and Paris' (1974) 7(2) *Cornell International Law Journal* 81

O'Neill, Kate, 'Against Dicta: A Legal Method for Rescuing Fair Use from the Right of First Publication' (2001) 89 *California Law Review* 371

Oxford Dictionary of National Biography (Oxford University Press, 2004) <www.oxforddnb.com/view/article/15070>

Oxford Dictionary of National Biography (Oxford University Press, online ed, 2009) <www.oxforddnb.com/view/article/5060>

Palmeter, N David, 'The Trade and Tariff Act of 1984: From the Customs Treatment of Manhole Covers to the Return of Goods from Outer Space' (1984) 11(3) *Syracuse Journal of International Law and Commerce* 487

Patterson, LR, *Copyright in Historical Perspective* (Vanderbilt University Press, 1968)

Paul, Lewis M, Gary F Simons and Charles D Fennig (eds), *Ethnologue: Language of the World* (SIL International, 18th ed, 2015) <www.ethnologue.com>
Peebles, Patrick, *The History of Sri Lanka* (Greenwood Press, 2006)
Peiris, PE, *Ceylon: The Portuguese Era: Being a History of the Island for the Period 1505–1658* (Tisara Prakashakayo, 2nd ed, 1992)
Perera, Marie, 'Coping with Student Heterogeneity in the English Language Classrooms: A Collaborative Action Research' (Report, National Education Commission, February 2010)
Pieris, Ralph, *Social Development and Planning in Asia* (Shakti Malik Abhinav Publications, 1976)
Poulsen, Lauge Skovgaard, 'The Importance of BITs for Foreign Direct Investment and Political Risk Insurance' (2009–2010) *Yearbook on International Investment Law & Policy* 539
Prasad, Akhil and Aditi Agrawala, *Copyright Law Desk Book: Knowledge Access and Development* (Universal Law Publishing, 2009)
Puckett, Lynne and William L Reynolds, 'Rules, Sanctions and Enforcement under Section 301: At Odds with WTO?' (1990) 90(4) *The American Journal of International Law* 675
Radwan, Ismail et al., 'Building the Sri Lankan Knowledge Economy' (Report, World Bank, March 2008)
Rajapaksa, Gotabaya, *Vistas of Prosperity and Splendour* (2019)
Rajapaksa, Mahinda, *Mahinda Chinthana—Vision for the Future* (2010)
Rajapaksha, Udaya, 'Ancient Food and Farming Systems in Sri Lanka' (1997) 19(1) *Vidurava* 41
Ranasinghe, P, YS Perera and AM Abeygunasekara, 'The Process and Costs of Publishing Medical Journals in Sri Lanka: An Economic Evaluation' (2011) 1(1) *BMJ Open* <http://bmjopen.bmj.com/content/1/1/e000057.full>
Records of the Diplomatic Conference for the Revision of the Berne Convention (Paris, 5–24 July 1971)
Records of the Intellectual Property Conference of Stockholm (11 June–14 July 1967) vol 2
Rens, Andrew and Rebecca Kahn (eds), *Access to Knowledge in South Africa* (Intellectual Property Research Unit, University of Cape Town and Information Society Project at Yale Law School, 2009)
Ricketson, Sam, *The Berne Convention for the Protection of Literary and Artistic Works: 1886–1986* (Kluwer, 1987)
Ricketson, Sam and Jane Ginsburg, *International Copyright and Neighbouring Rights: The Berne Convention and Beyond* (Oxford University Press, 2nd ed, 2006) vol 1 and 2
Rinehart, Christine Sixta, *Volatile Social Movements and the Origins of Terrorism: The Radicalization of Change* (Lexington Books, 2013)
Rodrigo, WD, 'Copyright Law in the Digital Era: A Comparative Study of Sri Lanka, Australia and the United States' (PhD Thesis, University of Queensland, 2007)
Rodrigo, WD, 'Access to Information for Educational Purposes: The Role of Educational Exceptions to Copyright in a Developing Country like Sri Lanka' (2008) 14(1) *The Bar Association Law Journal* 57
Rose, Mark, *Authors and Owners: The Invention of Copyright* (Harvard University Press, 1994)

Roy, Alpana, 'Copyright: A Colonial Doctrine in Postcolonial Age' (2008) 26(4) *Copyright Reporter* 112

Rupasinghe, S, 'The Role of English in Education, at School Level in Sri Lanka, as Perceived by Parents' (1983) *University of Colombo Review* 71

Ruse-Khan, Henning Grosse, 'The International Law Relation Between TRIPS and Subsequent TRIPS-Plus Free Trade Agreements: Towards Safeguarding TRIPS Flexibilities?' (2011) 18(2) *Journal of Intellectual Property Law* 1

Ryan, Michael P, *Knowledge Diplomacy: Global Competition and the Politics of Intellectual Property* (Brookings Institution Press, 1988)

Sag, Matthew, 'The Prehistory of Fair Use' (2011) 76(4) *Brooklyn Law Review* 1371

Sanderson, Michael, *Education and Economic Decline in Britain, 1870 to the 1990s* (Cambridge University Press, 1999)

Saunders, David, *Authorship and Copyright* (Routledge, 1992)

Sauvant, Karl P and Lisa E Sachs (eds), *The Effect of Treaties on Foreign Direct Investment: Bilateral Investment Treaties, Double Taxation Treaties, And Investment Flows* (Oxford University Press, 2009)

Schwartz, Eric J and David Nimmer, LexisNexis, *International Copyright Law and Practice*, vol 2 (at Release 25)

Schwartz, Warren F and Alan O Sykes, 'The Economic Structure of Renegotiation and Dispute Resolution in the World Trade Organisation' (2002) 31(S1) *The Journal of Legal Studies* S179

Schweitzer, Glenn (ed), *Science and Technology and the Future Development of Societies, International Workshop Proceedings* (The National Academic Press, 2008)

Scrutton, Thomas Edward, *The Law of Copyright* (William Clowes & Sons, 3rd ed, 1896)

Select Committee, House of Lords, *Report from the Select Committee of the House of Lords on the Copyright Bill and the Copyright (Artistic) Bill [HL]* (1899)

Seng, Daniel, 'WIPO Study on the Copyright Exceptions for the Benefit of Educational Activities for Asia and Australia' (SCCR/19/7, WIPO, 29 October 2009)

Seville, Catherine, *Literary Copyright Reform in Early Victorian England: The Framing of the 1842 Copyright Act* (Cambridge University Press, first published 1999, 2003 ed)

Seville, Catherine, *The Internationalisation of Copyright Law: Books, Buccaneers and the Black Flag in the Nineteenth Century* (Cambridge University Press, 2006)

Seville, Catherine, 'The Statute of Anne: Rhetoric and Reception in the Nineteenth Century' (2010–2011) 47 *Houston Law Review* 819

Shaheed, Farida, Special Rapporteur in field of Cultural Rights, *Report on Copyright Policy and the Right to Science and Culture* UN Doc A/HRC/28/57 (24 December 2014)

Shastri, Amita and A Jeyaratnam Wilson (eds), *The Post-Colonial States of South Asia: Democracy, Identity, Development and Security* (Routledge, 2001)

Shaver, Lea Bishop, 'Defining and Measuring A2K: A Blueprint for an Index of Access to Knowledge' (2008) 4(2) *I/S: A Journal of Law and Policy* 1

Shaver, Lea, 'Copyright and Inequality' (2014) 92 *Washington University Law Review* 117

Shaver, Lea, 'Local Language Limitations: Copyright and the Commons' (Working Paper, August 2014) <www.law.berkeley.edu/files/Shaver_Lea_IPSC_paper_2014.pdf>

Sherburn, George (ed), *The Correspondence of Alexander Pope* (Clarendon Press, 1956) vol 4

Sherman, Brad, 'Remembering and Forgetting: The Birth of Modern Copyright Law' (1995) 10 *Intellectual Property Journal* 1

Sherman, Brad and Lionel Bently, *The Making of Modern Intellectual Property Law: The British Experience, 1760–1911* (Cambridge University Press, first published 1999, 2003 ed)

Silva, Alberto Cerda, 'Beyond the Unrealistic Solution for Development Provided by the Appendix of the Berne Convention on Copyright' (Research Paper 8/2012, PIJIP, 2012) <http://digitalcommons.wcl.american.edu/research/30/>

Smith, Eric H, 'Worldwide Copyright Protection under the TRIPS Agreement' (1996) 29 *Vanderbilt Journal of Transnational Law* 559

Sorell, T, *Scientism: Philosophy and the Infatuation with Science* (Routledge, 1991)

Sorosky, Schuyler, 'United States v Forrester: An Unwarranted Narrowing of the Fourth Amendment' (2008) 41 *Loyola of Los Angeles Law Review* 1121

Special Committee on Education, *Report of the Special Committee on Education*, State Council of Ceylon Sessional Paper XXIV (1943)

Sri Lanka—Main Dedicated Intellectual Property Laws and Regulations Notified under Article 63.2 of the Agreement, WTO Doc IP/N/1/LKA/C/1/Add.1, IP/N/1/LKA/I/1/Add.1 (26 November 2001)

Sri Lanka—Responses from Sri Lanka to Questions Posed by the European Communities and Their Member States, WTO Doc IP/C/W/324/Add.4 (23 January 2002)

Sri Lanka—Review of Legislation, WTO Doc IP/Q/LKA1, IP/Q2/LKA1, IP/Q3/LKA1, IP/Q4/LKA1 (13 October 2003)

Sri Lanka (Ceylon), *Council Debates*, Ceylon Legislature, 9 September 1908

Sri Lanka, *Parliamentary Debates*, 25 May 1979

Sri Lanka, *Parliamentary Debates*, 23 July 2003

Sri Lanka, *Parliamentary Debates*, 25 July 2003

Sriyananda, Sahanika, 'Law's Delays—A Major Concern—Justice Ministry Secretary' *Sunday Observer* (online), 29 January 2012 <www.sundayobserver.lk/2012/01/29/fea06.asp>

Stephen, Leslie (ed), *Dictionary of National Biography* (Palgrave Macmillan, 1887) vol 10

Stern, Simon, 'From Author's Right to Property Right' (2012) 62(1) *University of Toronto Law Journal* 29

Stewart, Terence P (ed), *The GATT Uruguay Round: A Negotiating History (1986–1994)* (Kluwer Law International, 1999) vol 4

Stoll, Peter-Tobias, Jan Busche and Katrin Arend (eds), *WTO—Trade-Related Aspects of Intellectual Property Rights* (Martinus Nijhoff Publishers, 2009)

Strba, Susan Isiko, *International Copyright Law and Access to Education in Developing Countries: Exploring Multilateral Legal and Quasi-Legal Solutions* (Martinus Nijhoff Publishers, 2012)

Suarez, Michael F and Michael L Turner (eds), *The Cambridge History of the Book in Britain 1695–1830* (Cambridge University Press, 2009) vol 5

Suter, Keith, *Global Order and Global Disorder: Globalization and the Nation-State* (Praeger Publishers, 2003)

Swenson, Deborah L, 'Why do Developing Countries Sign BITs?' (2005) 12 *University of California, Davis Journal of International Law and Policy* 131

Talagala, Chamila, 'Translation and the International Copyright Crisis: The Sri Lankan Experience During the Early Years of Independence' (2017) 39(3) *European Intellectual Property Review* 153

Talagala, Chamila and Leanne Wiseman, 'Copyright, Open Access and Translation' (2015) 37(8) *European Intellectual Property Review* 498

Tambiah, SJ, *Sri Lanka: Ethnic Fratricide and the Dismantling of Democracy* (IB Tauris, 1986)

Tennent, JE, *Ceylon: An Account of the Island* (Longman, Green, Longman and Roberts, 1860) vol 1 and 2

Tenopir, Carol and Donald W King, 'Trends in Scientific Scholarly Journal Publishing in the United States' (1997) 28(3) *Journal of Scholarly Publishing* 135

Tian, YiJun, *Re-Thinking Intellectual Property: The Political Economy of Copyright Protection in the Digital Era* (Routledge-Cavendish, 2009)

Timmermans, Karin and Togi Hutadjulu (eds), 'The TRIPS Agreement and Pharmaceuticals' (Report of an ASEAN Workshop on the TRIPS Agreement and its Impact on Pharmaceuticals, Jakarta, 2–4 May 2000)

Toynbee, Arnold J, *A Study of History* (Oxford University Press, first published 1939, 1951 ed) vol 4

Tully, L Danielle, 'Prospects for Progress: The TRIPS Agreement and Developing Countries after the Doha Conference' (2003) 26 *Boston College International & Comparative Law Review* 129

UN Committee on Economic, Social and Cultural Rights, *General Comment No.13: The Right to Education (Art 13 of the Covenant)*, 21st sess. UN Doc E/C.12/1999/10 (8 December 1999)

UNDP, *Making Global Trade Work for People* (EARTHSCAN, 2003)

UNDP, *Sri Lanka Human Development Report 2012: Bridging Regional Disparities for Human Development* (2012)

UNDP, *Sri Lanka National Human Development Report 2014: Youth and Development: Towards a More Inclusive Future* (2014)

UNDP, 'Individual Consultant Procurement Notice' (Procurement Notice, 27 January 2015) <http://procurement-notices.undp.org/view_file.cfm?doc_id=45894>

UNESCO, 'Copyright Training Course for Nationals of Asian and Pacific States, Comparative Study of Copyright Laws in Force in the States of Asia and Pacific Region in relation to Tunis Model Law on Copyright for Developing Countries' (Paris, 15 September 1982)

UNESCO, 'Towards Knowledge Societies' (World Report, UNESCO, 2005)

UNESCO, *Science Report 2010: The Current Status of Science around the World* (2010)

UNESCO, *World Social Science Report 2010: Knowledge Divides* (2010)

UNESCO, *Adult and Youth Literacy, 1990–2015: Analysis of Data for 41 Selected Countries* (UNESCO Institute for Statistics, 2012)

UNESCO and WIPO, 'Tunis Model Law on Copyright for Developing Countries' (1976)

United Kingdom, *Cobbett's Parliamentary History of England*, 1774, vol 17

United Kingdom, *Hansard*, House of Commons, 14 December 1837, vol 39

United Kingdom, *Hansard*, House of Commons, 20 March 1838, vol 41

United Kingdom, *Hansard*, House of Commons, 20 April 1842, vol 62

United Kingdom, *Hansard*, House of Commons, 13 February 1852, vol 119

United Kingdom, *Hansard*, House of Lords, 30 April 1852, vol 121

United Kingdom, *Hansard*, House of Commons, 12 June 1879, vol 246

United Kingdom, *Hansard*, House of Commons, 29 July 1879, vol 248

United Kingdom, *Hansard*, House of Lords, 19 July 1897, vol 51

United Kingdom, Royal Commission to Make Inquiry with regard to the Laws and Regulations relating to Home, Colonial, and International Copyright, *Report of the Commissioners* (C 2036, 1878)

Vaddukoddai Resolution: The Resolution unanimously adopted at the First National Convention of the Tamil United Liberation Front held at Vaddukoddai on 14 May 1976

Vaidhyanathan, Siva, *Copyrights and Copywrongs: The Rise of Intellectual Property and How It Threatens Creativity* (New York University Press, 2001)

Venuti, L, *The Translator's Invisibility: A History of Translation* (Routledge, 1995)

Venuti, Lawrence, *The Scandals of Translation: Towards and Ethics of Difference* (Routledge, 1999)

Wagner, John A, *Encyclopaedia of the Wars of the Roses* (ABC-CLICO, 2001)

Waitley, Denis, *Empires of the Mind: Lessons to Lead and Succeed in a Knowledge-Based World* (William Morrow and Company, 1995)

Wansbrough, Dom Henry, 'The Bible in the Renaissance—William Tyndale' <http://users.ox.ac.uk/~sben0056/Tyndale.London.htm>

Ward, AW, GW Prothero and Stanley Leathes (eds), *The Cambridge Modern History* (Palgrave Macmillan, 1907) vol 2

Warnapala, WA Wiswa, *The Making of the System of Higher Education in Sri Lanka: An Evaluative Study* (2011)

Weedon, Alexis, *Victorian Publishing: The Economics of Book Production for a Mass Market, 1836–1916* (Ashgate, 2003)

Wijeyeratne, Roshan de Silva, *Nation, Constitutionalism and Buddhism in Sri Lanka* (Routledge, 2014)

Willinsky, John, *The Access Principle: The Case for Open Access to Research and Scholarship* (MIT Press, 2006)

Wilson, A Jeyaratnam, *Politics in Sri Lanka 1947–79* (Palgrave Macmillan, 2nd ed, 1979)

Wilson, A Jeyaratnam, *The Break-up of Sri Lanka: The Sinhalese-Tamil Conflict* (Orient Longman, 1988)

WIPO, *Berne Notification No 248: Berne Convention for the Protection of Literary Works and Artistic Works* <www.wipo.int/treaties/en/notifications/berne/treaty_berne_248.html>

WIPO, *Treaties and Contracting Parties: Contracting Parties—Berne Convention—Sri Lanka* <www.wipo.int/treaties/en/remarks.jsp?cnty_id=1028C>

WIPO, *WIPO-Administered Treaties—Contracting Parties: Berne Convention* <www.wipo.int/treaties/en/ShowResults.jsp?treaty_id=15>

WIPO, *WIPO-Administered Treaties—Notifications—Berne Convention*, Berne Notification No 92 <www.wipo.int/treaties/en/notifications/berne/treaty_berne_92.html>

Wirten, Eva Hemmungs, *No Trespassing: Authorship, Intellectual Property Rights, and Boundaries of Globalisation* (University of Toronto Press, 2004)

Wirten, Eva Hemmungs, *Cosmopolitan Copyright: Law and Language in the Translation Zone* (Uppsala Universitet, 2011)

Wiseman, Leanne Gaye, 'Making Copies: The Impact of Photocopying on Copyright Law in Australia' (PhD Thesis, University of Queensland, 2009)

World Bank, *Country and Lending Groups* <http://data.worldbank.org/about/country-and-lending-groups>

World Bank, 'South Asia Economic Focus: Making the Most of Cheap Oil' (Report, 2015)

World Bank, 'Sri Lanka Home: Overview' <www.worldbank.org/en/country/srilanka/overview>

World Bank, *Sri Lanka: Overview*, 'Context' (23 June 2015) <www.worldbank.org/en/country/srilanka/overview>

WTO, *Understanding the WTO: Settling Disputes*, 'A Unique Contribution' (2015) <www.wto.org/english/thewto_e/whatis_e/tif_e/disp1_e.htm>

WTO, *Understanding the WTO: The Organisation—Members and Observers* <www.wto.org/english/thewto_e/whatis_e/tif_e/org6_e.htm>

Yapa, Geetha, 'The Historical Development of Sri Lanka Scholarly Journal Publishing (1845–2010)' (2011) 4(3&4) *Sri Lankan Journal of Librarianship and Information Management* <http://sllim.sljol.info/article/abstract/10.4038/sllim.v4i3-4.4253/>

Yu, Juan, 'Can Developing Countries Benefit from Intellectual Property Protection' (2003) 10 *TFLR—IP Protection and Developing Countries* 359

Yu, Peter K, 'A Tale of Two Development Agendas' (2009) 35 *Ohio Northern University Law Review* 465

Index

For Product Safety Concerns and Information please contact our EU representative GPSR@taylorandfrancis.com
Taylor & Francis Verlag GmbH, Kaufingerstraße 24, 80331 München, Germany

www.ingramcontent.com/pod-product-compliance
Ingram Content Group UK Ltd.
Pitfield, Milton Keynes, MK11 3LW, UK
UKHW022133190926
475702UK00013B/1792

* 9 7 8 0 3 6 7 7 6 0 9 4 6 *